107 Hawkins Ave.
Sanford, N. C. 27330

ALFRED, LORD TENNYSON was born in 1809 at Somersby, Lincolnshire. Schooled at Louth and by his father, a rector, he began to write early, and at the age of twelve he composed "an epic of 6,000 lines." In 1828 he matriculated at Cambridge— but only after the elder Tennyson had approved his recitation by heart of the odes of Horace. *Poems, Chiefly Lyrical*, published in 1830, revealed Tennyson's swiftly maturing talent, a talent which was augmented by his friendship with Edward FitzGerald and A. H. Hallam. In 1830, the poet and Hallam volunteered in the army of a Spanish insurgent; and *Poems* (1833) derived largely from experience gained on the Continent. Hallam's death in the same year gave rise to *The Two Voices* (1834)—a critical turning point in Tennyson's optimism. After a lengthy silence he published *Poems* (1842), earning the admiration of Carlyle and Dickens. Eighteen-fifty witnessed his marriage to Emily Sarah Sellwood and his appointment as poet laureate, succeeding Wordsworth. The gravity with which he took his office was reflected in many poems on state occasions. His later years produced his acknowledged masterpieces: *In Memoriam* (1850), *Maud* (1855), *Ballads and Other Poems* (1880), *Locksley Hall Sixty Years After* (1886), and scattered sections of his eventual epic, *Idylls of the King* (1859-1885). In 1892, reading his favorite, Shakespeare, Tennyson quietly died at Aldworth and received a public funeral in Westminster Abbey.

Alfred Tennyson

Idylls of the King

AND

A SELECTION OF POEMS

LEE COUNTY LIBRARY
107 Hawkins Ave.
Sanford, N. C. 27330

With a Foreword by
GEORGE BARKER

A SIGNET CLASSIC

NEW AMERICAN LIBRARY

A DIVISION OF PENGUIN BOOKS USA INC., NEW YORK
PUBLISHED IN CANADA BY
PENGUIN BOOKS CANADA LIMITED, MARKHAM, ONTARIO

Copyright © 1961
by New American Library, a division of
Penguin Books USA Inc.

The selection of poems commencing
on page 257 was made of Oscar Williams

ℭ

SIGNET CLASSIC TRADEMARK REG. U.S. PAT. OFF. AND FOREIGN COUNTRIES

REGISTERED TRADEMARK—MARCA REGISTRADA

HECHO EN DRESDEN, TN, U.S.A.

SIGNET, SIGNET CLASSIC, MENTOR, ONYX, PLUME, MERIDIAN
and NAL BOOKS are published in the United States by New American Library,
a division of Penguin Books USA Inc.,
1633 Broadway, New York, New York 10019,
in Canada by Penguin Books Canada Limited,
2801 John Street, Markham, Ontario L3R 1B4

18   19   20   21   22   23   24   25   26

PRINTED IN THE UNITED STATES OF AMERICA

FOREWORD

His opinions too are not original, often not inde-
pendent even, and they sink into vulgarity: not only
"Locksley Hall" but "Maud" is an ungentlemanly
row and "The Princess" is an ungentlemanly row. . . .
But for all this he is a glorious poet and all he does
is chryselephantine.

—*Gerard Manley Hopkins*

THERE IS an arithmetic of poetry in which totals transcend all
enumerations; it is not possible to equate the figure of Ten-
nyson by adding together those elements that go to make up
either the poems or the name. Put conversely, if you disman-
tle the construction of Tennyson you will discover that the
sum of the parts does not equal the whole. To me it is as
though these poems and this reputation were in fact inhabited
by the presence of a superior power, a phenomenon of elec-
tricity, seemingly unwilling to subject itself to isolation or an-
alysis. I do not mean to refer to the Poetry in the poems or to
the Poet in the name; I mean to speak of a kind of authority
imbuing both which neither, upon examination, could wholly
account for. Tennyson's poems, unlike those of, say, Ben Jon-
son, transcend their own achievements and their own inten-
tions in such a way as to render a purely semantic criticism
of them quite specious. They call for an exercise in metaphysi-
cal permutations. For the Tennysonian characteristic is am-
bivalence. The poem is there in the hand; one examines its
colors and lines with much the same delight as if it were a king-
fisher; and then discovers that one has a salmon or a cheap
piece of Victorian cut glass in one's hand. And I am speak-
ing of more than the impression or effect of the poem upon the
reader; the ideas or intellectual specifications of the poems
seem to mutate as one looks at them, like the behavior of
water.

> Tears, idle tears, I know not what they mean,
> Tears from the depth of some divine despair
> Rise in the heart, and gather to the eyes,

> In looking on the happy Autumn-fields,
> And thinking of the days that are no more.

It is almost possible to watch such lines maneuvering their emphases like the lacunae of Lamia. When Tennyson is accused, as he has been, of silliness, of intellectual provinciality, of vulgarity of mind, what is happening, I think, is that his accusers are looking at the poems as though they were simply presenting a case. But Tennyson's poems never simply present a case, for even when these poems do present a case, it is by no means this presentation that matters most. What matters more is an expression on the face of the figure that makes this presentation, the never quite visible, but never invisible, presence of the poet himself. I think that this remark holds for poets other than Tennyson. The poems of Yeats, for example, and of Eliot even more so, draw part of their plenipotential dignity from the expression on the face of the poet as he presents the poem. Nor is this expression of the poetic face to be deduced directly or even obliquely from the emotion of the poem itself. Like Lewis Carroll's cat, it is very hard to place. And sometimes the effect (which may be the same thing as the meaning) of the poem occurs catalystically between the statements of the ostensible words and the expression of the invisible face. (This antiphonic effect is clearest, as I see it, in the satirical poem. We know that behind the machinations of the satire moves inevitably the love that seeks effects.)

So that the first of the metaphysical permutations of the Tennysonian mask is, I think, this plurality; the expression of the observed word and the expression of the invisible visage. To bring what evidence I may for these adumbrations, I suggest that recognizably the face behind the "Idylls of the King" hints at its own falsity, whereas the face behind "The Two Voices" acknowledges that it has removed its innermost mask. "The Two Voices" is not only a better poem, it is also a better Tennyson.

This notion has nothing to do with any speculative autobiographical correspondences between the poem and the poet. What I seek to describe is the permanence of that moment when the poet, perceiving the possible poem for the first time, modifies his approach to it in terms that strive to anticipate the poem's nature. I suggest that in the apocryphal street where poets pick up poems, there are laws that govern the behavior of both. The poet is not permitted to accost one kind of poem as though it were another; nor can he know what kind of poem he meets until he has met it. But he must behave as though he had in fact foreseen its nature, for his prognostication operates, in retrospect, as though it had actually had a hand in the evolution of the poem's nature. And this moment of what one could call categorical recognition is the moment immortalized ever afterwards in the expression on the face of the poet as it presides—as it must preside—over the poem. It is, finally, the act of imaginative domination which precipitates the poem's identity.

Thus the sonnets of Hopkins are dominated by an expression not so recognizably present in these sonnets themselves as in the mask, or face, that hangs like a cloud over them. It is a cloud not of anguish and not of personal passion but of a kind of ineffable regret. Not the individual regret of a creature for things done or for things not done, but the ineffable regret of the spirit aware that it can liberate itself only through its actions, which is torment, or through the intellect, which is inconclusive, or through theology, which is not viable. Thus, these sonnets have two subjects: the ostensible subject of the poet's despair, and the unspoken or masked subject, the tragic regret that this despair is not only possible, but, unforgivably, poetic. The poem hates the poetry.

Over Tennyson's beautiful and agonized poem "The Two Voices" no such profound regret (that the poem hates the poetry) presides as it does over the sonnets of Hopkins. Behind the nihilistic tergiversations of "The Two Voices" there echoes a private resentment rather than a tragic regret. Where the sonnets accuse the divine powers with a transcendental "How could you ever do this to us?", "The Two Voices" accuse those powers with a petulant "Why did you ever do this to me?"

But my purpose is not to try to make up an essay in comparative anatomy between Tennyson and Hopkins. What I seek to do is to demonstrate, if possible, the tenability of a theory of poetic possession, a conception of the face behind the poem, the hidden visage of its creator, that visage which, like an act of possession (in both senses), can never be dismissed from the poem, any more than the face of its father can be erased from that of the child.

I take it that a total poem is, in itself, the metaphor of an event. Since it is certainly not the mere description of an event (though it may be partly this), and since a poem cannot possibly exist without the event that engenders it, then I conclude that it operates or migrates between the inceptive event and the abstracted idea of the event enshrined in the eventual poem. I have to employ obscure terminology because this is the dark backward and abysm of the mind. Briefly, the subject of the poem is an occurrence in the moral or material his-

tory of the animal; the poem itself is such an event stolen from
temporal affairs and transferred to the altitude of the Ideal.
What I want to propose is that in this transference of the
event from the world of temporal affairs to the altitude of the
Ideal, the poet may (or may not) be aware of the almost su-
pernatural obligations of such a Promethean act—Promethean
in that it attempts to return this privilege whence it came.

Is there no bright reversion in the sky?

And upon the poem itself the presence of this awareness of
a supernatural prerogative or obligation may leave its distin-
guishing imprint, yet no more visible and no more verifiable,
save in between the lines, than that demigod who left his
hand mark on the first flame. Tennyson makes this—no, not
clear, because such a matter could never be that—a perhaps
tenable notion, and for the very reason that his poems contain
little except the fire and the dross, or the best and the worst.
Thus, this face wears the illuminated expression of a natural
man who is not a demigod but who is really playing with fire.
And this is the supernatural privilege, for among the Cauca-
sian Rocks of the mind this ontological fire can destroy as well
as animate. See William Blake.

What distinguishes a messenger from men who are simply
going from one place to another is more than the weight of
the message he carries. A glance at the melancholy postman
trudging down a damp lane with a neat packet of letters under
his arm unmistakably declares that Housman has merely a few
letters of condolence to deliver. If the address on these enve-
lopes were not quite so impressive, one has no doubt that he
could bring himself to chuck the lot under a hedge and go
home to bed. Conversely it would be excusable to assume from
his behavior that every word carried by Tennyson contained
state secrets. And this consciousness of a supremely responsible
communication (which is not the same thing as a supremely
important message) imparts to the poem its air of authority,
and presides over the total body of a poet's work like that face
or visage of congenita possession which I have tried to de-
scribe. Thus this consciousness of a supernatural privilege or
obligation so presides and so imparts the seeming authority.
And, as I see it, Tennyson acknowledged this privilege and
exercised this authority. What principally renders that sinister
figure a sympathetic, and at the same time an apparently sim-
ple, equation is his demonstrable conviction that even obscure
issues can be spoken of quite clearly.

A second voice was at mine ear,
A little whisper silver-clear,
A murmur, "Be of better cheer."
As from the blissful neighborhood,
A notice faintly understood,
"I see the end, and know the good."

But this is not to say that such obscure issues did not exist for
him. And by obscure issues I mean those remote but power-
ful enigmas in human affairs to whose elucidation the work-
ings of the creative intelligence have always been largely
directed: the ambiguities about ourselves, the gods and the
world that we do not understand and of whose very existence
we have only uncertain evidence.

Verlaine said of him, "When he should have been broken-
hearted he had reminiscences." But what In Memoriam lucidly
and veritably attests is that when one is brokenhearted, one
does in fact have reminiscences. It may not be honorable, it
may not be intelligent, it may not be French, but it is what
Tennyson knew more than Verlaine. What is it that we recol-
lect in tranquillity? Verlaine's remark is as irrelevant to In
Memoriam as Samuel Johnson's strictures are to Lycidas. For
Tennyson is not less prepared to be obvious in the services of
the poem than Whitman was prepared to be vulgar or John
Milton academic or W. H. Auden a boy scout or Yeats a Voro-
noff gland. What such poets have made out of their allegorical
instances is what truly matters. Nor can I recognize on what
authority we are to understand that poetry cannot be created
out of vulgarity, obviousness, reminiscences, or, indeed, as
William Shakespeare showed us, out of anything or nothing
at all.

For what I am really trying to write about is not so much
Lord Tennyson, whose shade is in no need of my administra-
tions, as about the art of poetry, whose identity has not, even
yet, been categorically disclosed. It is the great honor of Ten-
nyson that he was elected to glorify the simple, but never
simple-minded, operations of the common intelligence, whose
ardors and labors may be no less memorable than those of a
larger range but a smaller vulnerability. This most poetic of
poets speaks in truth not for those intellectual potentates who
can very well speak for themselves, but for the common or
sensible man.

As I see it, the speculative intelligence is to the poem what
the camouflage is to some species of animal: a function to
make one thing look like another. The function of speculative
intelligence in a poem is to make that poem look like a ra-

tional and comprehensible statement. But the poem is not this, or not merely this, because if it were it would in no way differ from the rational statements of prose. And we have it on the authority of I. A. Richards that prose makes statements and poems make "pseudo-statements." "Poetry is speech framed for contemplation of the mind by the way of hearing or speech framed to be heard for its own sake and interest even over and above its interest of meaning." No, the Dionysian beast whose nature is disguised by the camouflages of an intelligence is a hybrid monster uniting the instincts and the imagination of man. And these instincts and this imagination provide the real or sleeping subject of the poem, where to all appearances this subject is merely a collection of unverifiable assertions.

I believe that a poem does not finally appeal to the seat of rational judgment in mankind; it has other courts of judgment; the poem appeals to the analogical goddesses of memory, to the idols and incarnations of the human passions, to the instinctive responses of sensual conditions, as much as to common sense. And perhaps one of the reasons why Tennyson's poems wear what I have called an expression of ambivalent authority is that they utter the ejaculations of wonder which would be wrung from all perfectly normal intelligences if liberated in a world and underworld of such goddesses, such idols, such sensual conditions, and so little common sense.

—George Barker

CONTENTS

Idylls of the King

• •

IN TWELVE BOOKS

•

Flos Regum Arthurus — JOSEPH OF EXETER

DEDICATION

THESE to His Memory—since he held them dear,
Perchance as finding there unconsciously
Some image of himself—I dedicate,
I dedicate, I consecrate with tears—
These Idylls.

            And indeed he seems to me
Scarce other than my king's ideal knight,
"Who reverenced his conscience as his king;
Whose glory was, redressing human wrong;
Who spake no slander, no, nor listen'd to it;
Who loved one only and who clave to her"—
Her—over all whose realms to their last isle,
Commingled with the gloom of imminent war,
The shadow of his loss drew like eclipse,
Darkening the world. We have lost him; he is gone.
We know him now; all narrow jealousies
Are silent, and we see him as he moved,

How modest, kindly, all-accomplish'd, wise,
With what sublime repression of himself,
And in what limits, and how tenderly;
Not swaying to this faction or to that;
Not making his high place the lawless perch
Of wing'd ambitions, nor a vantage-ground
For pleasure; but thro' all this tract of years
Wearing the white flower of a blameless life,
Before a thousand peering littlenesses,
In that fierce light which beats upon a throne
And blackens every blot; for where is he
Who dares foreshadow for an only son
A lovelier life, a more unstain'd, than his?
Or how should England dreaming of *his* sons
Hope more for these than some inheritance
Of such a life, a heart, a mind as thine,
Thou noble Father of her Kings to be,
Laborious for her people and her poor—
Voice in the rich dawn of an ampler day—
Far-sighted summoner of War and Waste
To fruitful strifes and rivalries of peace—
Sweet nature gilded by the gracious gleam
Of letters, dear to Science, dear to Art,
Dear to thy land and ours, a Prince indeed,
Beyond all titles, and a household name,
Hereafter, thro' all times, Albert the Good.

Break not, O woman's-heart, but still endure;
Break not, for thou art royal, but endure,
Remembering all the beauty of that star
Which shone so close beside thee that ye made
One light together, but has past and leaves
The Crown a lonely sp.endor.

                    May all love,
His love, unseen but felt, o'ershadow thee,
The love of all thy sons encompass thee,
The love of all thy daughters cherish thee,
The love of all thy people comfort thee,
Till God's love set thee at his side again!

The Coming of Arthur

❖❖❖❖❖❖❖❖❖❖❖❖❖❖❖❖❖❖❖❖❖❖❖❖

LEODOGRAN, the king of Cameliard,
Had one fair daughter, and none other child;
And she was fairest of all flesh on earth,
Guinevere, and in her his one delight.

For many a petty king ere Arthur came
Ruled in this isle and, ever waging war
Each upon other, wasted all the land;
And still from time to time the heathen host
Swarm'd over-seas, and harried what was left.
And so there grew great tracts of wilderness,
Wherein the beast was ever more and more,
But man was less and less, till Arthur came.
For first Aurelius lived and fought and died,
And after him King Uther fought and died,
But either fail'd to make the kingdom one.
And after these King Arthur for a space,
And thro' the puissance of his Table Round,
Drew all their petty princedoms under him,
Their King and head, and made a realm and reign'd.

And thus the land of Cameliard was waste,
Thick with wet woods, and many a beast therein,
And none or few to scare or chase the beast;
So that wild dog and wolf and boar and bear
Came night and day, and rooted in the fields,
And wallow'd in the gardens of the King.
And ever and anon the wolf would steal
The children and devour, but now and then,
Her own brood lost or dead, lent her fierce teat
To human sucklings; and the children, housed
In her foul den, there at their meat would growl,
And mock their foster-mother on four feet,
Till, straighten'd, they grew up to wolf-like men,
Worse than the wolves. And King Leodogran
Groan'd for the Roman legions here again
And Cæsar's eagle. Then his brother king,

Urien, assail'd him; last a heathen horde,
Reddening the sun with smoke and earth with blood,
And on the spike that split the mother's heart
Spitting the child, brake on him, till, amazed,
He knew not whither he should turn for aid.

But—for he heard of Arthur newly crown'd,
Tho' not without an uproar made by those
Who cried, "He is not Uther's son"—the King
Sent to him, saying, "Arise, and help us thou!
For here between the man and beast we die."

And Arthur yet had done no deed of arms,
But heard the call and came; and Guinevere
Stood by the castle walls to watch him pass;
But since he neither wore on helm or shield
The golden symbol of his kinglihood,
But rode a simple knight among his knights,
And many of these in richer arms than he,
She saw him not, or mark'd not, if she saw,
One among many, tho' his face was bare.
But Arthur, looking downward as he past,
Felt the light of her eyes into his life
Smite on the sudden, yet rode on, and pitch'd
His tents beside the forest. Then he drave
The heathen; after, slew the beast, and fell'd
The forest, letting in the sun, and made
Broad pathways for the hunter and the knight,
And so return'd.

                    For while he linger'd there,
A doubt that ever smoulder'd in the hearts
Of those great lords and barons of his realm
Flash'd forth and into war; for most of these,
Colleaguing with a score of petty kings,
Made head against him, crying: "Who is he
That he should rule us? who hath proven him
King Uther's son? for lo! we look at him,
And find nor face nor bearing, limbs nor voice,
Are like to those of Uther whom we knew.
This is the son of Gorloïs, not the King;
This is the son of Anton, not the King."

And Arthur, passing thence to battle, felt
Travail, and throes and agonies of the life,
Desiring to be join'd with Guinevere,
And thinking as he rode: "Her father said

That there between the man and beast they die.
Shall I not lift her from this land of beasts
Up to my throne and side by side with me?
What happiness to reign a lonely king,
Vext—O ye stars that shudder over me,
O earth that soundest hollow under me,
Vext with waste dreams? for saving I be join'd
To her that is the fairest under heaven,
I seem as nothing in the mighty world,
And cannot will my will nor work my work
Wholly, nor make myself in mine own realm
Victor and lord. But were I join'd with her,
Then might we live together as one life,
And reigning with one will in everything
Have power on this dark land to lighten it,
And power on this dead world to make it live."

Thereafter—as he speaks who tells the tale—
When Arthur reach'd a field of battle bright
With pitch'd pavilions of his foe, the world
Was all so clear about him that he saw
The smallest rock far on the faintest hill,
And even in high day the morning star.
So when the King had set his banner broad,
At once from either side, with trumpet-blast,
And shouts and clarions shrilling unto blood,
The long-lanced battle let their horses run.
And now the barons and the kings prevail'd,
And now the King, as here and there that war
Went swaying; but the Powers who walk the world
Made lightnings and great thunders over him,
And dazed all eyes, till Arthur by main might,
And mightier of his hands with every blow,
And leading all his knighthood threw the kings,
Carádos, Urien, Cradlemont of Wales,
Claudius, and Clariance of Northumberland,
The King Brandagoras of Latangor,
With Anguisant of Erin, Morganore,
And Lot of Orkney. Then, before a voice
As dreadful as the shout of one who sees
To one who sins, and deems himself alone
And all the world asleep, they swerved and brake
Flying, and Arthur call'd to stay the brands
That hack'd among the flyers, "Ho! they yield!"
So like a painted battle the war stood
Silenced, the living quiet as the dead,

And in the heart of Arthur joy was lord.
He laugh'd upon his warrior whom he loved
And honor'd most. "Thou dost not doubt me King,
So well thine arm hath wrought for me to-day."
"Sir and my liege," he cried, "the fire of God
Descends upon thee in the battle-field.
I know thee for my King!" Whereat the two,
For each had warded either in the fight,
Sware on the field of death a deathless love.
And Arthur said, "Man's word is God in man;
Let chance what will, I trust thee to the death."

    Then quickly from the foughten field he sent
Ulfius, and Brastias, and Bedivere,
His new made knights, to King Leodogran,
Saying, "If I in aught have served thee well,
Give me thy daughter Guinevere to wife."

    Whom when he heard, Leodogran in heart
Debating—"How should I that am a king,
However much he holp me at my need,
Give my one daughter saving to a king,
And a king's son?"—lifted his voice, and call'd
A hoary man, his chamberlain, to whom
He trusted all things, and of him required
His counsel: "Knowest thou aught of Arthur's birth?"

    Then spake the hoary chamberlain and said:
"Sir King, there be but two old men that know;
And each is twice as old as I; and one
Is Merlin, the wise man that ever served
King Uther thro' his magic art, and one
Is Merlin's master—so they call him—Bleys,
Who taught him magic; but the scholar ran
Before the master, and so far that Bleys
Laid magic by, and sat him down, and wrote
All things and whatsoever Merlin did
In one great annal-book, where after-years
Will learn the secret of our Arthur's birth."

    To whom the King Leodogran replied:
"O friend, had I been holpen half as well
By this King Arthur as by thee today,
Then beast and man had had their share of me;
But summon here before us yet once more
Ulfius, and Brastias, and Bedivere."

    Then, when they came before him, the King said:

"I have seen the cuckoo chased by lesser fowl,
And reason in the chase; but wherefore now
Does these your lords stir up the heat of war,
Some calling Arthur born of Gorloïs,
Others of Anton? Tell me, ye yourselves,
Hold ye this Arthur for King Uther's son?"

And Ulfius and Brastias answer'd, "Ay."
Then Bedivere, the first of all his knights
Knighted by Arthur at his crowning, spake—
For bold in heart and act and word was he,
Whenever slander breathed against the King—

"Sir, there be many rumors on this head;
For there be those who hate him in their hearts,
Call him baseborn, and since his ways are sweet,
And theirs are bestial, hold him less than man;
And there be those who deem him more than man,
And dream he dropt from heaven. But my belief
In all this matter—so ye care to learn—
Sir, for ye know that in King Uther's time
The prince and warrior Gorloïs, he that held
Tintagil castle by the Cornish sea,
Was wedded with a winsome wife, Ygerne;
And daughters had she borne him,—one whereof,
Lot's wife, the Queen of Orkney, Bellicent,
Hath ever like a loyal sister cleaved
To Arthur,—but a son she had not borne.
And Uther cast upon her eyes of love;
But she, a stainless wife of Gorloïs,
So loathed the bright dishonor of his love
That Gorloïs and King Uther went to war,
And overthrown was Gorloïs and slain.
Then Uther in his wrath and heat besieged
Ygerne within Tintagil, where her men,
Seeing the mighty swarm about their walls,
Left her and fled, and Uther enter'd in,
And there was none to call to but himself.
So, compass'd by the power of the King,
Enforced she was to wed him in her tears,
And with a shameful swiftness; afterward,
Not many moons, King Uther died himself,
Moaning and wailing for an heir to rule
After him, lest the realm should go to wrack.
And that same night, the night of the new year,
By reason of the bitterness and grief
That vext his mother, all before his time

Was Arthur born, and all as soon as born
Deliver'd at a secret postern-gate
To Merlin, to be holden far apart
Until his hour should come, because the lords
Of that fierce day were as the lords of this,
Wild beasts, and surely would have torn the child
Piecemeal among them, had they known; for each
But sought to rule for his own self and hand,
And many hated Uther for the sake
Of Gorloïs. Wherefore Merlin took the child,
And gave him to Sir Anton, an old knight
And ancient friend of Uther; and his wife
Nursed the young prince, and rear'd him with her own;
And no man knew. And ever since the lords
Have foughten like wild beasts among themselves,
So that the realm has gone to wrack; but now,
This year, when Merlin—for his hour had come—
Brought Arthur forth, and set him in the hall,
Proclaiming, 'Here is Uther's heir, your king,'
A hundred voices cried: 'Away with him!
No king of ours! a son of Gorloïs he,
Or else the child of Anton, and no king,
Or else baseborn.' Yet Merlin thro' his craft,
And while the people clamor'd for a king,
Had Arthur crown'd; but after, the great lords
Banded, and so brake out in open war."

Then while the King debated with himself
If Arthur were the child of shamefulness,
Or born the son of Gorloïs after death,
Or Uther's son and born before his time,
Or whether there were truth in anything
Said by these three, there came to Cameliard,
With Gawain and young Modred, her two sons,
Lot's wife, the Queen of Orkney, Bellicent;
Whom as he could, not as he would, the King
Made feast for, saying, as they sat at meat:
"A doubtful throne is ice on summer seas.
Ye come from Arthur's court. Victor his men
Report him! Yea, but ye—think ye this king—
So many those that hate him, and so strong,
So few his knights, however brave they be—
Hath body enow to hold his foemen down?"

"O King," she cried, "and I will tell thee: few,
Few, but all brave, all of one mind with him;
For I was near him when the savage yells

Of Uther's peerage died, and Arthur sat
Crowned on the daïs, and his warriors cried,
'Be thou the king, and we will work thy will
Who love thee.' Then the King in low deep tones,
And simple words of great authority,
Bound them by so strait vows to his own self
That when they rose, knighted from kneeling, some
Were pale as at the passing of a ghost,
Some flush'd, and others dazed, as one who wakes
Half-blinded at the coming of a light.

"But when he spake, and cheer'd his Table Round
With large, divine, and comfortable words,
Beyond my tongue to tell thee—I beheld
From eye to eye thro' all their Order flash
A momentary likeness of the King;
And ere it left their faces, thro' the cross
And those around it and the Crucified,
Down from the casement over Arthur, smote
Flame-color, vert, and azure, in three rays,
One falling upon each of three fair queens
Who stood in silence near his throne, the friends
Of Arthur, gazing on him, tall, with bright
Sweet faces, who will help him at his need.

"And there I saw mage Merlin, whose vast wit
And hundred winters are but as the hands
Of loyal vassals toiling for their liege.

"And near him stood the Lady of the Lake.
Who knows a subtler magic than his own—
Clothed in white samite, mystic, wonderful.
She gave the King his huge cross-hilted sword,
Whereby to drive the heathen out. A mist
Of incense curl'd about her, and her face
Wellnigh was hidden in the minster gloom;
But there was heard among the holy hymns
A voice as of the waters, for she dwells
Down in a deep—calm, whatsoever storms
May shake the world—and when the surface rolls,
Hath power to walk the waters like our Lord.

"There likewise I beheld Excalibur
Before him at his crowning borne, the sword
That rose from out the bosom of the lake,
And Arthur row'd across and took it—rich
With jewels, elfin Urim, on the hilt,
Bewildering heart and eye—the blade so bright

That men are blinded by it—on one side,
Graven in the oldest tongue of all this world,
'Take me,' but turn the blade and ye shall see,
And written in the speech ye speak yourself,
'Cast me away!' And sad was Arthur's face
Taking it, but old Merlin counsell'd him,
'Take thou and strike! the time to cast away
Is yet far-off.' So this great brand the King
Took, and by this will beat his foemen down."

Thereat Leodogran rejoiced, but thought
To sift his doubtings to the last, and ask'd,
Fixing full eyes of question on her face,
"The swallow and the swift are near akin,
But thou art closer to this noble prince,
Being his own dear sister," and she said,
"Daughter of Gorloïs and Ygerne am I;"
"And therefore Arthur's sister?" ask'd the King.
She answer'd, "These be secret things," and sign'd
To those two sons to pass, and let them be.
And Gawain went, and breaking into song
Sprang out, and follow'd by his flying hair
Ran like a colt, and leapt at all he saw;
But Modred laid his ear beside the doors,
And there half-heard—the same that afterward
Struck for the throne, and striking found his doom.

And then the Queen made answer: "What know I?
For dark my mother was in eyes and hair,
And dark in hair and eyes am I; and dark
Was Gorloïs; yea, and dark was Uther too,
Wellnigh to blackness; but this king is fair
Beyond the race of Britons and of men.
Moreover, always in my mind I hear
A cry from out the dawning of my life,
A mother weeping, and I hear her say,
'O that ye had some brother, pretty one,
To guard thee on the rough ways of the world.'"

"Ay," said the King, "and hear ye such a cry?
But when did Arthur chance upon thee first?"

"O King!" she cried, "and I will tell thee true.
He found me first when yet a little maid.
Beaten I had been for a little fault
Whereof I was not guilty; and out I ran
And flung myself down on a bank of heath,
And hated this fair world and all therein,

And wept, and wish'd that I were dead; and he—
I know not whether of himself he came,
Or brought by Merlin, who, they say, can walk
Unseen at pleasure—he was at my side,
And spake sweet words, and comforted my heart,
And dried my tears, being a child with me.
And many a time he came, and evermore
As I grew greater grew with me; and sad
At times he seem'd, and sad with him was I,
Stern too at times, and then I loved him not,
But sweet again, and then I loved him well.
And now of late I see him less and less,
But those first days had golden hours for me,
For then I surely thought he would be king.

"But let me tell thee now another tale:
For Bleys, our Merlin's master, as they say,
Died but of late, and sent his cry to me,
To hear him speak before he left his life.
Shrunk like a fairy changeling lay the mage;
And when I enter'd told me that himself
And Merlin ever served about the King,
Uther, before he died; and on the night
When Uther in Tintagil past away
Moaning and wailing for an heir, the two
Left the still king, and passing forth to breathe,
Then from the castle gateway by the chasm
Descending thro' the dismal night—a night
In which the bounds of heaven and earth were lost—
Beheld, so high upon the dreary deeps
It seem'd in heaven, a ship, the shape thereof
A dragon wing'd, and all from stem to stern
Bright with a shining people on the decks,
And gone as soon as seen. And then the two
Dropt to the cove, and watch'd the great sea fall,
Wave after wave, each mightier than the last,
Till last, a ninth one, gathering half the deep
And full of voices, slowly rose and plunged
Roaring, and all the wave was in a flame;
And down the wave and in the flame was borne
A naked babe, and rode to Merlin's feet,
Who stoopt and caught the babe, and cried, 'The King!
Here is an heir for Uther!' And the fringe
Of that great breaker, sweeping up the strand,
Lash'd at the wizard as he spake the word,
And all at once all round him rose in fire,

So that the child and he were clothed in fire.
And presently thereafter follow'd calm,
Free sky and stars. 'And this same child,' he said,
'Is he who reigns; nor could I part in peace
Till this were told.' And saying this the seer
Went thro' the strait and dreadful pass of death,
Not ever to be question'd any more
Save on the further side; but when I met
Merlin, and ask'd him if these things were truth—
The shining dragon and the naked child
Descending in the glory of the seas—
He laugh'd as is his wont, and answer'd me
In riddling triplets of old time, and said:—

    " 'Rain, rain, and sun! a rainbow in the sky!
A young man will be wiser by and by;
An old man's wit may wander ere he die.

    " 'Rain, rain, and sun! a rainbow on the lea!
And truth is this to me, and that to thee;
And truth or clothed or naked let it be.

    " 'Rain, sun, and rain! and the free blossom blows;
Sun, rain, and sun! and where is he who knows?
From the great deep to the great deep he goes.'

    "So Merlin riddling anger'd me; but thou
Fear not to give this King thine only child,
Guinevere; so great bards of him will sing
Hereafter; and dark sayings from of old
Ranging and ringing thro' the minds of men,
And echo'd by old folk beside their fires
For comfort after their wage-work is done,
Speak of the King; and Merlin in our time
Hath spoken also, not in jest, and sworn
Tho' men may wound him that he will not die,
But pass, again to come, and then or now
Utterly smite the heathen underfoot,
Till these and all men hail him for their king."

    She spake and King Leodogran rejoiced,
But musing "Shall I answer yea or nay?"
Doubted, and drowsed, nodded and slept, and saw,
Dreaming, a slope of land that ever grew,
Field after field, up to a height, the peak
Haze-hidden, and thereon a phantom king,
Now looming, and now lost; and on the slope
The sword rose, the hind fell, the herd was driven,
Fire glimpsed; and all the land from roof and rick,

In drifts of smoke before a rolling wind,
Stream'd to the peak, and mingled with the haze
And made it thicker; while the phantom king
Sent out at times a voice; and here or there
Stood one who pointed toward the voice, the rest
Slew on and burnt, crying, "No king of ours,
No son of Uther, and no king of ours;"
Till with a wink his dream was changed, the haze
Descended, and the solid earth became
As nothing, but the King stood out in heaven,
Crown'd. And Leodogran awoke, and sent
Ulfius, and Brastias, and Bedivere,
Back to the court of Arthur answering yea.

Then Arthur charged his warrior whom he loved
And honor'd most, Sir Lancelot, to ride forth
And bring the Queen, and watch'd him from the gates;
And Lancelot past away among the flowers—
For then was latter April—and return'd
Among the flowers, in May, with Guinevere.
To whom arrived, by Dubric the high saint,
Chief of the church in Britain, and before
The stateliest of her altar-shrines, the King
That morn was married, while in stainless white,
The fair beginners of a nobler time,
And glorying in their vows and him, his knights
Stood round him, and rejoicing in his joy.
Far shone the fields of May thro' open door,
The sacred altar blossom'd white with May,
The sun of May descended on their King,
They gazed on all earth's beauty in their Queen,
Roll'd incense, and there past along the hymns
A voice as of the waters, while the two
Sware at the shrine of Christ a deathless love.
And Arthur said, "Behold, thy doom is mine.
Let chance what will, I love thee to the death!"
To whom the Queen replied with drooping eyes,
"King and my lord, I love thee to the death!"
And holy Dubric spread his hands and spake:
"Reign ye, and live and love, and make the world
Other, and may thy Queen be one with thee,
And all this Order of thy Table Round
Fulfil the boundless purpose of their King!"

So Dubric said; but when they left the shrine
Great lords from Rome before the portal stood.
In scornful stillness gazing as they past;

Then while they paced a city all on fire
With sun and cloth of gold, the trumpets blew,
And Arthur's knighthood sang before the King:—

"Blow trumpet, for the world is white with May!
Blow trumpet, the long night hath roll'd away!
Blow thro' the living world—'Let the King reign!'

"Shall Rome or Heathen rule in Arthur's realm?
Flash brand and lance, fall battle-axe upon helm,
Fall battle-axe, and flash brand! Let the King reign!

"Strike for the King and live! his knights have heard
That God hath told the King a secret word.
Fall battle-axe, and flash brand! Let the King reign!

"Blow trumpet! he will lift us from the dust.
Blow trumpet! live the strength, and die the lust!
Clang battle-axe, and clash brand! Let the King reign!

"Strike for the King and die! and if thou diest,
The King is king, and ever wills the highest.
Clang battle-axe, and clash brand! Let the King reign!

"Blow, for our Sun is mighty in his May!
Blow, for our Sun is mightier day by day!
Clang battle-axe, and clash brand! Let the King reign!

"The King will follow Christ, and we the King,
In whom high God hath breathed a secret thing.
Fall battle-axe, and clash brand! Let the King reign!"

So sang the knighthood, moving to their hall.
There at the banquet those great lords from Rome,
The slowly-fading mistress of the world,
Strode in and claim'd their tribute as of yore.
But Arthur spake: "Behold, for these have sworn
To wage my wars, and worship me their King;
The old order changeth, yielding place to new,
And we that fight for our fair father Christ,
Seeing that ye be grown too weak and old
To drive the heathen from your Roman wall,
No tribute will we pay." So those great lords
Drew back in wrath, and Arthur strove with Rome.

And Arthur and his knighthood for a space
Were all one will, and thro' that strength the King
Drew in the petty princedoms under him,
Fought, and in twelve great battles overcame
The heathen hordes, and made a realm and reign'd.

The Round Table

GARETH AND LYNETTE
THE MARRIAGE OF GERAINT
GERAINT AND ENID
BALIN AND BALAN
MERLIN AND VIVIEN

LANCELOT AND ELAINE
THE HOLY GRAIL
PELLEAS AND ETTARRE
THE LAST TOURNAMENT
GUINEVERE

✠✠✠✠ GARETH AND LYNETTE ✠✠✠✠

THE last tall son of Lot and Bellicent,
And tallest, Gareth, in a showerful spring
Stared at the spate. A slender-shafted pine
Lost footing, fell, and so was whirl'd away.
"How he went down," said Gareth, "as a false knight
Or evil king before my lance, if lance
Were mine to use—O senseless cataract,
Bearing all down in thy precipitancy—
And yet thou art but swollen with cold snows
And mine is living blood. Thou dost His will,
The Maker's, and not knowest, and I that know,
Have strength and wit, in my good mother's hall
Linger with vacillating obedience,
Prison'd, and kept and coax'd and whistled to—
Since the good mother holds me still a child!
Good mother is bad mother unto me!
A worse were better; yet no worse would I.
Heaven yield her for it, but in me put force
To weary her ears with one continuous prayer,
Until she let me fly discaged to sweep
In ever-highering eagle-circles up
To the great Sun of Glory, and thence swoop

Down upon all things base, and dash them dead,
A knight of Arthur, working out his will,
To cleanse the world. Why, Gawain, when he came
With Modred hither in the summertime,
Ask'd me to tilt with him, the proven knight.
Modred for want of worthier was the judge.
Then I so shook him in the saddle, he said,
'Thou hast half prevail'd against me,' said so—he—
Tho' Modred biting his thin lips was mute,
For he is always sullen—what care I?"

And Gareth went, and hovering round her chair
Ask'd, "Mother, tho' ye count me still the child,
Sweet mother, do ye love the child?" She laughed,
"Thou art but a wild-goose to question it."
"Then, mother, an ye love the child," he said,
"Being a goose and rather tame than wild,
Hear the child's story." "Yea, my well-beloved,
An 't were but of the goose and golden eggs."

And Gareth answer'd her with kindling eyes:
"Nay, nay, good mother, but this egg of mine
Was finer gold than any goose can lay;
For this is an eagle, a royal eagle, laid
Almost beyond eye-reach, on such a palm
As glitters gilded in thy Book of Hours.
And there was ever haunting round the palm
A lusty youth, but poor, who often saw
The splendor sparkling from aloft, and thought,
'An I could climb and lay my hand upon it,
Then were I wealthier than a leash of kings.'
But ever when he reach'd a hand to climb,
One that had loved him from his childhood caught
And stay'd him, 'Climb not lest thou break thy neck,
I charge thee by my love,' and so the boy,
Sweet mother, neither clomb nor brake his neck,
But brake his very heart in pining for it,
And past away."

              To whom the mother said,
"True love, sweet son, had risk'd himself and climb'd,
And handed down the golden treasure to him."

And Gareth answer'd her with kindling eyes:
"Gold? said I gold?—ay then, why he, or she,
Or whosoe'er it was, or half the world
Had ventured—had the thing I spake of been

Mere gold—but this was all of that true steel
Whereof they forged the brand Excalibur,
And lightnings play'd about it in the storm,
And all the little fowl were flurried at it,
And there were cries and clashings in the nest,
That sent him from his senses. Let me go."

Then Bellicent bemoan'd herself and said:
"Hast thou no pity upon my loneliness?
Lo, where thy father Lot beside the hearth
Lies like a log, and all but smoulder'd out!
For ever since when traitor to the King
He fought against him in the barons' war,
And Arthur gave him back his territory,
His age hath slowly droopt, and now lies there
A yet-warm corpse, and yet unburiable,
No more; nor sees, nor hears, nor speaks, nor knows.
And both thy brethren are in Arthur's hall,
Albeit neither loved with that full love
I feel for thee, nor worthy such a love.
Stay therefore thou; red berries charm the bird,
And thee, mine innocent, the jousts, the wars,
Who never knewest finger-ache, nor pang
Of wrench'd or broken limb—an often chance
In those brain-stunning shocks, and tourney-falls,
Frights to my heart. But stay; follow the deer
By these tall firs and our fast-falling burns;
So make thy manhood mightier day by day.
Sweet is the chase; and I will seek thee out
Some comfortable bride and fair, to grace
Thy climbing life, and cherish my prone year,
Till falling into Lot's forgetfulness
I know not thee, myself, nor anything.
Stay, my best son! ye are yet more boy than man."

Then Gareth: "An ye hold me yet for child,
Hear yet once more the story of the child.
For, mother, there was once a king, like ours.
The prince his heir, when tall and marriageable,
Ask'd for a bride; and thereupon the king
Set two before him. One was fair, strong, arm'd—
But to be won by force—and many men
Desired her; one, good lack, no man desired.
And these were the conditions of the King:
That save he won the first by force, he needs
Must wed that other, whom no man desired,
A red-faced bride who knew herself so vile

That evermore she long'd to hide herself,
Nor fronted man or woman, eye to eye—
Yea—some she cleaved to, but they died of her.
And one—they call'd her Fame; and one—O mother,
How can ye keep me tether'd to you?—Shame.
Man am I grown, a man's work must I do.
Follow the deer? follow the Christ, the King,
Live pure, speak true, right wrong, follow the King—
Else, wherefore born?"

        To whom the mother said:
"Sweet son, for there be many who deem him not,
Or will not deem him, wholly proven king—
Albeit in mine own heart I knew him King
When I was frequent with him in my youth,
And heard him kingly speak, and doubted him
No more than he, himself; but felt him mine,
Of closest kin to me. Yet—wilt thou leave
Thine easeful biding here, and risk thine all,
Life, limbs, for one that is not proven king?
Stay, till the cloud that settles round his birth
Hath lifted but a little. Stay, sweet son."

    And Gareth answer'd quickly: "Not an hour,
So that ye yield me—I will walk thro' fire,
Mother, to gain it—your full leave to go.
Not proven, who swept the dust of ruin'd Rome
From off the threshold of the realm, and crush'd
The idolaters, and made the people free?
Who should be king save him who makes us free?"

    So when the Queen, who long had sought in vain
To break him from intent to which he grew,
Found her son's will unwaveringly one,
She answer'd craftily: "Will ye walk thro' fire?
Who walks thro' fire will hardly heed the smoke.
Ay, go then, an ye must; only one proof,
Before thou ask the King to make thee knight,
Of thine obedience and thy love to me,
Thy mother,—I demand."

        And Gareth cried:
"A hard one, or a hundred, so I go.
Nay—quick! the proof to prove me to the quick!"

    But slowly spake the mother looking at him:
"Prince, thou shalt go disguised to Arthur's hall,
And hire thyself to serve for meats and drinks

Among the scullions and the kitchen-knaves,
And those that hand the dish across the bar.
Nor shalt thou tell thy name to any one.
And thou shalt serve a twelvemonth and a day."

For so the Queen believed that when her son
Beheld his only way to glory lead
Low down thro' villain kitchen-vassalage,
Her own true Gareth was too princely-proud
To pass thereby; so should he rest with her,
Closed in her castle from the sound of arms.

Silent awhile was Gareth, then replied:
"The thrall in person may be free in soul,
And I shall see the jousts. Thy son am I,
And, since thou art my mother, must obey.
I therefore yield me freely to thy will;
For hence will I, disguised, and hire myself
To serve with scullions and with kitchen-knaves;
Nor tell my name to any—no, not the King."

Gareth awhile linger'd. The mother's eye
Full of wistful fear that he would go,
And turning toward him wheresoe'er he turn'd,
Perplext his outward purpose, till an hour
When, waken'd by the wind which with full voice
Swept bellowing thro' the darkness on to dawn,
He rose, and out of slumber calling two
That still had tended on him from his birth,
Before the wakeful mother heard him, went.

The three were clad like tillers of the soil.
Southward they set their faces. The birds made
Melody on branch and melody in mid air.
The damp hill-slopes were quicken'd into green,
And the live green had kindled into flowers,
For it was past the time of Easter-day.

So, when their feet were planted on the plain
That broaden'd toward the base of Camelot,
Far off they saw the silver-misty morn
Rolling her smoke about the royal mount,
That rose between the forest and the field.
At times the summit of the high city flash'd;
At times the spires and turrets halfway down
Prick'd thro' the mist; at times the great gate shone
Only, that open'd on the field below;
Anon, the whole fair city had disappear'd.

Then those who went with Gareth were amazed,
One crying, "Let us go no further, lord;
Here is a city of enchanters, built
By fairy kings." The second echo'd him,
"Lord, we have heard from our wise man at home
To northward, that this king is not the King,
But only changeling out of Fairyland,
Who drave the heathen hence by sorcery
And Merlin's glamour." Then the first again,
"Lord, there is no such city anywhere,
But all a vision."

          Gareth answer'd them
With laughter, swearing he had glamour enow
In his own blood, his princedom, youth, and hopes,
To plunge old Merlin in the Arabian sea;
So push'd them all unwilling toward the gate.
And there was no gate like it under heaven.
For barefoot on the keystone, which was lined
And rippled like an ever-fleeting wave,
The Lady of the Lake stood; all her dress
Wept from her sides as water flowing away;
But like the cross her great and goodly arms
Stretch'd under all the cornice and upheld.
And drops of water fell from either hand;
And down from one a sword was hung, from one
A censer, either worn with wind and storm;
And o'er her breast floated the sacred fish;
And in the space to left of her, and right,
Were Arthur's wars in weird devices done,
New things and old co-twisted, as if Time
Were nothing, so inveterately that men
Were giddy gazing there; and over all
High on the top were those three queens, the friends
Of Arthur, who should help him at his need.

Then those with Gareth for so long a space
Stared at the figures that at last it seem'd
The dragon-boughts and elvish emblemings
Began to move, seethe, twine, and curl. They call'd
To Gareth, "Lord, the gateway is alive."

And Gareth likewise on them fixt his eyes
So long that even to him they seem'd to move.
Out of the city a blast of music peal'd.
Back from the gate started the three, to whom
From out thereunder came an ancient man,
Long-bearded, saying, "Who be ye, my sons?"

Then Gareth: "We be tillers of the soil,
Who leaving share in furrow come to see
The glories of our King; but these, my men,—
Your city moved so weirdly in the mist—
Doubt if the King be king at all, or come
From Fairyland; and whether this be built
By magic, and by fairy kings and queens;
Or whether there be any city at all,
Or all a vision; and this music now
Hath scared them both, but tell thou these the truth."

Then that old Seer made answer, playing on him
And saying: "Son, I have seen the good ship sail
Keel upward, and mast downward, in the heavens,
And solid turrets topsy-turvy in air;
And here is truth, but an it please thee not,
Take thou the truth as thou hast told it me.
For truly, as thou sayest, a fairy king
And fairy queens have built the city, son;
They came from out a sacred mountain-cleft
Toward the sunrise, each with harp in hand,
And built it to the music of their harps.
And, as thou sayest, it is enchanted, son,
For there is nothing in it as it seems
Saving the King; tho' some there be that hold
The King a shadow, and the city real.
Yet take thou heed of him, for, so thou pass
Beneath this archway, then wilt thou become
A thrall to his enchantments, for the King
Will bind thee by such vows as is a shame
A man should not be bound by, yet the which
No man can keep; but, so thou dread to swear,
Pass not beneath this gateway, but abide
Without, among the cattle of the field.
For an ye heard a music, like enow
They are building still, seeing the city is built
To music, therefore never built at all,
And therefore built for ever."

Gareth spake
Anger'd: "Old master, reverence thine own beard
That looks as white as utter truth, and seems
Wellnigh as long as thou art statured tall!
Why mockest thou the stranger that hath been
To thee fair-spoken?"

But the Seer replied:
"Know ye not then the Riddling of the Bards:
'Confusion, and illusion, and relation,
Elusion, and occasion, and evasion'?
I mock thee not but as thou mockest me,
And all that see thee, for thou art not who
Thou seemest, but I know thee who thou art.
And now thou goest up to mock the King,
Who cannot brook the shadow of any lie."

Unmockingly the mocker ending here
Turn'd to the right, and past along the plain;
Whom Gareth looking after said: "My men,
Our one white lie sits like a little ghost
Here on the threshold of our enterprise.
Let love be blamed for it, not she, nor I.
Well, we will make amends."

          With all good cheer
He spake and laugh'd, then enter'd with his twain
Camelot, a city of shadowy palaces
And stately, rich in emblem and the work
Of ancient kings who did their days in stone;
Which Merlin's hand, the Mage at Arthur's court,
Knowing all arts, had touch'd, and everywhere,
At Arthur's ordinance, tipt with lessening peak
And pinnacle, and had made it spire to heaven.
And ever and anon a knight would pass
Outward, or inward to the hall; his arms
Clash'd, and the sound was good to Gareth's ear.
And out of bower and casement shyly glanced
Eyes of pure women, wholesome stars of love;
And all about a healthful people stept
As in the presence of a gracious king.

Then into hall Gareth ascending heard
A voice, the voice of Arthur, and beheld
Far over heads in that long-vaulted hall
The splendor of the presence of the King
Throned, and delivering doom—and look'd no more—
But felt his young heart hammering in his ears,
And thought, "For this half-shadow of a lie
The truthful King will doom me when I speak."
Yet pressing on, tho' all in fear to find
Sir Gawain or Sir Modred, saw nor one
Nor other, but in all the listening eyes
Of those tall knights that ranged about the throne

Clear honor shining like the dewy star
Of dawn, and faith in their great King, with pure
Affection, and the light of victory,
And glory gain'd, and evermore to gain.

Then came a widow crying to the King:
"A boon, Sir King! Thy father, Uther, reft
From my dead lord a field with violence;
For howsoe'er at first he proffer'd gold,
Yet, for the field was pleasant in our eyes,
We yielded not; and then he reft us of it
Perforce and left us neither gold nor field."

Said Arthur, "Whether would ye, gold or field?"
To whom the woman weeping, "Nay, my lord,
The field was pleasant in my husband's eye."

And Arthur: "Have thy pleasant field again,
And thrice the gold for Uther's use thereof,
According to the years. No boon is here,
But justice, so thy say be proven true.
Accursed, who from the wrongs his father did
Would shape himself a right!"

And while she past,
Came yet another widow crying to him:
"A boon, Sir King! Thine enemy, King, am I.
With thine own hand thou slewest my dear lord,
A knight of Uther in the barons' war,
When Lot and many another rose and fought
Against thee, saying thou wert basely born.
I held with these, and loathe to ask thee aught.
Yet lo! my husband's brother had my son
Thrall'd in his castle, and hath starved him dead.
And standeth seized of that inheritance
Which thou that slewest the sire hast left the son.
So, tho' I scarce can ask it thee for hate,
Grant me some knight to do the battle for me,
Kill the foul thief, and wreak me for my son."

Then strode a good knight forward, crying to him,
"A boon, Sir King! I am her kinsman, I.
Give me to right her wrong, and slay the man."

Then came Sir Kay, the seneschal, and cried,
"A boon, Sir King! even that thou grant her none,
This railer, that hath mock'd thee in full hall—
None; or the wholesome boon of gyve and gag."

But Arthur: "We sit King, to help the wrong'd
Thro' all our realm. The woman loves her lord.
Peace to thee, woman, with thy loves and hates!
The kings of old had doom'd thee to the flames;
Aurelius Emrys would have scourged thee dead,
And Uther slit thy tongue; but get thee hence—
Lest that rough humor of the kings of old
Return upon me! Thou that art her kin,
Go likewise; lay him low and slay him not,
But bring him here, that I may judge the right,
According to the justice of the King.
Then, be he guilty, by that deathless King
Who lived and died for men, the man shall die."

Then came in hall the messenger of Mark,
A name of evil savor in the land,
The Cornish king. In either hand he bore
What dazzled all, and shone far-off as shines
A field of charlock in the sudden sun
Between two showers, a cloth of palest gold,
Which down he laid before the throne, and knelt,
Delivering that his lord, the vassal king,
Was even upon his way to Camelot;
For having heard that Arthur of his grace
Had made his goodly cousin Tristram knight,
And, for himself was of the greater state,
Being a king, he trusted his liege-lord
Would yield him this large honor all the more;
So pray'd him well to accept this cloth of gold,
In token of true heart and fealty.

Then Arthur cried to rend the cloth, to rend
In pieces, and so cast it on the hearth.
An oak-tree smoulder'd there. "The goodly knight!
What! shall the shield of Mark stand among these?"
For, midway down the side of that long hall,
A stately pile,—whereof along the front,
Some blazon'd, some but carven, and some blank,
There ran a treble range of stony shields,—
Rose, and high-arching overbrow'd the hearth.
And under every shield a knight was named.
For this was Arthur's custom in his hall:
When some good knight had done one noble deed,
His arms were carven only; but if twain,
His arms were blazon'd also; but if none,
The shield was blank and bare, without a sign
Saving the name beneath. And Gareth saw

The shield of Gawain blazon'd rich and bright,
And Modred's blank as death; and Arthur cried
To rend the cloth and cast it on the hearth.

"More like are we to reave him of his crown
Than make him knight because men call him king.
The kings we found, ye know we stay'd their hands
From war among themselves, but left them kings;
Of whom were any bounteous, merciful,
Truth-speaking, brave, good livers, them we enroll'd
Among us, and they sit within our hall.
But Mark hath tarnish'd the great name of king,
As Mark would sully the low state of churl;
And, seeing he hath sent us cloth of gold,
Return, and meet, and hold him from our eyes,
Lest we should lap him up in cloth of lead,
Silenced for ever—craven—a man of plots,
Craft, poisonous counsels, wayside ambushings—
No fault of thine; let Kay the seneschal
Look to thy wants, and send thee satisfied—
Accursed, who strikes nor lets the hand be seen!"

And many another suppliant crying came
With noise of ravage wrought by beast and man,
And evermore a knight would ride away.

Last, Gareth leaning both hands heavily
Down on the shoulders of the twain, his men,
Approach'd between them toward the King, and ask'd,
"A boon, Sir King,"—his voice was all ashamed,—
"For see ye not how weak and hunger worn
I seem—leaning on these? grant me to serve
For meat and drink among thy kitchen-knaves
A twelvemonth and a day, nor seek my name.
Hereafter I will fight."

                    To him the King:
"A goodly youth and worth a goodlier boon!
But so thou wilt no goodlier, then must Kay,
The master of the meats and drinks, be thine."

He rose and past; then Kay, a man of mien
Wan-sallow as the plant that feels itself
Root-bitten by white lichen:

                    "Lo, ye now!
This fellow hath broken from some abbey, where,
God wot, he had not beef and brewis enow,

However that might chance! but an he work,
Like any pigeon will I cram his crop,
And sleeker shall he shine than any hog."

Then Lancelot standing near: "Sir Seneschal,
Sleuth-hound thou knowest, and gray, and all the hounds;
A horse thou knowest, a man thou dost not know.
Broad brows and fair, a fluent hair and fine,
High nose, a nostril large and fine, and hands
Large, fair, and fine!—Some young lad's mystery—
But, or from sheepcot or king's hall, the boy
Is noble-natured. Treat him with all grace,
Lest he should come to shame thy judging of him."

Then Kay: "What murmurest thou of mystery?
Think ye this fellow will poison the King's dish?
Nay, for he spake too fool-like—mystery!
Tut, an the lad were noble, he had ask'd
For horse and armor. Fair and fine, forsooth!
Sir Fine-face, Sir Fair-hands? but see thou to it
That thine own fineness, Lancelot, some fine day
Undo thee not—and leave my man to me."

So Gareth all for glory underwent
The sooty yoke of kitchen-vassalage,
Ate with young lads his portion by the door,
And couch'd at night with grimy kitchen-knaves.
And Lancelot ever spake him pleasantly,
But Kay the seneschal, who loved him not,
Would hustle and harry him, and labor him
Beyond his comrades of the hearth, and set
To turn the broach, draw water, or hew wood,
Or grosser tasks; and Gareth bow'd himself
With all obedience to the King, and wrought
All kind of service with a noble ease
That graced the lowliest act in doing it.
And when the thralls had talk among themselves,
And one would praise the love that linkt the King
And Lancelot—how the King had saved his life
In battle twice, and Lancelot once the King's—
For Lancelot was first in the tournament,
But Arthur mightiest on the battlefield—
Gareth was glad. Or if some other told
How once the wandering forester at dawn,
Far over the blue tarns and hazy seas,
On Caer-Eryri's highest found the King,
A naked babe, of whom the Prophet spake,

"He passes to the Isle Avilion,
He passes and is heal'd and cannot die"—
Gareth was glad. But if their talk were foul,
Then would he whistle rapid as any lark,
Or carol some old roundelay, and so loud
That first they mock'd, but, after, reverenced him.
Or Gareth, telling some prodigious tale
Of knights who sliced a red life-bubbling way
Thro' twenty folds of twisted dragon, held
All in a gap-mouth'd circle his good mates
Lying or sitting round him, idle hands,
Charm'd; till Sir Kay, the seneschal, would come
Blustering upon them, like a sudden wind
Among dead leaves, and drive them all apart.
Or when the thralls had sport among themselves,
So there were any trial of mastery,
He, by two yards in casting bar or stone,
Was counted best; and if there chanced a joust,
So that Sir Kay nodded him leave to go,
Would hurry thither, and when he saw the knights
Clash like the coming and retiring wave,
And the spear spring, and good horse reel, the boy
Was half beyond himself for ecstasy.

So for a month he wrought among the thralls;
But in the weeks that follow'd the good Queen,
Repentant of the word she made him swear,
And saddening in her childless castle, sent,
Between the in-crescent and de-crescent moon,
Arms for her son, and loosed him from his vow.

This, Gareth hearing from a squire of Lot
With whom he used to play at tourney once,
When both were children, and in lonely haunts
Would scratch a ragged oval on the sand,
And each at either dash from either end—
Shame never made girl redder than Gareth joy.
He laugh'd, he sprang. "Out of the smoke, at once
I leap from Satan's foot to Peter's knee—
These news be mine, none other's—nay, the King's—
Descend into the city;" whereon he sought
The King alone, and found, and told him all.

"I have stagger'd thy strong Gawain in a tilt
For pastime; yea, he said it; joust can I.
Make me thy knight—in secret! let my name

Be hidden, and give me the first quest, I spring
Like flame from ashes."

                    Here the King's calm eye
Fell on, and check'd, and made him flush, and bow
Lowly, to kiss his hand, who answer'd him:
"Son, the good mother let me know thee here,
And sent her wish that I would yield thee thine.
Make thee my knight? my knights are sworn to vows
Of utter hardihood, utter gentleness,
And, loving, utter faithfulness in love,
And uttermost obedience to the King."

    Then Gareth, lightly springing from his knees:
"My King, for hardihood I can promise thee.
For uttermost obedience make demand
Of whom ye gave me to, the seneschal,
No mellow master of the meats and drinks!
And as for love, God wot, I love not yet,
But love I shall, God willing."

                    And the King:
"Make thee my knight in secret? yea, but he,
Our noblest brother, and our truest man,
And one with me in all, he needs must know."

    "Let Lancelot know, my King, let Lancelot know,
Thy noblest and thy truest!"

                    And the King:
"But wherefore would ye men should wonder at you?
Nay, rather for the sake of me, their King,
And the deed's sake my knighthood do the deed,
Than to be noised of."

                    Merrily Gareth ask'd:
"Have I not earn'd my cake in baking of it?
Let be my name until I make my name!
My deeds will speak; it is but for a day."
So with a kindly hand on Gareth's arm
Smiled the great King, and half-unwillingly
Loving his lusty youthhood yielded to him.
Then, after summoning Lancelot privily:
"I have given him the first quest; he is not proven.
Look therefore, when he calls for this in hall,
Thou get to horse and follow him far away.

Cover the lions on thy shield, and see,
Far as thou mayest, he be nor ta'en nor slain."

Then that same day there past into the hall
A damsel of high lineage, and a brow
May-blossom, and a cheek of apple-blossom,
Hawk-eyes; and lightly was her slender nose
Tip-tilted like the petal of a flower.
She into hall past with her page and cried:

"O King, for thou hast driven the foe without,
See to the foe within! bridge, ford, beset
By bandits, every one that owns a tower
The lord for half a league. Why sit ye there?
Rest would I not, Sir King, an I were king,
Till even the lonest hold were all as free
From cursed bloodshed as thine altar-cloth
From that best blood it is a sin to spill."

"Comfort thyself," said Arthur, "I nor mine
Rest; so my knighthood keep the vows they swore,
The wastest moorland of our realm shall be
Safe, damsel, as the centre of this hall.
What is thy name? thy need?"

                              "My name?" she said—
"Lynette, my name; noble; my need, a knight
To combat for my sister, Lyonors,
A lady of high lineage, of great lands,
And comely, yea, and comelier than myself.
She lives in Castle Perilous. A river
Runs in three loops about her living-place;
And o'er it are three passings, and three knights
Defend the passings, brethren, and a fourth,
And of that four the mightiest, holds her stay'd
In her own castle, and so besieges her
To break her will, and make her wed with him;
And but delays his purport till thou send
To do the battle with him thy chief man
Sir Lancelot, whom he trusts to overthrow,
Then wed, with glory; but she will not wed
Save whom she loveth, or a holy life.
Now therefore have I come for Lancelot."

Then Arthur mindful of Sir Gareth ask'd:
"Damsel, ye know this Order lives to crush
All wrongers of the realm. But say, these four,
Who be they? What the fashion of the men?"

"They be of foolish fashion, O Sir King,
The fashion of that old knight-errantry
Who ride abroad, and do but what they will;
Courteous or bestial from the moment, such
As have nor law nor king; and three of these
Proud in their fantasy call themselves the Day,
Morning-Star, and Noon-Sun, and Evening-Star,
Being strong fools; and never a whit more wise
The fourth, who alway rideth arm'd in black,
A huge man-beast of boundless savagery.
He names himself the Night and oftener Death;
And wears a helmet mounted with a skull,
And bears a skeleton figured on his arms,
To show that who may slay or scape the three,
Slain by himself, shall enter endless night.
And all these four be fools, but mighty men,
And therefore am I come for Lancelot."

Hereat Sir Gareth call'd from where he rose,
A head with kindling eyes above the throng,
"A boon, Sir King—this quest!" then—for he mark'd
Kay near him groaning like a wounded bull—
"Yea, King, thou knowest thy kitchen-knave am I,
And mighty thro' thy meats and drinks am I,
And I can topple over a hundred such.
Thy promise, King," and Arthur glancing at him,
Brought down a momentary brow. "Rough, sudden,
And pardonable, worthy to be knight—
Go therefore," and all hearers were amazed.

But on the damsel's forehead shame, pride, wrath
Slew the may-white. She lifted either arm,
"Fie on thee, King! I ask'd for thy chief knight,
And thou hast given me but a kitchen-knave."
Then ere a man in hall could stay her, turn'd,
Fled down the lane of access to the King,
Took horse, descended the slope street, and past
The weird white gate, and paused without, beside
The field of tourney, murmuring "kitchen-knave!"

Now two great entries open'd from the hall,
At one end one that gave upon a range
Of level pavement where the King would pace
At sunrise, gazing over plain and wood;
And down from this a lordly stairway sloped
Till lost in blowing trees and tops of towers;
And out by this main doorway past the King.

But one was counter to the hearth, and rose
High that the highest-crested helm could ride
Therethro' nor graze; and by this entry fled
The damsel in her wrath, and on to this
Sir Gareth strode, and saw without the door
King Arthur's gift, the worth of half a town,
A war-horse of the best, and near it stood
The two that out of north had follow'd him.
This bare a maiden shield, a casque; that held
The horse, the spear; whereat Sir Gareth loosed
A cloak that dropt from collar-bone to heel,
A cloth of roughest web, and cast it down,
And from it, like a fuel-smother'd fire
That lookt half-dead, brake bright, and flash'd as those
Dull-coated things, that making slide apart
Their dusk wing-cases, all beneath there burns
A jewell'd harness, ere they pass and fly.
So Gareth ere he parted flash'd in arms.
Then as he donn'd the helm, and took the shield
And mounted horse and graspt a spear, of grain
Storm-strengthen'd on a windy site, and tipt
With trenchant steel, around him slowly prest
The people, while from out of kitchen came
The thralls in throng, and seeing who had work'd
Lustier than any, and whom they could but love,
Mounted in arms, threw up their caps and cried,
"God bless the King, and all his fellowship!"
And on thro' lanes of shouting Gareth rode
Down the slope street, and past without the gate.

    So Gareth past with joy; but as the cur
Pluckt from the cur he fights with, ere his cause
Be cool'd by fighting, follows, being
His owner, but remembers all, and growls
Remembering, so Sir Kay beside the door
Mutter'd in scorn of Gareth whom he used
To harry and hustle.

                        "Bound upon a quest
With horse and arms—the king hath past his time—
My scullion knave! Thralls, to your work again,
For an your fire be low ye kindle mine!
Will there be dawn in West and eve in East?
Begone!—my knave!—belike and like enow
Some old head-blow not heeded in his youth
So shook his wits they wander in his prime—
Crazed! How the villain lifted up his voice,

Nor shamed to bawl himself a kitchen-knave!
Tut, he was tame and meek enow with me,
Till peacock'd up with Lancelot's noticing.
Well—I will after my loud knave, and learn
Whether he know me for his master yet.
Out of the smoke he came, and so my lance
Hold, by God's grace, he shall into the mire—
Thence, if the King awaken from his craze,
Into the smoke again."

                    But Lancelot said:
"Kay, wherefore wilt thou go against the King,
For that did never he whereon ye rail,
But ever meekly served the King in thee?
Abide; take counsel, for this lad is great
And lusty, and knowing both of lance and sword."
"Tut, tell not me," said Kay, "ye are overfine
To mar stout knaves with foolish courtesies;"
Then mounted, on thro' silent faces rode
Down the slope city, and out beyond the gate.

    But by the field of tourney lingering yet
Mutter'd the damsel: "Wherefore did the King
Scorn me? for, were Sir Lancelot lackt, at least
He might have yielded to me one of those
Who tilt for lady's love and glory here,
Rather than—O sweet heaven! O, fie upon him!—
His kitchen-knave."

                    To whom Sir Gareth drew—
And there were none but few goodlier than he—
Shining in arms, "Damsel, the quest is mine.
Lead, and I follow." She thereat, as one
That smells a foul-flesh'd agaric in the holt,
And deems it carrion of some woodland thing,
Or shrew or weasel, nipt her slender nose
With petulant thumb and finger, shrilling, "Hence!
Avoid, thou smellest all of kitchen-grease.
And look who come behind;" for there was Kay.
"Knowest thou not me? thy master? I am Kay.
We lack thee by the hearth."

                    And Gareth to him,
"Master no more! too well I know thee, ay—
The most ungentle knight in Arthur's hall."
"Have at thee then," said Kay; they shock'd, and Kay
Fell shoulder-slipt, and Gareth cried again,
"Lead, and I follow," and fast away she fled.

But after sod and shingle ceased to fly
Behind her, and the heart of her good horse
Was nigh to burst with violence of the beat,
Perforce she stay'd, and overtaken spoke:

"What doest thou, scullion, in my fellowship?
Deem'st thou that I accept thee aught the more
Or love thee better, that by some device
Full cowardly, or by mere unhappiness,
Thou hast overthrown and slain thy master—thou!—
Dish-washer and broach-turner, loon!—to me
Thou smellest all of kitchen as before."

"Damsel," Sir Gareth answer'd gently, "say
Whate'er ye will, but whatsoe'er ye say,
I leave not till I finish this fair quest,
Or die therefore."

              "Ay, wilt thou finish it?
Sweet lord, how like a noble knight he talks!
The listening rogue hath caught the manner of it.
But, knave, anon thou shalt be met with, knave,
And then by such a one that thou for all
The kitchen brewis that was ever supt
Shalt not once dare to look him in the face."

"I shall assay," said Gareth with a smile
That madden'd her, and away she flash'd again
Down the long avenues of a boundless wood;
And Gareth following was again beknaved:

"Sir Kitchen-knave, I have miss'd the only way
Where Arthur's men are set along the wood;
The wood is nigh as full of thieves as leaves.
If both be slain, I am rid of thee; but yet,
Sir Scullion, canst thou use that spit of thine?
Fight, an thou canst; I have miss'd the only way."

So till the dusk that follow'd even-song
Rode on the two, reviler and reviled;
Then after one long slope was mounted, saw,
Bowl-shaped, thro' tops of many thousand pines
A gloomy-gladed hollow slowly sink
To westward—in the deeps whereof a mere,
Round as the red eye of an eagle-owl,
Under the half-dead sunset glared; and shouts
Ascended, and there brake a serving-man
Flying from out of the black wood, and crying,

"They have bound my lord to cast him in the mere."
Then Gareth, "Bound am I to right the wrong'd,
But straitlier bound am I to bide with thee."
And when the damsel spake contemptuously,
"Lead, and I follow," Gareth cried again,
"Follow, I lead!" so down among the pines
He plunged; and there, black-shadow'd nigh the mere,
And mid-thigh-deep in bulrushes and reed,
Saw six tall men haling a seventh along,
A stone about his neck to drown him in it.
Three with good blows he quieted, but three
Fled thro' the pines; and Gareth loosed the stone
From off his neck, then in the mere beside
Tumbled it; oilily bubbled up the mere.
Last, Gareth loosed his bonds and on free feet
Set him, a stalwart baron, Arthur's friend.

"Well that ye came, or else these caitiff rogues
Had wreak'd themselves on me; good cause is theirs
To hate me, for my wont hath ever been
To catch my thief, and then like vermin here
Drown him, and with a stone about his neck;
And under this wan water many of them
Lie rotting, but at night let go the stone,
And rise, and flickering in a grimly light
Dance on the mere. Good now, ye have saved a life
Worth somewhat as the cleanser of this wood.
And fain would I reward thee worshipfully.
What guerdon will ye?"

                    Gareth sharply spake:
"None! for the deed's sake have I done the deed,
In uttermost obedience to the King.
But wilt thou yield this damsel harborage?"

    Whereat the baron saying, "I well believe
You be of Arthur's Table," a light laugh
Broke from Lynette: "Ay, truly of a truth,
And in a sort, being Arthur's kitchen-knave!—
But deem not I accept thee aught the more,
Scullion, for running sharply with thy spit
Down on a rout of craven foresters.
A thresher with his flail had scatter'd them.
Nay—for thou smellest of the kitchen still.
But an this lord will yield us harborage,
Well."

So she spake. A league beyond the wood,
All in a full-fair manor and a rich,
His towers, where that day a feast had been
Held in high hall, and many a viand left,
And many a costly cate, received the three.
And there they placed a peacock in his pride
Before the damsel, and the baron set
Gareth beside her, but at once she rose.

"Meseems, that here is much discourtesy,
Setting this knave, Lord Baron, at my side.
Hear me—this morn I stood in Arthur's hall,
And pray'd the King would grant me Lancelot
To fight the brotherhood of Day and Night—
The last a monster unsubduable
Of any save of him for whom I call'd—
Suddenly bawls this frontless kitchen-knave,
'The quest is mine; thy kitchen-knave am I,
And mighty thro' thy meats and drinks am I.'
Then Arthur all at once gone mad replies,
'Go therefore,' and so gives the quest to him—
Him—here—a villain fitter to stick swine
Than ride abroad redressing women's wrong,
Or sit beside a noble gentlewoman."

Then half-ashamed and part-amazed, the lord
Now look'd at one and now at other, left
The damsel by the peacock in his pride,
And, seating Gareth at another board,
Sat down beside him, ate and then began:

"Friend, whether thou be kitchen-knave, or not,
Or whether it be the maiden's fantasy,
And whether she be mad, or else the King,
Or both or neither, or thyself be mad,
I ask not; but thou strikest a strong stroke,
For strong thou art and godly there-withal,
And saver of my life; and therefore now,
For here be mighty men to joust with, weigh
Whether thou wilt not with thy damsel back
To crave again Sir Lancelot of the King.
Thy pardon; I but speak for thine avail,
The saver of my life."

And Gareth said,
"Full pardon, but I follow up the quest,
Despite of Day and Night and Death and Hell."

So when, next morn, the lord whose life he saved
Had, some brief space, convey'd them on their way
And left them with God-speed, Sir Gareth spake,
"Lead, and I follow." Haughtily she replied:

"I fly no more; I allow thee for an hour.
Lion and stoat have isled together, knave,
In time of flood. Nay, furthermore, methinks
Some ruth is mine for thee. Back wilt thou, fool?
For hard by here is one will overthrow
And slay thee; then will I to court again,
And shame the King for only yielding me
My champion from the ashes of his hearth."

To whom Sir Gareth answer'd courteously:
"Say thou thy say, and I will do my deed.
Allow me for mine hour, and thou wilt find
My fortunes all as fair as hers who lay
Among the ashes and wedded the King's son."

Then to the shore of one of those long loops
Wherethro' the serpent river coil'd, they came.
Rough-thicketed were the banks and steep; the stream
Full, narrow; this a bridge of single arc
Took at a leap; and on the further side
Arose a silk pavilion, gay with gold
In streaks and rays, and all Lent-lily in hue,
Save that the dome was purple, and above,
Crimson, a slender banneret fluttering.
And therebefore the lawless warrior paced
Unarm'd, and calling, "Damsel, is this he,
The champion thou hast brought from Arthur's hall,
For whom we let thee pass?" "Nay, nay," she said,
"Sir Morning-Star. The King in utter scorn
Of thee and thy much folly hath sent thee here
His kitchen-knave; and look thou to thyself.
See that he fall not on thee suddenly,
Any slay thee unarm'd; he is not knight but knave."

Then at his call, "O daughters of the Dawn,
And servants of the Morning-Star, approach,
Arm me," from out the silken curtain-folds
Bare-footed and bare-headed three fair girls
In gilt and rosy raiment came. Their feet
In dewy grasses glisten'd; and the hair
All over glanced with dewdrop or with gem
Like sparkles in the stone Avanturine,
These arm'd him in blue arms, and gave a shield

Blue also, and thereon the morning star.
And Gareth silent gazed upon the knight,
Who stood a moment, ere his horse was brought,
Glorying; and in the stream beneath him shone,
Immingled with heaven's azure waveringly,
The gay pavilion and the naked feet,
His arms, the rosy raiment, and the star.

Then she that watch'd him: "Wherefore stare ye so?
Thou shakest in thy fear. There yet is time;
Flee down the valley before he get to horse.
Who will cry shame? Thou art not knight but knave."

Said Gareth: "Damsel, whether knave or knight,
Far liefer had I fight a score of times
Than hear thee so missay me and revile.
Fair words were best for him who fights for thee;
But truly foul are better, for they send
That strength of anger thro' mine arms, I know
That I shall overthrow him."

                                And he that bore
The star, when mounted, cried from o'er the bridge:
"A kitchen-knave, and sent in scorn of me!
Such fight not I, but answer scorn with scorn.
For this were shame to do him further wrong
Than set him on his feet, and take his horse
And arms, and so return him to the King.
Come, therefore, leave thy lady lightly, knave.
Avoid; for it beseemeth not a knave
To ride with such a lady."

                                "Dog, thou liest!
I spring from loftier lineage than thine own."
He spake; and all at fiery speed the two
Shock'd on the central bridge, and either spear
Bent but not brake, and either knight at once,
Hurl'd as a stone from out of a catapult
Beyond his horse's crupper and the bridge,
Fell, as if dead; but quickly rose and drew,
And Gareth lash'd so fiercely with his brand
He drave his enemy backward down the bridge,
The damsel crying, "Well-stricken, kitchen-knave!"
Till Gareth's shield was cloven; but one stroke
Laid him that clove it grovelling on the ground.

Then cried the fallen, "Take not my life; I yield."
And Gareth, "So this damsel ask it of me
Good—I accord it easily as a grace."

She reddening, "Insolent scullion! I of thee?
I bound to thee for any favor ask'd!"
"Then shall he die." And Gareth there unlaced
His helmet as to slay him, but she shriek'd,
"Be not so hardy, scullion, as to slay
One nobler than thyself." "Damsel, thy charge
Is an abounding pleasure to me. Knight,
Thy life is thine at her command. Arise
And quickly pass to Arthur's hall, and say
His kitchen-knave hath sent thee. See thou crave
His pardon for thy breaking of his laws.
Myself when I return will plead for thee.
Thy shield is mine—farewell; and damsel, thou,
Lead, and I follow."

And fast away she fled;
Then when he came upon her, spake: "Methought,
Knave, when I watch'd thee striking on the bridge,
The savor of thy kitchen came upon me
A little faintlier; but the wind hath changed,
I scent it twenty-fold." And then she sang,
" 'O morning star'—not that tall felon there
Whom thou, by sorcery or unhappiness
Or some device, hast foully overthrown,—

" 'O morning star that smilest in the blue,
O star, my morning dream hath proven true,
Smile sweetly, thou! my love hath smiled on me.'

"But thou begone, take counsel, and away,
For hard by here is one that guards a ford—
The second brother in their fool's parable—
Will pay thee all thy wages, and to boot.
Care not for shame; thou art not knight but knave."

To whom Sir Gareth answer'd, laughingly:
"Parables? Hear a parable of the knave.
When I was kitchen-knave among the rest,
Fierce was the hearth, and one of my co-mates
Own'd a rough dog, to whom he cast his coat,
'Guard it,' and there was none to meddle with it.
And such a coat art thou, and thee the King
Gave me to guard, and such a dog am I,
To worry, and not to flee—and—knight or knave—
The knave that doth thee service as full knight
Is all as good, meseems, as any knight
Toward thy sister's freeing."

"Ay, Sir Knave!
Ay, knave, because thou strikest as a knight,
Being but knave, I hate thee all the more."

"Fair damsel, you should worship me the more,
That, being but knave, I throw thine enemies."

"Ay, ay," she said, "but thou shalt meet thy match."

So when they touch'd the second river-loop,
Huge on a huge red horse, and all in mail
Burnish'd to blinding, shone the Noon-day Sun
Beyond a raging shallow. As if the flower
That blows a globe of after arrowlets
Ten-thousand-fold had grown, flash'd the fierce shield,
All sun; and Gareth's eyes had flying blots
Before them when he turn'd from watching him.
He from beyond the roaring shallow roar'd,
"What doest thou, brother, in my marches here?"
And she athwart the shallow shrill'd again,
"Here is a kitchen-knave from Arthur's hall
Hath overthrown thy brother, and hath his arms."
"Ugh!" cried the Sun, and, vizoring up a red
And cipher face of rounded foolishness,
Push'd horse across the foamings of the ford,
Whom Gareth met mid-stream; no room was there
For lance or tourney-skill. Four strokes they struck
With sword, and these were mighty; the new knight
Had fear he might be shamed; but as the Sun
Heaved up a ponderous arm to strike the fifth,
The hoof of his horse slipt in the stream, the stream
Descended, and the Sun was wash'd away.

Then Gareth laid his lance athwart the ford;
So drew him home; but he that fought no more,
As being all bone-batter'd on the rock,
Yielded, and Gareth sent him to the King.
"Myself when I return will plead for thee.
Lead, and I follow." Quietly she led.
"Hath not the good wind, damsel, changed again?"
"Nay, not a point; nor art thou victor here.
There lies a ridge of slate across the ford;
His horse thereon stumbled—ay, for I saw it.

" 'O sun'—not this strong fool whom thou, Sir Knave,
Hast overthrown thro' mere unhappiness—

" 'O sun, that wakenest all to bliss or pain,

O moon, that layest all to sleep again,
Shine sweetly; twice my love hath smiled on me.'

"What knowest thou of love-song or of love?
Nay, nay, God wot, so thou wert nobly born,
Thou hast a pleasant presence. Yea, perchance,—

" 'O dewy flowers that open to the sun,
O dewy flowers that close when day is done,
Blow sweetly; twice my love hath smiled on me.'

"What knowest thou of flowers, except, belike,
To garnish meats with? hath not our good King
Who lent me thee, the flower of kitchendom,
A foolish love for flowers? what stick ye round
The pasty? wherewithal deck the boar's head?
Flowers? nay, the boar hath rosemaries and bay.

" 'O birds that warble to the morning sky,
O birds that warble as the day goes by,
Sing sweetly; twice my love hath smiled on me.'

"What knowest thou of birds, lark, mavis, merle,
Linnet? what dream ye when they utter forth
May-music growing with the growing light,
Their sweet sun-worship? these be for the snare—
So runs thy fancy—these be for the spit,
Larding and basting. See thou have not now
Larded thy last, except thou turn and fly.
There stands the third fool of their allegory."

For there beyond a bridge of treble bow,
All in a rose-red from the west, and all
Naked it seem'd, and glowing in the broad
Deep-dimpled current underneath, the knight
That named himself the Star of Evening stood.

And Gareth, "Wherefore waits the madman there
Naked in open dayshine?" "Nay," she cried,
"Not naked, only wrapt in harden'd skins
That fit him like his own; and so ye cleave
His armor off him, these will turn the blade."

Then the third brother shouted o'er the bridge,
"O brother-star, why shine ye here so low?
Thy ward is higher up; but have ye slain
The damsel's champion?" and the damsel cried:

"No star of thine, but shot from Arthur's heaven
With all disaster unto thine and thee!

For both thy younger brethren have gone down
Before this youth; and so wilt thou, Sir Star.
Art thou not old?"

           "Old, damsel, old and hard,
Old, with the might and breath of twenty boys."
Said Gareth, "Old, and over-bold in brag!
But that same strength which threw the Morning Star
Can throw the Evening."

           Then that other blew
A hard and deadly note upon the horn.
"Approach and arm me!" With slow steps from out
An old storm-beaten, russet, many-stain'd
Pavilion, forth a grizzled damsel came,
And arm'd him in old arms, and brought a helm
With but a drying evergreen for crest,
And gave a shield whereon the star of even
Half-tarnish'd and half-bright, his emblem, shone.
But when it glitter'd o'er the saddle-bow,
They madly hurl'd together on the bridge;
And Gareth overthrew him, lighted, drew,
There met him drawn, and overthrew him again,
But up like fire he started; and as oft
As Gareth brought him grovelling on his knees,
So many a time he vaulted up again;
Till Gareth panted hard, and his great heart,
Foredooming all his trouble was in vain,
Labor'd within him, for he seem'd as one
That all in later, sadder age begins
To war against ill uses of a life,
But these from all his life arise, and cry,
"Thou hast made us lords, and canst not put us down!"
He half despairs; so Gareth seem'd to strike
Vainly, the damsel clamoring all the while,
"Well done, knave-knight, well stricken, O good knight-
    knave—
O knave, as noble as any of all the knights—
Shame me not, shame me not. I have prophesied—
Strike, thou art worthy of the Table Round—
His arms are old, he trusts the harden'd skin—
Strike—strike—the wind will never change again."
And Gareth hearing ever stronglier smote,
And hew'd great pieces of his armor off him,
But lash'd in vain against the harden'd skin,
And could not wholly bring him under, more

Than loud Southwesterns, rolling ridge on ridge,
The buoy that rides at sea, and dips and springs
For ever; till at length Sir Gareth's brand
Clash'd his, and brake it utterly to the hilt.
"I have thee now;" but forth that other sprang,
And, all unknightlike, writhed his wiry arms
Around him, till he felt, despite his mail,
Strangled, but straining even his uttermost
Cast, and so hurl'd him headlong o'er the bridge
Down to the river, sink or swim, and cried,
"Lead, and I follow."

                    But the damsel said:
"I lead no longer; ride thou at my side;
Thou art the kingliest of all kitchen-knaves.

   " 'O trefoil, sparkling on the rainy plain,
O rainbow with three colors after rain,
Shine sweetly; thrice my love hath smiled on me.'

   "Sir—and, good faith, I fain had added—Knight,
But that I heard thee call thyself a knave,—
Shamed am I that I so rebuked, reviled,
Missaid thee. Noble I am, and thought the King
Scorn'd me and mine; and now thy pardon, friend,
For thou hast ever answer'd courteously,
And wholly bold thou art, and meek withal
As any of Arthur's best, but, being knave,
Hast maz'd my wit. I marvel what thou art."

   "Damsel," he said, "you be not all to blame,
Saving that you mistrusted our good King
Would handle scorn, or yield you, asking, one
Not fit to cope your quest. You said your say;
Mine answer was my deed. Good sooth! I hold
He scarce is knight, yea but half-man, nor meet
To fight for gentle damsel, he, who lets
His heart be stirr'd with any foolish heat
At any gentle damsel's waywardness.
Shamed? care not! thy foul sayings fought for me;
And seeing now thy words are fair, methinks
There rides no knight, not Lancelot, his great self,
Hath force to quell me."

                    Nigh upon that hour
When the lone hern forgets his melancholy,
Lets down his other leg, and stretching dreams
Of goodly supper in the distant pool,

Then turn'd the noble damsel smiling at him,
And told him of a cavern hard at hand,
Where bread and baken meats and good red wine
Of Southland, which the Lady Lyonors
Had sent her coming champion, waited him.

    Anon they past a narrow comb wherein
Were slabs of rock with figures, knights on horse
Sculptured, and deckt in slowly-waning hues.
"Sir Knave, my knight, a hermit once was here,
Whose holy hand hath fashion'd on the rock
The war of Time against the soul of man.
And yon four fools have suck'd their allegory
From these damp walls, and taken but the form.
Know ye not these?" and Gareth lookt and read—
In letters like to those the vexillary
Hath left crag-carven o'er the streaming Gelt—
"PHOSPHORUS," then "MERIDIES,"—"HESPERUS"—
"NOX"—"MORS," beneath five figures, armed men,
Slab after slab, their faces forward all,
And running down the Soul, a shape that fled
With broken wings, torn raiment, and loose hair,
For help and shelter to the hermit's cave.
"Follow the faces, and we find it. Look,
Who comes behind?"

        For one—delay'd at first
Thro' helping back the dislocated Kay
To Camelot, then by what thereafter chanced,
The damsel's headlong error thro' the wood—
Sir Lancelot, having swum the river-loops—
His blue shield-lions cover'd—softly drew
Behind the twain, and when he saw the star
Gleam, on Sir Gareth's turning to him, cried,
"Stay, felon knight, I avenge me for my friend."
And Gareth crying prick'd against the cry;
But when they closed—in a moment—at one touch
Of that skill'd spear, the wonder of the world—
Went sliding down so easily, and fell,
That when he found the grass within his hands
He laugh'd. The laughter jarr'd upon Lynette.
Harshly she ask'd him, "Shamed and overthrown,
And tumbled back into the kitchen-knave,
Why laugh ye? that ye blew your boast in vain?"
"Nay, noble damsel, but that I, the son
Of old King Lot and good Queen Bellicent,

And victor of the bridges and the ford,
And knight of Arthur, here lie thrown by whom
I know not, all thro' mere unhappiness—
Device and sorcery and unhappiness—
Out, sword; we are thrown!" And Lancelot answer'd: "Prince,
O Gareth—thro' the mere unhappiness
Of one who came to help thee, not to harm,
Lancelot, and all as glad to find thee whole
As on the day when Arthur knighted him."

Then Gareth: "Thou—Lancelot!—thine the hand
That threw me? An some chance to mar the boast
Thy brethren of thee make—which could not chance—
Had sent thee down before a lesser spear,
Shamed had I been, and sad—O Lancelot—thou!"

Whereat the maiden, petulant: "Lancelot,
Why came ye not, when call'd? and wherefore now
Come ye, not call'd? I gloried in my knave,
Who being still rebuked would answer still
Courteous as any knight—but now, if knight,
The marvel dies, and leaves me fool'd and trick'd,
And only wondering wherefore play'd upon;
And doubtfu. whether I and mine be scorn'd.
Where should be truth if not in Arthur's hall,
In Arthur's presence? Knight, knave, prince and fool,
I hate thee and forever."

And Lancelot said:
"Blessed be thou, Sir Gareth! knight art thou
To the King's best wish. O damsel, be you wise,
To call him shamed who is but overthrown?
Thrown have I been, nor once, but many a time.
Victor from vanquish'd issues at the last,
And overthrower from being overthrown.
With sword we have not striven, and thy good horse
And thou art weary; yet not less I left
Thy manhood thro' that wearied lance of thine.
Well hast thou done; for all the stream is freed,
And thou hast wreak'd his justice on his foes,
And when reviled hast answer'd graciously,
And makest merry when overthrown. Prince, knight,
Hail, knight and prince, and of our Table Round!"

And then when turning to Lynette he told
The tale of Gareth, petulantly she said:
"Ay, well—ay, well—for worse than being fool'd

Of others, is to fool one's self. A cave,
Sir Lancelot, is hard by, with meats and drinks
And forage for the horse, and flint for fire.
But all about it flies a honeysuckle.
Seek, till we find." And when they sought and found,
Sir Gareth drank and ate, and all his life
Past into sleep; on whom the maiden gazed:
"Sound sleep be thine! sound cause to sleep hast thou.
Wake lusty! Seem I not as tender to him
As any mother? Ay, but such a one
As all day long hath rated at her child,
And vext his day, but blesses him asleep—
Good lord, how sweetly smells the honeysuckle
In the hush'd night, as if the world were one
Of utter peace, and love, and gentleness!
O Lancelot, Lancelot," and she clapt her hands—
"Full merry am I to find my goodly knave
Is knight and noble. See now, sworn have I,
Else yon black felon had not let me pass,
To bring thee back to do the battle with him.
Thus an thou goest, he will fight thee first;
Who doubts thee victor? so will my knight-knave
Miss the full flower of this accomplishment."

Said Lancelot: "Peradventure he you name
May know my shield. Let Gareth, an he will,
Change his for mine, and take my charger, fresh,
Not to be spurr'd, loving the battle as well
As he that rides him." "Lancelot-like," she said,
"Courteous in this, Lord Lancelot, as in all."

And Gareth, wakening, fiercely clutch'd the shield:
"Ramp, ye lance-splintering lions, on whom all spears
Are rotten sticks! ye seem agape to roar!
Yea, ramp and roar at leaving of your lord!—
Care not, good beasts, so well I care for you.
O noble Lancelot, from my hold on these
Streams virtue—fire—thro' one that will not shame
Even the shadow of Lancelot under shield.
Hence; let us go."

Silent the silent field
They traversed. Arthur's Harp tho' summer-wan,
In counter motion to the clouds, allured
The glance of Gareth dreaming on his liege.
A star shot: "Lo," said Gareth, "the foe falls!"
An owl whoopt: "Hark the victor pealing there!"

Suddenly she that rode upon his left
Clung to the shield that Lancelot lent him, crying:
"Yield, yield him this again; 't is he must fight:
I curse the tongue that all thro' yesterday
Reviled thee, and hath wrought on Lancelot now
To lend thee horse and shield. Wonders ye have done,
Miracles ye cannot. Here is glory enow
In having flung the three. I see thee maim'd,
Mangled; I swear thou canst not fling the fourth."

"And wherefore, damsel? tell me all ye know.
You cannot scare me; nor rough face, or voice,
Brute bulk of limb, or boundless savagery
Appal me from the quest."

              "Nay, prince," she cried,
"God wot, I never look'd upon the face,
Seeing he never rides abroad by day,
But watch'd him have I like a phantom pass
Chilling the night; nor have I heard the voice.
Always he made his mouthpiece of a page
Who came and went, and still reported him
As closing in himself the strength of ten,
And when his anger tare him, massacring
Man, woman, lad, and girl—yea, the soft babe!
Some hold that he hath swallow'd infant flesh,
Monster! O prince, I went for Lancelot first,
The quest is Lancelot's; give him back the shield."

Said Gareth laughing, "An he fight for this,
Belike he wins it as the better man;
Thus—and not else!"

              But Lancelot on him urged
All the devisings of their chivalry
When one might meet a mightier than himself;
How best to manage horse, lance, sword, and shield,
And so fill up the gap where force might fail
With skill and fineness. Instant were his words.

Then Gareth: "Here be rules. I know but one—
To dash against mine enemy and to win.
Yet have I watch'd thee victor in the joust,
And seen thy way." "Heaven help thee!" sigh'd Lynette.

Then for a space, and under cloud that grew
To thunder-gloom palling all stars, they rode
In converse till she made her palfrey halt,

Lifted an arm, and softly whisper'd, "There."
And all the three were silent seeing, pitch'd
Beside the Castle Perilous on flat field,
A huge pavilion like a mountain peak
Sunder the glooming crimson on the marge,
Black, with black banner, and a long black horn
Beside it hanging; which Sir Gareth graspt,
And so, before the two could hinder him,
Sent all his heart and breath thro' all the horn.
Echo'd the walls; a light twinkled; anon
Came lights and lights, and once again he blew;
Whereon were hollow tramplings up and down
And muffled voices heard, and shadows past;
Till high above him, circled with her maids,
The Lady Lyonors at a window stood,
Beautiful among lights, and waving to him
White hands and courtesy. But when the prince
Three times had blown—after long hush—at last—
The huge pavilion slowly yielded up,
Thro' those black foldings, that which housed therein.
High on a night-black horse, in night-black arms,
With white breast-bone, and barren ribs of Death,
And crown'd with fleshless laughter—some ten steps—
In the half-light—thro' the dim dawn—advanced
The monster, and then paused, and spake no word.

But Gareth spake and all indignantly:
"Fool, for thou hast, men say, the strength of ten,
Canst thou not trust the limbs thy God hath given,
But must, to make the terror of thee more,
Trick thyself out in ghastly imageries
Of that which Life hath done with, and the clod,
Less dull than thou, will hide with mantling flowers
As if for pity?" But he spake no word;
Which set the horror higher. A maiden swoon'd;
The Lady Lyonors wrung her hands and wept,
As doom'd to be the bride of Night and Death;
Sir Gareth's head prickled beneath his helm;
And even Sir Lancelot thro' his warm blood felt
Ice strike, and all that mark'd him were aghast.

At once Sir Lancelot's charger fiercely neigh'd,
And Death's dark war-horse bounded forward with him.
Then those that did not blink the terror saw
That Death was cast to ground, and slowly rose.
But with one stroke Sir Gareth split the skull.

Half fell to right and half to left and lay.
Then with a stronger buffet he clove the helm
As throughly as the skull; and out from this
Issued the bright face of a blooming boy
Fresh as a flower new-born, and crying, "Knight,
Slay me not; my three brethren bade me do it,
To make a horror all about the house,
And stay the world from Lady Lyonors.
They never dream'd the passes would be past."
Answer'd Sir Gareth graciously to one
Not many a moon his younger, "My fair child,
What madness made thee challenge the chief knight
Of Arthur's hall?" "Fair Sir, they bade me do it.
They hate the King and Lancelot, the King's friend;
They hoped to slay him somewhere on the stream,
They never dream'd the passes could be past."

Then sprang the happier day from underground;
And Lady Lyonors and her house, with dance
And revel and song, made merry over Death,
As being after all their foolish fears
And horrors only proven a blooming boy.
So large mirth lived, and Gareth won the quest.

And he that told the tale in older times
Says that Sir Gareth wedded Lyonors,
But he that told it later says Lynette.

✠✠✠ THE MARRIAGE OF GERAINT ✠✠✠

THE brave Geraint, a knight of Arthur's court,
A tributary prince of Devon, one
Of that great Order of the Table Round,
Had married Enid, Yniol's only child,
And loved her as he loved the light of heaven.
And as the light of heaven varies, now
At sunrise, now at sunset, now by night
With moon and trembling stars, so loved Geraint
To make her beauty vary day by day,
In crimsons and in purples and in gems.
And Enid, but to please her husband's eye,
Who first had found and loved her in a state

Of broken fortunes, daily fronted him
In some fresh splendor; and the Queen herself,
Grateful to Prince Geraint for service done,
Loved her, and often with her own white hands
Array'd and deck'd her, as the loveliest,
Next after her own self, in all the court.
And Enid loved the Queen, and with true heart
Adored her, as the stateliest and the best
And loveliest of all women upon earth.
And seeing them so tender and so close,
Long in their common love rejoiced Geraint.
But when a rumor rose about the Queen,
Touching her guilty love for Lancelot,
Tho' yet there lived no proof, nor yet was heard
The world's loud whisper breaking into storm,
Not less Geraint believed it; and there fell
A horror on him lest his gentle wife,
Thro' that great tenderness for Guinevere,
Had suffer'd or should suffer any taint
In nature. Wherefore, going to the King,
He made this pretext, that his princedom lay
Close on the borders of a territory
Wherein were bandit earls, and caitiff knights,
Assassins, and all flyers from the hand
Of Justice, and whatever loathes a law;
And therefore, till the King himself should please
To cleanse this common sewer of all his realm,
He craved a fair permission to depart,
And there defend his marches. And the King
Mused for a little on his plea, but, last,
Allowing it, the prince and Enid rode,
And fifty knights rode with them, to the shores
Of Severn, and they past to their own land;
Where, thinking that, if ever yet was wife
True to her lord, mine shall be so to me,
He compass'd her with sweet observances
And worship, never leaving her, and grew
Forgetful of his promise to the King,
Forgetful of the falcon and the hunt,
Forgetful of the tilt and tournament,
Forgetful of his glory and his name,
Forgetful of his princedom and its cares.
And this forgetfulness was hateful to her.
And by and by the people, when they met
In twos and threes, or fuller companies,

Began to scoff and jeer and babble of him
As of a prince whose manhood was all gone,
And molten down in mere uxoriousness.
And this she gather'd from the people's eyes;
This too the women who attired her head,
To please her, dwelling on his boundless love,
Told Enid, and they sadden'd her the more;
And day by day she thought to tell Geraint,
But could not out of bashful delicacy,
While he, that watch'd her sadden, was the more
Suspicious that her nature had a taint.

At last, it chanced that on a summer morn—
They sleeping each by either—the new sun
Beat thro' the blindless casement of the room,
And heated the strong warrior in his dreams;
Who, moving, cast the coverlet aside,
And bared the knotted column of his throat,
The massive square of his heroic breast,
And arms on which the standing muscle sloped,
As slopes a wild brook o'er a little stone,
Running too vehemently to break upon it.
And Enid woke and sat beside the couch,
Admiring him, and thought within herself,
Was ever man so grandly made as he?
Then, like a shadow, past the people's talk
And accusation of uxoriousness
Across her mind, and bowing over him,
Low to her own heart piteously she said:

"O noble breast and all-puissant arms,
Am I the cause, I the poor cause that men
Reproach you, saying all your force is gone?
I am the cause, because I dare not speak
And tell him what I think and what they say.
And yet I hate that he should linger here;
I cannot love my lord and not his name.
Far liefer had I gird his harness on him,
And ride with him to battle and stand by,
And watch his mightful hand striking great blows
At caitiffs and at wrongers of the world.
Far better were I laid in the dark earth,
Not hearing any more his noble voice,
Not to be folded more in these dear arms,
And darken'd from the high light in his eyes,
Than that my lord thro' me should suffer shame.

Am I so bold, and could I so stand by,
And see my dear lord wounded in the strife,
Or maybe pierced to death before mine eyes,
And yet not dare to tell him what I think,
And how men slur him, saying all his force
Is melted into mere effeminacy?
O me, I fear that I am no true wife!"

Half inwardly, half audibly she spoke,
And the strong passion in her made her weep
True tears upon his broad and naked breast,
And these awoke him, and by great mischance
He heard but fragments of her later words,
And that she fear'd she was not a true wife.
And then he thought, "In spite of all my care,
For all my pains, poor man, for all my pains,
She is not faithful to me, and I see her
Weeping for some gay knight in Arthur's hall."
Then, tho' he loved and reverenced her too much
To dream she could be guilty of foul act,
Right thro' his manful breast darted the pang
That makes a man, in the sweet face of her
Whom he loves most, lonely and miserable.
At this he hurl'd his huge limbs out of bed,
And shook his drowsy squire awake and cried,
"My charger and her palfrey;" then to her,
"I will ride forth into the wilderness,
For, tho' it seems my spurs are yet to win,
I have not fallen so low as some would wish.
And thou, put on thy worst and meanest dress
And ride with me." And Enid ask'd, amazed,
"If Enid errs, let Enid learn her fault."
But he, "I charge thee, ask not, but obey."
Then she bethought her of a faded silk,
A faded mantle and a faded veil,
And moving toward a cedarn cabinet,
Wherein she kept them folded reverently
With sprigs of summer laid between the folds,
She took them, and array'd herself therein,
Remembering when first he came on her
Drest in that dress, and how he loved her in it,
And all her foolish fears about the dress,
And all his journey to her, as himself
Had told her, and their coming to the court.

For Arthur on the Whitsuntide before
Held court at old Caerleon upon Usk.

There on a day, he sitting high in hall,
Before him came a forester of Dean,
Wet from the woods, with notice of a hart
Taller than all his fellows, milky-white,
First seen that day; these things he told the King.
Then the good King gave order to let blow
His horns for hunting on the morrow morn,
And when the Queen petition'd for his leave
To see the hunt, allow'd it easily.
So with the morning all the court were gone.
But Guinevere lay late into the morn,
Lost in sweet dreams, and dreaming of her love
For Lancelot, and forgetful of the hunt,
But rose at last, a single maiden with her,
Took horse, and forded Usk, and gain'd the wood;
There, on a little knoll beside it, stay'd
Waiting to hear the hounds, but heard instead
A sudden sound of hoofs, for Prince Geraint,
Late also, wearing neither hunting-dress
Nor weapon save a golden-hilted brand,
Came quickly flashing thro' the shallow ford
Behind them, and so gallop'd up the knoll.
A purple scarf, at either end whereof
There swung an apple of the purest gold,
Sway'd round about him, as he gallop'd up
To join them, glancing like a dragonfly
In summer suit and silks of holiday.
Low bow'd the tributary prince, and she,
Sweetly and statelily, and with all grace
Of womanhood and queenhood, answer'd him:
"Late, late, Sir Prince," she said, "later than we!"
"Yea, noble Queen," he answer'd, "and so late
That I but come like you to see the hunt,
Not join it." "Therefore wait with me," she said;
"For on this little knoll, if anywhere,
There is good chance that we shall hear the hounds:
Here often they break covert at our feet."

    And while they listen'd for the distant hunt,
And chiefly for the baying of Cavall,
King Arthur's hound of deepest mouth, there rode
Full slowly by a knight, lady, and dwarf;
Whereof the dwarf lagg'd latest, and the knight
Had vizor up, and show'd a youthful face,
Imperious, and of haughtiest lineaments.
And Guinevere, not mindful of his face

In the King's hall, desired his name, and sent
Her maiden to demand it of the dwarf,
Who being vicious, old, and irritable,
And doubling all his master's vice of pride,
Made answer sharply that she should not know.
"Then will I ask it of himself," she said.
"Nay, by my faith, thou shalt not," cried the dwarf;
"Thou art not worthy even to speak of him;"
And when she put her horse toward the knight,
Struck at her with his whip, and she return'd
Indignant to the Queen; whereat Geraint
Exclaiming, "Surely I will learn the name,"
Made sharply to the dwarf, and ask'd it of him,
Who answer'd as before; and when the prince
Had put his horse in motion toward the knight,
Struck at him with his whip, and cut his cheek.
The prince's blood spirted upon the scarf,
Dyeing it; and his quick, instinctive hand
Caught at the hilt, as to abolish him:
But he, from his exceeding manfulness
And pure nobility of temperament,
Wroth to be wroth at such a worm, refrain'd
From even a word, and so returning said:

"I will avenge this insult, noble Queen,
Done in your maiden's person to yourself,
And I will track this vermin to their earths;
For tho' I ride unarm'd, I do not doubt
To find, at some place I shall come at, arms
On loan, or else for pledge; and, being found,
Then will I fight him, and will break his pride,
And on the third day will again be here,
So that I be not fallen in fight. Farewell."

"Farewell, fair prince," answer'd the stately Queen.
"Be prosperous in this journey, as in all;
And may you light on all things that you love,
And live to wed with her whom first you love.
But ere you wed with any, bring your bride,
And I, were she the daughter of a king,
Yea, tho' she were a beggar from the hedge,
Will clothe her for her bridals like the sun."

And Prince Geraint, now thinking that he heard
The noble hart at bay, now the far horn,
A little vext at losing of the hunt,
A little at the vile occasion, rode,

By ups and downs, thro' many a grassy glade
And valley, with fixt eye following the three.
At last they issued from the world of wood,
And climb'd upon a fair and even ridge,
And show'd themselves against the sky, and sank.
And thither came Geraint, and underneath
Beheld the long street of a little town
In a long valley, on one side whereof,
White from the mason's hand, a fortress rose;
And on one side a castle in decay,
Beyond a bridge that spann'd a dry ravine.
And out of town and valley came a noise
As of a broad brook o'er a shingly bed
Brawling, or like a clamor of the rooks
At distance, ere they settle for the night.

And onward to the fortress rode the three,
And enter'd, and were lost behind the walls.
"So," thought Geraint, "I have track'd him to his earth."
And down the long street riding wearily,
Found every hostel full, and everywhere
Was hammer laid to hoof, and the hot hiss
And bustling whistle of the youth who scour'd
His master's armor; and of such a one
He ask'd, "What means the tumult in the town?"
Who told him, scouring still, "The sparrow-hawk!"
Then riding close behind an ancient churl,
Who, smitten by the dusty sloping beam,
Went sweating underneath a sack of corn,
Ask'd yet once more what meant the hubbub here?
Who answer'd gruffly, "Ugh! the sparrow-hawk!"
Then riding further past an armorer's,
Who, with back turn'd, and bow'd above his work,
Sat riveting a helmet on his knee,
He put the selfsame query, but the man
Not turning round, nor looking at him, said:
"Friend, he that labors for the sparrow-hawk
Has little time for idle questioners."
Whereat Geraint flash'd into sudden spleen:
"A thousand pips eat up your sparrow-hawk!
Tits, wrens, and all wing'd nothings peck him dead!
Ye think the rustic cackle of your bourg
The murmur of the world! What is it to me?
O wretched set of sparrows, one and all,
Who pipe of nothing but of sparrow-hawks!
Speak, if ye be not like the rest, hawk-mad,

Where can I get me harborage for the night?
And arms, arms, arms to fight my enemy? Speak!"
Whereat the armorer turning all amazed
And seeing one so gay in purple silks,
Came forward with the helmet yet in hand
And answer'd: "Pardon me, O stranger knight;
We hold a tourney here to-morrow morn,
And there is scantly time for half the work.
Arms? truth! I know not; all are wanted here.
Harborage? truth, good truth, I know not, save,
It may be, at Earl Yniol's, o'er the bridge
Yonder." He spoke and fell to work again.

Then rode Geraint, a little spleenful yet,
Across the bridge that spann'd the dry ravine.
There musing sat the hoary-headed earl—
His dress a suit of fray'd magnificence,
Once fit for feasts of ceremony—and said:
"Whither, fair son?" to whom Geraint replied,
"O friend, I seek a harborage for the night."
Then Yniol, "Enter therefore and partake
The slender entertainment of a house
Once rich, now poor, but ever open-door'd."
"Thanks, venerable friend," replied Geraint;
"So that ye do not serve me sparrow-hawks
For supper, I will enter, I will eat
With all the passion of a twelve hours' fast."
Then sigh'd and smiled the hoary-headed earl,
And answer'd, "Graver cause than yours is mine
To curse this hedgerow thief, the sparrow-hawk.
But in, go in; for save yourself desire it,
We will not touch upon him even in jest."

Then rode Geraint into the castle court,
His charger trampling many a prickly star
Of sprouted thistle on the broken stones.
He look'd and saw that all was ruinous.
Here stood a shatter'd archway plumed with fern;
And here had fallen a great part of a tower,
Whole, like a crag that tumbles from the cliff,
And like a crag was gay with wilding flowers;
And high above a piece of turret stair,
Worn by the feet that now were silent, wound
Bare to the sun, and monstrous ivy-stems
Claspt the gray walls with hairy-fibred arms,
And suck'd the joining of the stones, and look'd
A knot, beneath, of snakes, aloft, a grove.

And while he waited in the castle court,
The voice of Enid, Yniol's daughter, rang
Clear thro' the open casement of the hall,
Singing; and as the sweet voice of a bird,
Heard by the lander in a lonely isle,
Moves him to think what kind of bird it is
That sings so delicately clear, and make
Conjecture of the plumage and the form,
So the sweet voice of Enid moved Geraint,
And made him like a man abroad at morn
When first the liquid note beloved of men
Comes flying over many a windy wave
To Britain, and in April suddenly
Breaks from a coppice gemm'd with green and red,
And he suspends his converse with a friend,
Or it may be the labor of his hands,
To think or say, "There is the nightingale:"
So fared it with Geraint, who thought and said,
"Here, by God's grace, is the one voice for me."

It chanced the song that Enid sang was one
Of Fortune and her wheel, and Enid sang:

"Turn, Fortune, turn thy wheel, and lower the proud;
Turn thy wild wheel thro' sunshine, storm, and cloud;
Thy wheel and thee we neither love nor hate.

"Turn, Fortune, turn thy wheel with smile or frown;
With that wild wheel we go not up or down;
Our hoard is little, but our hearts are great.

"Smile and we smile, the lords of many lands;
Frown and we smile, the lords of our own hands;
For man is man and master of his fate.

"Turn, turn thy wheel above the staring crowd;
Thy wheel and thou are shadows in the cloud;
Thy wheel and thee we neither love nor hate."

"Hark, by the bird's song ye may learn the nest,"
Said Yniol; "enter quickly." Entering then,
Right o'er a mount of newly-fallen stones,
The dusky-rafter'd many-cobweb'd hall,
He found an ancient dame in dim brocade;
And near her, like a blossom vermeil-white
That lightly breaks a faded flower-sheath,
Moved the fair Enid, all in faded silk,
Her daughter. In a moment thought Geraint,
"Here, by God's rood, is the one maid for me."
But none spake word except the hoary earl:

"Enid, the good knight's horse stands in the court;
Take him to stall, and give him corn, and then
Go to the town and buy us flesh and wine;
And we will make us merry as we may.
Our hoard is little, but our hearts are great."

He spake; the prince, as Enid past him, fain
To follow, strode a stride, but Yniol caught
His purple scarf, and held, and said, "Forbear!
Rest! the good house, tho' ruin'd, O my son,
Endures not that her guest should serve himself."
And reverencing the custom of the house
Geraint, from utter courtesy, forbore.

So Enid took his charger to the stall,
And after went her way across the bridge,
And reach'd the town, and while the prince and earl
Yet spoke together, came again with one,
A youth that, following with a costrel, bore
The means of goodly welcome, flesh and wine.
And Enid brought sweet cakes to make them cheer,
And, in her veil enfolded, manchet bread.
And then, because their hall must also serve
For kitchen, boil'd the flesh, and spread the board,
And stood behind, and waited on the three.
And, seeing her so sweet and serviceable,
Geraint had longing in him evermore
To stoop and kiss the tender little thumb
That crost the trenches as she laid it down.
But after all had eaten, then Geraint,
For now the wine made summer in his veins,
Let his eye rove in following, or rest
On Enid at her lowly handmaid-work,
Now here, now there, about the dusky hall;
Then suddenly addrest the hoary earl:

"Fair host and earl, I pray your courtesy;
This sparrow-hawk, what is he? tell me of him.
His name? but no, good faith, I will not have it;
For if he be the knight whom late I saw
Ride into that new fortress by your town,
White from the mason's hand, then have I sworn
From his own lips to have it—I am Geraint
Of Devon—for this morning when the Queen
Sent her own maiden to demand the name,
His dwarf, a vicious under-shapen thing,
Struck at her with his whip, and she return'd

Indignant to the Queen; and then I swore
That I would track this caitiff to his hold,
And fight and break his pride, and have it of him.
And all unarm'd I rode, and thought to find
Arms in your town, where all the men are mad;
They take the rustic murmur of their bourg
For the great wave that echoes round the world.
They would not hear me speak; but if ye know
Where I can light on arms, or if yourself
Should have them, tell me, seeing I have sworn
That I will break his pride and learn his name,
Avenging this great insult done the Queen."

Then cried Earl Yniol: "Art thou he indeed,
Geraint, a name far-sounded among men
For noble deeds? and truly I, when first
I saw you moving by me on the bridge,
Felt ye were somewhat, yea, and by your state
And presence might have guess'd you one of those
That eat in Arthur's hall at Camelot.
Nor speak I now from foolish flattery;
For this dear child hath often heard me praise
Your feats of arms, and often when I paused
Hath ask'd again, and ever loved to hear;
So grateful is the noise of noble deeds
To noble hearts who see but acts of wrong.
O, never yet had woman such a pair
Of suitors as this maiden; first Limours,
A creature wholly given to brawls and wine,
Drunk even when he woo'd; and be he dead
I know not, but he past to the wild land.
The second was your foe, the sparrow-hawk,
My curse, my nephew—I will not let his name
Slip from my lips if I can help it—he,
When I that knew him fierce and turbulent
Refused her to him, then his pride awoke;
And since the proud man often is the mean,
He sow'd a slander in the common ear,
Affirming that his father left him gold,
And in my charge, which was not render'd to him;
Bribed with large promises the men who served
About my person, the more easily
Because my means were somewhat broken into
Thro' open doors and hospitality;
Raised my own town against me in the night
Before my Enid's birthday, sack'd my house;
From my own earldom foully ousted me;

Built that new fort to overawe my friends,
For truly there are those who love me yet;
And keeps me in this ruinous castle here,
Where doubtless he would put me soon to death
But that his pride too much despises me.
And I myself sometimes despise myself;
For I have let men be and have their way,
Am much too gentle, have not used my power;
Nor know I whether I be very base
Or very manful, whether very wise
Or very foolish; only this I know,
That whatsoever evil happen to me,
I seem to suffer nothing heart or limb,
But can endure it all most patiently."

"Well said, true heart," replied Geraint, "but arms,
That if the sparrow-hawk, this nephew, fight
In next day's tourney I may break his pride."

And Yniol answer'd: "Arms, indeed, but old
And rusty, old and rusty, Prince Geraint,
Are mine, and therefore, at thine asking, thine.
But in this tournament can no man tilt,
Except the lady he loves best be there.
Two forks are fixt into the meadow ground,
And over these is placed a silver wand,
And over that a golden sparrow-hawk,
The prize of beauty for the fairest there.
And this, what knight soever be in field
Lays claim to for the lady at his side,
And tilts with my good nephew thereupon,
Who being apt at arms and big of bone
Has ever won it for the lady with him,
And toppling over all antagonism
Has earn'd himself the name of sparrow-hawk.
But thou, that has no lady, canst not fight."

To whom Geraint with eyes all bright replied,
Leaning a little toward him: "Thy leave!
Let me lay lance in rest, O noble host,
For this dear child, because I never saw,
Tho' having seen all beauties of our time,
Nor can see elsewhere, anything so fair.
And if I fall her name will yet remain
Untarnish'd as before; but if I live,
So aid me heaven when at mine uttermost
As I will make her truly my true wife!"

Then, howsoever patient, Yniol's heart
Danced in his bosom, seeing better days.
And looking round he saw not Enid there—
Who hearing her own name had stolen away—
But that old dame, to whom full tenderly
And fondling all her hand in his he said:
"Mother, a maiden is a tender thing,
And best by her that bore her understood.
Go thou to rest, but ere thou go to rest
Tell her, and prove her heart toward the prince."

So spake the kindly-hearted earl, and she
With frequent smile and nod departing found,
Half disarray'd as to her rest, the girl;
Whom first she kiss'd on either cheek, and then
On either shining shoulder laid a hand,
And kept her off and gazed upon her face,
And told her all their converse in the hall,
Proving her heart. But never light and shade
Coursed one another more on open ground
Beneath a troubled heaven than red and pale
Across the face of Enid hearing her;
While slowly falling as a scale that falls,
When weight is added only grain by grain,
Sank her sweet head upon her gentle breast;
Nor did she lift an eye nor speak a word,
Rapt in the fear and in the wonder of it.
So moving without answer to her rest
She found no rest, and ever fail'd to draw
The quiet night into her blood, but lay
Contemplating her own unworthiness;
And when the pale and bloodless east began
To quicken to the sun, arose, and raised
Her mother too, and hand in hand they moved
Down to the meadow where the jousts were held,
And waited there for Yniol and Geraint.

And thither came the twain, and when Geraint
Beheld her first in field, awaiting him,
He felt, were she the prize of bodily force,
Himself beyond the rest pushing could move
The Chair of Idris. Yniol's rusted arms
Were on his princely person, but thro' these
Prince-like his bearing shone; and errant knights
And ladies came, and by and by the town
Flow'd in and settling circled all the lists.
And there they fixt the forks into the ground,

And over these they placed the silver wand,
And over that the golden sparrow-hawk.
Then Yniol's nephew, after trumpet blown,
Spake to the lady with him and proclaim'd,
"Advance and take, the fairest of the fair,
What I these two years past have won for thee,
The prize of beauty." Loudly spake the prince,
"Forbear; there is a worthier," and the knight
With some surprise and thrice as much disdain
Turn'd, and beheld the four, and all his face
Glow'd like the heart of a great fire at Yule,
So burnt he was with passion, crying out,
"Do battle for it then," no more; and thrice
They clash'd together, and thrice they brake their spears.
Then each, dishorsed and drawing, lash'd at each
So often and with such blows that all the crowd
Wonder'd, and now and then from distant walls
There came a clapping as of phantom hands.
So twice they fought, and twice they breathed, and still
The dew of their great labor and the blood
Of their strong bodies, flowing, drain'd their force.
But either's force was match'd till Yniol's cry,
"Remember that great insult done the Queen,"
Increased Geraint's, who heaved his blade aloft,
And crack'd the helmet thro', and bit the bone,
And fell'd him, and set foot upon his breast,
And said, "Thy name?" To whom the fallen man
Made answer, groaning: "Edyrn, son of Nudd!
Ashamed am I that I should tell it thee.
My pride is broken; men have seen my fall."
"Then, Edyrn, son of Nudd," replied Geraint,
"These two things shalt thou do, or else thou diest.
First, thou thyself, with damsel and with dwarf,
Shalt ride to Arthur's court and, coming there,
Crave pardon for that insult done the Queen,
And shalt abide her judgment on it; next,
Thou shalt give back their earldom to thy kin.
These two things shalt thou do, or thou shalt die."
And Edyrn answer'd, "These things will I do,
For I have never yet been overthrown,
And thou hast overthrown me, and my pride
Is broken down, for Enid sees my fall!"
And rising up he rode to Arthur's court,
And there the Queen forgave him easily.
And, being young, he changed and came to loathe

His crime of traitor, slowly drew himself
Bright from his old dark life, and fell at last
In the great battle fighting for the King.

But when the third day from the hunting-morn
Made a low splendor in the world, and wings
Moved in her ivy, Enid, for she lay
With her fair head in the dim-yellow light,
Among the dancing shadows of the birds,
Woke and bethought her of her promise given
No later than last eve to Prince Geraint—
So bent he seem'd on going the third day,
He would not leave her till her promise given—
To ride with him this morning to the court,
And there be made known to the stately Queen,
And there be wedded with all ceremony.
At this she cast her eyes upon her dress,
And thought it never yet had look'd so mean.
For as a leaf in mid-November is
To what it was in mid-October, seem'd
The dress that now she look'd on to the dress
She look'd on ere the coming of Geraint.
And still she look'd, and still the terror grew
Of that strange bright and dreadful thing, a court,
All staring at her in her faded silk;
And softly to her own sweet heart she said:

"This noble prince who won our earldom back,
So splendid in his acts and his attire,
Sweet heaven, how much I shall discredit him!
Would he could tarry with us here awhile,
But being so beholden to the prince,
It were but little grace in any of us,
Bent as he seem'd on going this third day,
To seek a second favor at his hands,
Yet if he could but tarry a day or two,
Myself would work eye dim and finger lame
Far liefer than so much discredit him."

And Enid fell in longing for a dress
All branch'd and flower'd with gold, a costly gift
Of her good mother, given her on the night
Before her birthday, three sad years ago,
That night of fire, when Edyrn sack'd their house
And scatter'd all they had to all the winds;
For while the mother show'd it, and the two
Were turning and admiring it, the work

To both appear'd so costly, rose a cry
That Edyrn's men were on them, and they fled
With little save the jewels they had on,
Which being sold and sold had bought them bread.
And Edyrn's men had caught them in their flight,
And placed them in this ruin; and she wish'd
The prince had found her in her ancient home;
Then let her fancy flit across the past,
And roam the goodly places that she knew;
And last bethought her how she used to watch,
Near that old home, a pool of golden carp;
And one was patch'd and blurr'd and lustreless
Among his burnish'd brethren of the pool;
And half asleep she made comparison
Of that and these to her own faded self
And the gay court, and fell asleep again,
And dreamt herself was such a faded form
Among her burnish'd sisters of the pool.
But this was in the garden of a king,
And tho' she lay dark in the pool she knew
That all was bright; that all about were birds
Of sunny plume in gilded trellis-work;
That all the turf was rich in plots that look'd
Each like a garnet or a turkis in it;
And lords and ladies of the high court went
In silver tissue talking things of state;
And children of the King in cloth of gold
Glanced at the doors or gambol'd down the walks.
And while she thought, "They will not see me," came
A stately queen whose name was Guinevere,
And all the children in their cloth of gold
Ran to her, crying, "If we have fish at all
Let them be gold; and charge the gardeners now
To pick the faded creature from the pool,
And cast it on the mixen that it die."
And therewithal one came and seized on her,
And Enid started waking, with her heart
All overshadowed by the foolish dream,
And lo! it was her mother grasping her
To get her well awake; and in her hand
A suit of bright apparel, which she laid
Flat on the couch, and spoke exultingly:

"See here, my child, how fresh the colors look,
How fast they hold, like colors of a shell
That keeps the wear and polish of the wave.

Why not? It never yet was worn, I trow:
Look on it, child, and tell me if ye know it."

    And Enid look'd, but, all confused at first,
Could scarce divide it from her foolish dream.
Then suddenly she knew it and rejoiced,
And answer'd, "Yea, I know it; your good gift,
So sadly lost on that unhappy night;
Your own good gift!" "Yea, surely," said the dame,
"And gladly given again this happy morn.
For when the jousts were ended yesterday,
Went Yniol thro' the town, and everywhere
He found the sack and plunder of our house
All scatter'd thro' the houses of the town,
And gave command that all which once was ours
Should now be ours again; and yester-eve,
While ye were talking sweetly with your prince,
Came one with this and laid it in my hand,
For love or fear, or seeking favor of us,
Because we have our earldom back again.
And yester-eve I would not tell you of it,
But kept it for a sweet surprise at morn.
Yea, truly is it not a sweet surprise?
For I myself unwillingly have worn
My faded suit, as you, my child, have yours,
And, howsoever patient, Yniol his.
Ah, dear, he took me from a goodly house,
With store of rich apparel, sumptuous fare,
And page, and maid, and squire, and seneschal,
And pastime both of hawk and hound, and all
That appertains to noble maintenance.
Yea, and he brought me to a goodly house;
But since our fortune swerved from sun to shade,
And all thro' that young traitor, cruel need
Constrain'd us, but a better time has come.
So clothe yourself in this, that better fits
Our mended fortunes and a prince's bride;
For tho' ye won the prize of fairest fair,
And tho' I heard him call you fairest fair,
Let never maiden think, however fair,
She is not fairer in new clothes than old.
And should some great court-lady say, the prince
Hath pick'd a ragged-robin from the hedge,
And like a madman brought her to the court,
Then were ye shamed, and, worse, might shame the prince
To whom we are beholden; but I know,

When my dear child is set forth at her best,
That neither court nor country, tho' they sought
Thro' all the provinces like those of old
That lighted on Queen Esther, has her match."

Here ceased the kindly mother out of breath,
And Enid listen'd brightening as she lay;
Then, as the white and glittering star of morn
Parts from a bank of snow, by and by
Slips into golden cloud, the maiden rose,
And left her maiden couch, and robed herself,
Help'd by the mother's careful hand and eye,
Without a mirror, in the gorgeous gown;
Who, after, turn'd her daughter round, and said
She never yet had seen her half so fair;
And call'd her like that maiden in the tale,
Whom Gwydion made by glamour out of flowers,
And sweeter than the bride of Cassivelaun,
Flur, for whose love the Roman Cæsar first
Invaded Britain: "But we beat him back,
As this great prince invaded us, and we,
Not beat him back, but welcomed him with joy.
And I can scarcely ride with you to court,
For old am I, and rough the ways and wild;
But Yniol goes, and I full oft shall dream
I see my princess as I see her now,
Clothed with my gift and gay among the gay."

But while the women thus rejoiced, Geraint
Woke where he slept in the high hall, and call'd
For Enid, and when Yniol made report
Of that good mother making Enid gay
In such apparel as might well beseem
His princess, or indeed the stately Queen,
He answer'd: "Earl, entreat her by my love,
Albeit I give no reason but my wish,
That she ride with me in her faded silk."
Yniol with that hard message went; it fell
Like flaws in summer laying lusty corn;
For Enid, all abash'd, she knew not why,
Dared not to glance at her good mother's face,
But silently, in all obedience,
Her mother silent too, nor helping her,
Laid from her limbs the costly-broider'd gift,
And robed them in her ancient suit again,
And so descended. Never man rejoiced
More than Geraint to greet her thus attired;

And glancing all at once as keenly at her
As careful robins eye the delver's toil,
Made her cheek burn and either eyelid fall,
But rested with her sweet face satisfied;
Then seeing cloud upon the mother's brow,
Her by both hands he caught, and sweetly said:

"O my new mother, be not wroth or grieved
At thy new son, for my petition to her.
When late I left Caerleon, our great Queen,
In words whose echo lasts, they were so sweet,
Made promise that, whatever bride I brought,
Herself would clothe her like the sun in heaven.
Thereafter, when I reach'd this ruin'd hall,
Beholding one so bright in dark estate,
I vow'd that, could I gain her, our fair Queen,
No hand but hers, should make your Enid burst
Sunlike from cloud—and likewise thought perhaps,
That service done so graciously would bind
The two together; fain I would the two
Should love each other. How can Enid find
A nobler friend? Another thought was mine:
I came among you here so suddenly
That tho' her gentle presence at the lists
Might well have served for proof that I was loved,
I doubted whether daughter's tenderness,
Or easy nature, might not let itself
Be moulded by your wishes for her weal;
Or whether some false sense in her own self
Of my contrasting brightness overbore
Her fancy dwelling in this dusky hall,
And such a sense might make her long for court
And all its perilous glories; and I thought,
That could I someway prove such force in her
Link'd with such love for me that at a word,
No reason given her, she could cast aside
A splendor dear to women, new to her,
And therefore dearer; or if not so new,
Yet therefore tenfold dearer by the power
Of intermitted usage; then I felt
That I could rest, a rock in ebbs and flows,
Fixt on her faith. Now, therefore, I do rest,
A prophet certain of my prophecy,
That never shadow of mistrust can cross
Between us. Grant me pardon for my thoughts;
And for my strange petition I will make

Amends hereafter by some gaudy-day,
When your fair child shall wear your costly gift
Beside your own warm hearth, with, on her knees,
Who knows? another gift of the high God,
Which, maybe, shall have learn'd to lisp you thanks."

He spoke; the mother smiled, but half in tears,
Then brought a mantle down and wrapt her in it,
And claspt and kiss'd her, and they rode away.

Now thrice that morning Guinevere had climb'd
The giant tower, from whose high crest, they say,
Men saw the goodly hills of Somerset,
And white sails flying on the yellow sea;
But not to goodly hill or yellow sea
Look'd the fair Queen, but up the vale of Usk,
By the flat meadow, till she saw them come;
And then descending met them at the gates,
Embraced her with all welcome as a friend,
And did her honor as the prince's bride,
And clothed her for her bridals like the sun;
And all that week was old Caerleon gay,
For by the hands of Dubric, the high saint,
They twain were wedded with all ceremony.

And this was on the last year's Whitsuntide.
But Enid ever kept the faded silk,
Remembering how first he came on her
Drest in that dress, and how he loved her in it,
And all her foolish fears about the dress,
And all his journey toward her, as himself
Had told her, and their coming to the court.

And now this morning when he said to her,
"Put on your worst and meanest dress," she found
And took it, and array'd herself therein.

✠✠✠✠✠✠ GERAINT AND ENID ✠✠✠✠✠✠

O PURBLIND race of miserable men,
How many among us at this very hour
Do forge a lifelong trouble for ourselves,
By taking true for false, or false for true;

Here, thro' the feeble twilight of this world
Groping, how many, until we pass and reach
That other where we see as we are seen!

So fared it with Geraint, who issuing forth
That morning, when they both had got to horse,
Perhaps because he loved her passionately,
And felt that tempest brooding round his heart
Which, if he spoke at all, would break perforce
Upon a head so dear in thunder, said:
"Not at my side. I charge thee ride before,
Ever a good way on before; and this
I charge thee, on thy duty as a wife,
Whatever happens, not to speak to me,
No, not a word!" and Enid was aghast;
And forth they rode, but scarce three paces on,
When crying out, "Effeminate as I am,
I will not fight my way with gilded arms,
All shall be iron;" he loosed a mighty purse,
Hung at his belt, and hurl'd it toward the squire.
So the last sight that Enid had of home
Was all the marble threshold flashing, strown
With gold and scatter'd coinage, and the squire
Chafing his shoulder. Then he cried again,
"To the wilds!" and Enid leading down the tracks
Thro' which he bade her lead him on, they past
The marches, and by bandit-haunted holds,
Gray swamps and pools, waste places of the hern,
And wildernesses, perilous paths, they rode.
Round was their pace at first, but slacken'd soon.
A stranger meeting them had surely thought,
They rode so slowly and they look'd so pale,
That each had suffer'd some exceeding wrong.
For he was ever saying to himself,
"O, I that wasted time to tend upon her,
To compass her with sweet observances,
To dress her beautifully and keep her true"—
And there he broke the sentence in his heart
Abruptly, as a man upon his tongue
May break it when his passion masters him.
And she was ever praying the sweet heavens
To save her dear lord whole from any wound.
And ever in her mind she cast about
For that unnoticed failing in herself
Which made him look so cloudy and so cold;
Till the great plover's human whistle amazed

Her heart, and glancing round the waste she fear'd
In every wavering brake an ambuscade;
Then thought again, "If there be such in me,
I might amend it by the grace of Heaven,
If he would only speak and tell me of it."

But when the fourth part of the day was gone,
Then Enid was aware of three tall knights
On horseback, wholly arm'd, behind a rock
In shadow, waiting for them, caitiffs all;
And heard one crying to his fellow, "Look,
Here comes a laggard hanging down his head,
Who seems no bolder than a beaten hound;
Come, we will slay him and will have his horse
And armor, and his damsel shall be ours."

Then Enid ponder'd in her heart, and said:
"I will go back a little to my lord,
And I will tell him all their caitiff talk;
For, be he wroth even to slaying me,
Far liefer by his dear hand had I die
Than that my lord should suffer loss or shame."

Then she went back some paces of return,
Met his full frown timidly firm, and said:
"My lord, I saw three bandits by the rock
Waiting to fall on you, and heard them boast
That they would slay you, and possess your horse
And armor, and your damsel should be theirs."

He made a wrathful answer: "Did I wish
Your warning or your silence? one command
I laid upon you, not to speak to me,
And thus ye keep it! Well then, look—for now,
Whether ye wish me victory or defeat,
Long for my life or hunger for my death,
Yourself shall see my vigor is not lost."

Then Enid waited pale and sorrowful,
And down upon him bare the bandit three.
And at the midmost charging, Prince Geraint
Drave the long spear a cubit thro' his breast
And out beyond; and then against his brace
Of comrades, each of whom had broken on him
A lance that splinter'd like an icicle,
Swung from his brand a windy buffet out
Once, twice, to right, to left, and stunn'd the twain

Or slew them, and dismounting, like a man
That skins the wild beast after slaying him,
Stript from the three dead wolves of woman born
The three gay suits of armor which they wore,
And let the bodies lie, but bound the suits
Of armor on their horses, each on each,
And tied the bridle-reins of all the three
Together, and said to her, "Drive them on
Before you;" and she drove them thro' the waste.

He follow'd nearer; ruth began to work
Against his anger in him, while he watch'd
The being he loved best in all the world,
With difficulty in mild obedience
Driving them on. He fain had spoken to her,
And loosed in words of sudden fire the wrath
And smoulder'd wrong that burnt him all within;
But evermore it seem'd an easier thing
At once without remorse to strike her dead
Than to cry "Halt," and to her own bright face
Accuse her of the least immodesty:
And thus tongue-tied, it made him wroth the more
That she could speak whom his own ear had heard
Call herself false, and suffering thus he made
Minutes an age; but in scarce longer time
Than at Caerleon the full-tided Usk,
Before he turn to fall seaward again,
Pauses, did Enid, keeping watch, behold
In the first shallow shade of a deep wood,
Before a gloom of stubborn-shafted oaks,
Three other horsemen waiting, wholly arm'd,
Whereof one seem'd far larger than her lord,
And shook her pulses, crying, "Look, a prize!
Three horses and three goodly suits of arms,
And all in charge of whom? a girl! set on."
"Nay," said the second, "yonder comes a knight."
The third, "A craven; how he hangs his head!"
The giant answer'd merrily, "Yea, but one?
Wait here, and when he passes fall upon him!"

And Enid ponder'd in her heart and said:
"I will abide the coming of my lord,
And I will tell him all their villainy.
My lord is weary with the fight before,
And they will fall upon him unawares.
I needs must disobey him for his good;

How should I dare obey him to his harm?
Needs must I speak, and tho' he kill me for it,
I save a life dearer to me than mine."

And she abode his coming, and said to him
With timid firmness, "Have I leave to speak?"
He said, "Ye take it, speaking," and she spoke:

"There lurk three villains yonder in the wood,
And each of them is wholly arm'd, and one
Is larger-limb'd than you are, and they say
That they will fall upon you while ye pass."

To which he flung a wrathful answer back:
"And if there were an hundred in the wood,
And every man were larger-limb'd than I,
And all at once should sally out upon me,
I swear it would not ruffle me so much
As you that not obey me. Stand aside,
And if I fall, cleave to the better man."

And Enid stood aside to wait the event,
Not dare to watch the combat, only breathe.
Short fits of prayer, at every stroke a breath,
And he she dreaded most bare down upon him.
Aim'd at the helm, his lance err'd; but Geraint's,
A little in the late encounter strain'd,
Struck thro' the bulky bandit's corselet home,
And then brake short, and down his enemy roll'd,
And there lay still; as he that tells the tale
Saw once a great piece of a promontory,
That had a sapling growing on it, slide
From the long shore-cliff's windy walls to the beach,
And there lie still, and yet the sapling grew;
So lay the man transfixt. His craven pair
Of comrades making slowlier at the prince,
When now they saw their bulwark fallen, stood;
On whom the victor, to confound them more,
Spurr'd with his terrible war-cry; for as one,
That listens near a torrent mountain-brook,
All thro' the crash of the near cataract hears
The drumming thunder of the huger fall
At distance, were the soldiers wont to hear
His voice in battle, and be kindled by it,
And foemen scared, like that false pair who turn'd
Flying, but, overtaken, died the death
Themselves had wrought on many an innocent.

Thereon Geraint, dismounting, pick'd the lance
That pleased him best, and drew from those dead wolves
Their three gay suits of armor, each from each,
And bound them on their horses, each on each,
And tied the bridle-reins of all the three
Together, and said to her, "Drive them on
Before you," and she drove them thro' the wood.

He follow'd nearer still. The pain she had
To keep them in the wild ways of the wood,
Two sets of three laden with jingling arms,
Together, served a little to disedge
The sharpness of that pain about her heart;
And they themselves, like creatures gently born
But into bad hands fallen, and now so long
By bandits groom'd, prick'd their light ears, and felt
Her low firm voice and tender government.

So thro' the green gloom of the wood they past,
And issuing under open heavens beheld
A little town with towers, upon a rock,
And close beneath, a meadow gemlike chased
In the brown wild, and mowers mowing in it;
And down a rocky pathway from the place
There came a fair-hair'd youth, that in his hand
Bare victual for the mowers; and Geraint
Had ruth again on Enid looking pale.
Then, moving downward to the meadow ground,
He, when the fair-hair'd youth came by him, said,
"Friend, let her eat; the damsel is so faint."
"Yea, willingly," replied the youth; "and thou,
My lord, eat also, tho' the fare is coarse,
And only meet for mowers;" then set down
His basket, and dismounting on the sward
They let the horses graze, and ate themselves.
And Enid took a little delicately,
Less having stomach for it than desire
To close with her lord's pleasure, but Geraint
Ate all the mowers' victual unawares,
And when he found all empty was amazed;
And "Boy," said he, "I have eaten all, but take
A horse and arms for guerdon; choose the best."
He, reddening in extremity of delight,
"My lord, you overpay me fifty-fold."
"Ye will be all the wealthier," cried the prince.
"I take it as free gift, then," said the boy,

"Not guerdon; for myself can easily,
While your good damsel rests, return and fetch
Fresh victual for these mowers of our earl;
For these are his, and all the field is his,
And I myself am his; and I will tell him
How great a man thou art. He loves to know
When men of mark are in his territory;
And he will have thee to his palace here,
And serve thee costlier than with mowers' fare."

Then said Geraint: "I wish no better fare;
I never ate with angrier appetite
Than when I left your mowers dinnerless.
And into no earl's palace will I go.
I know, God knows, too much of palaces!
And if he want me, let him come to me.
But hire us some fair chamber for the night,
And stalling for the horses, and return
With victual for these men, and let us know."

"Yea, my kind lord," said the glad youth, and went,
Held his head high, and thought himself a knight,
And up the rocky pathway disappear'd,
Leading the horse, and they were left alone.

But when the prince had brought his errant eyes
Home from the rock, sideways he let them glance
At Enid, where she droopt. His own false doom,
That shadow of mistrust should never cross
Betwixt them, came upon him, and he sigh'd;
Then with another humorous ruth remark'd
The lusty mowers laboring dinnerless,
And watch'd the sun blaze on the turning scythe,
And after nodded sleepily in the heat.
But she, remembering her old ruin'd hall,
And all the windy clamor of the daws
About her hollow turret, pluck'd the grass
There growing longest by the meadow's edge,
And into many a listless annulet,
Now over, now beneath her marriage ring,
Wove and unwove it, till the boy return'd
And told them of a chamber, and they went;
Where, after saying to her, "If ye will,
Call for the woman of the house," to which
She answer'd, "Thanks, my lord;" the two remain'd
Apart by all the chamber's width, and mute
As creatures voiceless thro' the fault of birth,

Or two wild men supporters of a shield,
Painted, who stare at open space, nor glance
The one at other, parted by the shield.

On a sudden, many a voice along the street,
And heel against the pavement echoing, burst
Their drowse; and either started while the door,
Push'd from without, drave backward to the wall,
And midmost of a rout of roisterers,
Femininely fair and dissolutely pale,
Her suitor in old years before Geraint
Enter'd, the wild lord of the place, Limours.
He moving up with pliant courtliness
Greeted Geraint full face, but stealthily,
In the mid-warmth of welcome and graspt hand,
Found Enid with the corner of his eye,
And knew her sitting sad and solitary.
Then cried Geraint for wine and goodly cheer
To feed the sudden guest, and sumptuously,
According to his fashion, bade the host
Call in what men soever were his friends,
And feast with these in honor of their earl;
"And care not for the cost; the cost is mine."

And wine and food were brought, and Earl Limours
Drank till he jested with all ease, and told
Free tales, and took the word and play'd upon it,
And made it of two colors; for his talk,
When wine and free companions kindled him,
Was wont to glance and sparkle like a gem
Of fifty facets; thus he moved the prince
To laughter and his comrades to applause.
Then when the prince was merry, ask'd Limours,
"Your leave, my lord, to cross the room, and speak
To your good damsel there who sits apart,
And seems so lonely?" "My free leave," he said;
"Get her to speak; she doth not speak to me."
Then rose Limours, and looking at his feet,
Like him who tries the bridge he fears may fail,
Crost and came near, lifted adoring eyes,
Bow'd at her side and utter'd whisperingly:

"Enid, the pilot star of my lone life,
Enid, my early and my only love,
Enid, the loss of whom hath turn'd me wild—
What chance is this? how is it I see you here?
Ye are in my power at last, are in my power.

Yet fear me not; I call mine own self wild,
But keep a touch of sweet civility
Here in the heart of waste and wilderness.
I thought, but that your father came between,
In former days you saw me favorably.
And if it were so do not keep it back.
Make me a little happier; let me know it.
Owe you me nothing for a life half-lost?
Yea, yea, the whole dear debt of all you are.
And, Enid, you and he, I see with joy,
Ye sit apart, you do not speak to him,
You come with no attendance, page or maid,
To serve you—doth he love you as of old?
For, call it lovers' quarrels, yet I know
Tho' men may bicker with the things they love,
They would not make them laughable in all eyes,
Not while they loved them; and your wretched dress,
A wretched insult on you, dumbly speaks
Your story, that this man loves you no more.
Your beauty is no beauty to him now.
A common chance—right well I know it—pall'd—
For I know men; nor will ye win him back,
For the man's love once gone never returns.
But here is one who loves you as of old;
With more exceeding passion than of old.
Good, speak the word; my followers ring him round.
He sits unarm'd; I hold a finger up;
They understand. Nay, I do not mean blood;
Nor need ye look so scared at what I say.
My malice is no deeper than a moat,
No stronger than a wall. There is the keep;
He shall not cross us more; speak but the word.
Or speak it not; but then by Him that made me
The one true lover whom you ever own'd,
I will make use of all the power I have.
O, pardon me! the madness of that hour
When first I parted from thee moves me yet."

At this the tender sound of his own voice
And sweet self-pity, or the fancy of it,
Made his eye moist; but Enid fear'd his eyes,
Moist as they were, wine-heated from the feast,
And answer'd with such craft as women use,
Guilty or guiltless, to stave off a chance
That breaks upon them perilously, and said:

"Earl, if you love me as in former years,
And do not practise on me, come with morn,
And snatch me from him as by violence.
Leave me to-night; I am weary to the death."

Low at leave-taking, with his brandish'd plume
Brushing his instep, bow'd the all-amorous earl,
And the stout prince bade him a loud good-night.
He moving homeward babbled to his men,
How Enid never loved a man but him,
Nor cared a broken egg-shell for her lord.

But Enid left alone with Prince Geraint,
Debating his command of silence given,
And that she now perforce must violate it,
Held commune with herself, and while she held
He fell asleep, and Enid had no heart
To wake him, but hung o'er him wholly pleased
To find him yet unwounded after fight,
And hear him breathing low and equally.
Anon she rose and, stepping lightly, heap'd
The pieces of his armor in one place,
All to be there against a sudden need;
Then dozed awhile herself, but, over toil'd
By that day's grief and travel, evermore
Seem'd catching at a rootless thorn, and then
Went slipping down horrible precipices,
And strongly striking out her limbs awoke;
Then thought she heard the wild earl at the door,
With all his rout of random followers.
Sound on a dreadful trumpet, summoning her;
Which was the red cock shouting to the light,
As the gray dawn stole o'er the dewy world
And glimmer'd on his armor in the room.
And once again she rose to look at it,
But touch'd it unawares; jangling, the casque
Fell, and he started up and stared at her.
Then breaking his command of silence given,
She told him all that Earl Limours had said,
Except the passage that he loved her not;
Nor left untold the craft herself had used,
But ended with apology so sweet,
Low-spoken, and of so few words, and seem'd
So justified by that necessity,
That tho' he thought, "Was it for him she wept
In Devon?" he but gave a wrathful groan,

Saying, "Your sweet faces make good fellows fools
And traitors. Call the host and bid him bring
Charger and palfrey." So she glided out
Among the heavy breathings of the house,
And like a household spirit at the walls
Beat, till she woke the sleepers, and return'd;
Then tending her rough lord, tho' all unask'd,
In silence, did him service as a squire;
Till issuing arm'd he found the host and cried,
"Thy reckoning, friend?" and ere he learnt it, "Take
Five horses and their armors;" and the host,
Suddenly honest, answer'd in amaze,
"My lord, I scarce have spent the worth of one!"
"Ye will be all the wealthier," said the prince,
And then to Enid, "Forward! and today
I charge you, Enid, more especially,
What thing soever ye may hear, or see,
Or fancy—tho' I count it of small use
To charge you—that ye speak not but obey."

And Enid answer'd: "Yea, my lord, I know
Your wish and would obey; but, riding first,
I hear the violent threats you do not hear,
I see the danger which you cannot see.
Then not to give you warning, that seems hard,
Almost beyond me; yet I would obey."

"Yea so," said he, "do it; be not too wise,
Seeing that ye are wedded to a man,
Not all mismated with a yawning clown,
But one with arms to guard his head and yours,
With eyes to find you out however far,
And ears to hear you even in his dreams."

With that he turn'd and look'd as keenly at her
As careful robins eye the delver's toil;
And that within her which a wanton fool
Or hasty judger would have call'd her guilt
Made her cheek burn and either eyelid fall.
And Geraint look'd and was not satisfied.

Then forward by a way which, beaten broad,
Led from the territory of false Limours
To the waste earldom of another earl,
Doorm, whom his shaking vassals call'd the Bull,
Went Enid with her sullen follower on.
Once she look'd back, and when she saw him ride

More near by many a rood than yester-morn,
It wellnigh made her cheerful; till Geraint,
Waving an angry hand as who should say,
"Ye watch me," sadden'd all her heart again.
But while the sun yet beat a dewy blade,
The sound of many a heavily-galloping hoof
Smote on her ear, and turning round she saw
Dust, and the points of lances bicker in it.
Then, not to disobey her lord's behest,
And yet to give him warning, for he rode
As if he heard not, moving back she held
Her finger up, and pointed to the dust.
At which the warrior in his obstinacy,
Because she kept the letter of his word,
Was in a manner pleased, and turning stood.
And in the moment after, wild Limours,
Borne on a black horse, like a thundercloud
Whose skirts are loosen'd by the breaking storm,
Half ridden off with by the thing he rode,
And all in passion uttering a dry shriek,
Dash'd on Geraint, who closed with him, and bore
Down by the length of lance and arm beyond
The crupper, and so left him stunn'd or dead,
And overthrew the next that follow'd him,
And blindly rush'd on all the rout behind.
But at the flash and motion of the man
They vanish'd panic-stricken, like a shoal
Of darting fish, that on a summer morn
Adown the crystal dykes at Camelot
Come slipping o'er their shadows on the sand,
But if a man who stands upon the brink
But lift a shining hand against the sun,
There is not left the twinkle of a fin
Betwixt the cressy islets white in flower;
So, scared but at the motion of the man,
Fled all the boon companions of the earl,
And left him lying in the public way;
So vanish friendships only made in wine.

Then like a stormy sunlight smiled Geraint,
Who saw the chargers of the two that fell
Start from their fallen lords and wildly fly,
Mixt with the flyers. "Horse and man," he said,
"All of one mind and all right-honest friends!
Not a hoof left! and I methinks till now
Was honest—paid with horses and with arms;

I cannot steal or plunder, no, nor beg.
And so what say ye, shall we strip him there,
Your lover? has your palfrey heart enough
To bear his armor? shall we fast or dine?
No?—then do thou, being right honest, pray
That we may meet the horsemen of Earl Doorm;
I too would still be honest." Thus he said;
And sadly gazing on her bridle-reins,
And answering not one word, she led the way.

But as a man to whom a dreadful loss
Falls in a far land and he knows it not,
But coming back he learns it, and the loss
So pains him that he sickens nigh to death;
So fared it with Geraint, who, being prick'd
In combat with the followers of Limours,
Bled underneath his armor secretly,
And so rode on, nor told his gentle wife
What ail'd him, hardly knowing it himself,
Till his eye darken'd and his helmet wagg'd;
And at a sudden swerving of the road,
Tho' happily down on a bank of grass,
The prince, without a word, from his horse fell.

And Enid heard the clashing of his fall,
Suddenly came, and at his side all pale
Dismounting loosed the fastenings of his arms,
Nor let her true hand falter, nor blue eye
Moisten, till she had lighted on his wound,
And tearing off her veil of faded silk
Had bared her forehead to the blistering sun,
And swathed the hurt that drain'd her dear lord's life.
Then, after all was done that hand could do,
She rested, and her desolation came
Upon her, and she wept beside the way.

And many past, but none regarded her,
For in that realm of lawless turbulence
A woman weeping for her murder'd mate
Was cared as much for as a summer shower.
One took him for a victim of Earl Doorm,
Nor dared to waste a perilous pity on him.
Another hurrying past, a man-at-arms,
Rode on a mission to the bandit earl;
Half whistling and half singing a coarse song,
He drove the dust against her veilless eyes.
Another, flying from the wrath of Doorm

Before an ever-fancied arrow, made
The long way smoke beneath him in his fear;
At which her palfrey whinnying lifted heel,
And scour'd into the coppices and was lost,
While the great charger stood, grieved like a man.

But at the point of noon the huge Earl Doorm,
Broad-faced with under-fringe of russet beard,
Bound on a foray, rolling eyes of prey,
Came riding with a hundred lances up;
But ere he came, like one that hails a ship,
Cried out with a big voice, "What, is he dead?"
"No, no, not dead!" she answer'd in all haste.
"Would some of your kind people take him up,
And bear him hence out of this cruel sun?
Most sure am I, quite sure, he is not dead."

Then said Earl Doorm: "Well, if he be not dead,
Why wail ye for him thus? ye seem a child.
And be he dead, I count you for a fool;
Your wailing will not quicken him; dead or not,
Ye mar a comely face with idiot tears.
Yet, since the face is comely—some of you,
Here, take him up, and bear him to our hall.
And if he live, we will have him of our band;
And if he die, why earth has earth enough
To hide him. See ye take the charger too,
A noble one."

He spake and past away,
But left two brawny spearmen, who advanced,
Each growling like a dog, when his good bone
Seems to be pluck'd at by the village boys
Who love to vex him eating, and he fears
To lose his bone, and lays his foot upon it,
Gnawing and growling; so the ruffians growl'd,
Fearing to lose, and all for a dead man,
Their chance of booty from the morning's raid,
Yet raised and laid him on a litter-bier,
Such as they brought upon their forays out
For those that might be wounded; laid him on it
All in the hollow of his shield, and took
And bore him to the naked hall of Doorm—
His gentle charger following him unled—
And cast him and the bier in which he lay
Down on an oaken settle in the hall,
And then departed, hot in haste to join

Their luckier mates, but growling as before,
And cursing their lost time, and the dead man,
And their own earl, and their own souls, and her.
They might as well have blest her; she was deaf
To blessing or to cursing save from one.

So for long hours sat Enid by her lord
There in the naked hall, propping his head,
And chafing his pale hands, and calling to him,
Till at the last he waken'd from his swoon,
And found his own dear bride propping his head,
And chafing his faint hands, and calling to him;
And felt the warm tears falling on his face,
And said to his own heart, "She weeps for me;"
And yet lay still, and feign'd himself as dead,
That he might prove her to the uttermost,
And say to his own heart, "She weeps for me."

But in the falling afternoon return'd
The huge Earl Doorm with plunder to the hall.
His lusty spearmen follow'd him with noise:
Each hurling down a heap of things that rang
Against the pavement, cast his lance aside,
And doff'd his helm; and then there flutter'd in,
Half-bold, half-frighted, with dilated eyes,
A tribe of women, dress'd in many hues,
And mingled with the spearmen; and Earl Doorm
Struck with a knife's haft hard against the board.
And call'd for flesh and wine to feed his spears.
And men brought in whole hogs and quarter beeves,
And all the hall was dim with steam of flesh.
And none spake word, but all sat down at once,
And ate with tumult in the naked hall,
Feeding like horses when you hear them feed;
Till Enid shrank far back into herself,
To shun the wild ways of the lawless tribe.
But when Earl Doorm had eaten all he would,
He roll'd his eyes about the hall, and found
A damsel drooping in a corner of it.
Then he remember'd her and how she wept.
And out of her there came a power upon him;
And rising on the sudden he said: "Eat!
I never yet beheld a thing so pale.
God's curse, it makes me mad to see you weep.
Eat! Look yourself. Good luck had your good man,
For were I dead who is it would weep for me?
Sweet lady, never since I first drew breath

Have I beheld a lily like yourself.
And so there lived some color in your cheek,
There is not one among my gentlewomen
Were fit to wear your slipper for a glove.
But listen to me, and by me be ruled,
And I will do the thing I have not done,
For ye shall share my earldom with me, girl,
And we will live like two birds in one nest,
And I will fetch you forage from all fields,
For I compel all creatures to my will."

He spoke; the brawny spearman let his cheek
Bulge with the unswallow'd piece, and turning stared;
While some, whose souls the old serpent long had drawn
Down, as the worm draws in the wither'd leaf
And makes it earth, hiss'd each at other's ear
What shall not be recorded—women they,
Women, or what had been those gracious things,
But now desired the humbling of their best,
Yea, would have help'd him to it; and all at once
They hated her, who took no thought of them,
But answer'd in low voice, her meek head yet
Drooping, "I pray you of your courtesy,
He being as he is, to let me be."

She spake so low he hardly heard her speak,
But like a mighty patron, satisfied
With what himself had done so graciously,
Assumed that she had thank'd him, adding, "Yea,
Eat and be glad, for I account you mine."

She answer'd meekly, "How should I be glad
Henceforth in all the world at anything,
Until my lord arise and look upon me?"

Here the huge earl cried out upon her talk,
As all but empty heart and weariness
And sickly nothing; suddenly seized on her,
And bare her by main violence to the board,
And thrust the dish before her, crying, "Eat."

"No, no," said Enid, vext, "I will not eat
Till yonder man upon the bier arise,
And eat with me." "Drink, then," he answer'd. "Here!"—
And fill'd a horn with wine and held it to her,—
"Lo! I, myself, when flush'd with fight or hot,
God's curse, with anger—often I myself,
Before I well have drunken, scarce can eat;
Drink therefore, and the wine will change your will."

"Not so," she cried, "by Heaven, I will not drink
Till my dear lord arise and bid me do it,
And drink with me; and if he rise no more,
I will not look at wine until I die."

At this he turn'd all red and paced his hall,
Now gnaw'd his under, now his upper lip,
And coming up close to her, said at last:
"Girl, for I see ye scorn my courtesies,
Take warning; yonder man is surely dead,
And I compel all creatures to my will.
Not eat nor drink? And wherefore wail for one
Who put your beauty to this flout and scorn
By dressing it in rags? Amazed am I,
Beholding how ye butt against my wish,
That I forbear you thus; cross me no more.
At least put off to please me this poor gown,
This silken rag, this beggar-woman's weed.
I love that beauty should go beautifully;
For see ye not my gentlewomen here,
How gay, how suited to the house of one
Who loves that beauty should go beautifully?
Rise therefore; robe yourself in this; obey."

He spoke, and one among his gentlewomen
Display'd a splendid silk of foreign loom,
Where like a shoaling sea the lovely blue
Play'd into green, and thicker down the front
With jewels than the sward with drops of dew,
When all night long a cloud clings to the hill,
And with the dawn ascending lets the day
Strike where it clung; so thickly shone the gems.

But Enid answer'd, harder to be moved
Than hardest tyrants in their day of power,
With lifelong injuries burning unavenged,
And now their hour has come; and Enid said:

"In this poor gown my dear lord found me first,
And loved me serving in my father's hall;
In this poor gown I rode with him to court,
And there the Queen array'd me like the sun;
In this poor gown he bade me clothe myself,
When now we rode upon this fatal quest
Of honor, where no honor can be gain'd;
And this poor gown I will not cast aside
Until himself arise a living man,
And bid me cast it. I have griefs enough;

Pray you be gentle, pray you let me be.
I never loved, can never love but him.
Yea, God, I pray you of your gentleness,
He being as he is, to let me be."

Then strode the brute earl up and down his hall,
And took his russet beard between his teeth;
Last, coming up quite close, and in his mood
Crying, "I count it of no more avail,
Dame, to be gentle than ungentle with you;
Take my salute," unknightly with flat hand,
However lightly, smote her on the cheek.

Then Enid, in her utter helplessness,
And since she thought, "He had not dared to do it,
Except he surely knew my lord was dead,"
Sent forth a sudden sharp and bitter cry,
As of a wild thing taken in the trap,
Which sees the trapper coming thro' the wood.

This heard Geraint, and grasping at his sword,—
It lay beside him in the hollow shield,—
Made but a single bound, and with a sweep of it
Shore thro' the swarthy neck, and like a ball
The russet-bearded head roll'd on the floor.
So died Earl Doorm by him he counted dead.
And all the men and women in the hall
Rose when they saw the dead man rise, and fled
Yelling as from a spectre, and the two
Were left alone together, and he said:

"Enid, I have used you worse than that dead man,
Done you more wrong; we both have undergone
That trouble which has left me thrice your own.
Henceforward I will rather die than doubt.
And here I lay this penance on myself,
Not, tho' mine own ears heard you yestermorn—
You thought me sleeping, but I heard you say,
I heard you say, that you were no true wife,
I swear I will not ask your meaning in it.
I do believe yourself against yourself,
And will henceforward rather die than doubt."

And Enid could not say one tender word,
She felt so blunt and stupid at the heart.
She only pray'd him, "Fly, they will return
And slay you; fly, your charger is without,
My palfrey lost." "Then, Enid, shall you ride

Behind me." "Yea," said Enid, "let us go."
And moving out they found the stately horse,
Who now no more a vassal to the thief,
But free to stretch his limbs in lawful fight,
Neigh'd with all gladness as they came, and stoop'd
With a low whinny toward the pair; and she
Kiss'd the white star upon his noble front,
Glad also; then Geraint upon the horse
Mounted, and reach'd a hand, and on his foot
She set her own and climb'd; he turn'd his face
And kiss'd her climbing, and she cast her arms
About him, and at once they rode away.

And never yet, since high in Paradise
O'er the four rivers the first roses blew,
Came purer pleasure unto mortal kind
Than lived thro' her who in that perilous hour
Put hand to hand beneath her husband's heart,
And felt him hers again. She did not weep,
But o'er her meek eyes came a happy mist
Like that which kept the heart of Eden green
Before the useful trouble of the rain.
Yet not so misty were her meek blue eyes
As not to see before them on the path,
Right in the gateway of the bandit hold,
A knight of Arthur's court, who laid his lance
In rest and made as if to fall upon him.
Then, fearing for his hurt and loss of blood,
She, with her mind all full of what had chanced,
Shriek'd to the stranger, "Slay not a dead man!"
"The voice of Enid," said the knight; but she,
Beholding it was Edyrn, son of Nudd,
Was moved so much the more, and shriek'd again,
"O cousin, slay not him who gave you life."
And Edyrn moving frankly forward spake:
"My lord Geraint, I greet you with all love;
I took you for a bandit knight of Doorm;
And fear not, Enid, I should fall upon him,
Who love you, prince, with something of the love
Wherewith we love the Heaven that chastens us.
For once, when I was up so high in pride
That I was halfway down the slope to hell,
By overthrowing me you threw me higher.
Now, made a knight of Arthur's Table Round,
And since I knew this earl when I myself

Was half a bandit in my lawless hour,
I come the mouthpiece of our King to Doorm—
The King is close behind me—bidding him
Disband himself, and scatter all his powers,
Submit, and hear the judgment of the King."

"He hears the judgment of the King of kings,"
Cried the wan prince; "and lo, the powers of Doorm
Are scatter'd!" and he pointed to the field,
Where, huddled here and there on mound and knoll,
Were men and women staring and aghast,
While some yet fled; and then he plainlier told
How the huge earl lay slain within his hall.
But when the knight besought him, "Follow me,
Prince, to the camp, and in the King's own ear
Speak what has chanced; ye surely have endured
Strange chances here alone;" that other flush'd,
And hung his head, and halted in reply,
Fearing the mild face of the blameless King,
And after madness acted question ask'd;
Till Edyrn crying, "If ye will not go
To Arthur, then will Arthur come to you."
"Enough," he said, "I follow," and they went.
But Enid in their going had two fears,
One from the bandit scatter'd in the field,
And one from Edyrn. Every now and then,
When Edyrn rein'd his charger at her side,
She shrank a little. In a hollow land,
From which old fires have broken, men may fear
Fresh fire and ruin. He, perceiving, said:

"Fair and dear cousin, you that most had cause
To fear me, fear no longer, I am changed.
Yourself were first the blameless cause to make
My nature's prideful sparkle in the blood
Break into furious flame; being repulsed
By Yniol and yourself, I schemed and wrought
Until I overturn'd him; then set up—
With one main purpose ever at my heart—
My haughty jousts, and took a paramour;
Did her mock-honor as the fairest fair,
And, toppling over all antagonism,
So wax'd in pride that I believed myself
Unconquerable, for I was wellnigh mad;
And, but for my main purpose in these jousts,
I should have slain your father, seized yourself.

I lived in hope that sometime you would come
To these my lists with him whom best you loved,
And there, poor cousin, with your meek blue eyes,
The truest eyes that ever answer'd heaven,
Behold me overturn and trample on him.
Then, had you cried, or knelt, or pray'd to me,
I should not less have kill'd him. And you came,—
But once you came,—and with your own true eyes
Beheld the man you loved—I speak as one
Speaks of a service done him—overthrow
My proud self, and my purpose three years old,
And set his foot upon me, and give me life.
There was I broken down, there was I saved;
Tho' thence I rode all-shamed, hating the life
He gave me, meaning to be rid of it.
And all the penance the Queen laid upon me
Was but to rest awhile within her court;
Where first as sullen as a beast new-caged,
And waiting to be treated like a wolf,
Because I knew my deeds were known, I found,
Instead of scornful pity or pure scorn,
Such fine reserve and noble reticence,
Manners so kind, yet stately, such a grace
Of tenderest courtesy, that I began
To glance behind me at my former life,
And find that it had been the wolf's indeed.
And oft I talk'd with Dubric, the high saint,
Who, with mild heat of holy oratory,
Subdued me somewhat to that gentleness
Which, when it weds with manhood, makes a man.
And you were often there about the Queen,
But saw me not, or mark'd not if you saw;
Nor did I care or dare to speak with you,
But kept myself aloof till I was changed;
And fear not, cousin, I am changed indeed."

He spoke, and Enid easily believed,
Like simple noble natures, credulous
Of what they long for, good in friend or foe,
There most in those who most have done them ill.
And when they reach'd the camp the King himself
Advanced to greet them, and beholding her
Tho' pale, yet happy, ask'd her not a word,
But went apart with Edyrn, whom he held

In converse for a little, and return'd,
And, gravely smiling, lifted her from horse,
And kiss'd her with all pureness, brother-like
And show'd an empty tent allotted her,
And glancing for a minute, till he saw her
Pass into it, turn'd to the prince, and said:

"Prince, when of late ye pray'd me for my leave
To move to your own land and there defend
Your marches, I was prick'd with some reproof,
As one that let foul wrong stagnate and be,
By having look'd too much thro' alien eyes,
And wrought too long with delegated hands,
Not used mine own; but now behold me come
To cleanse this common sewer of all my realm,
With Edyrn and with others. Have ye look'd
At Edyrn? have ye seen how nobly changed?
This work of his is great and wonderful.
His very face with change of heart is changed.
The world will not believe a man repents;
And this wise world of ours is mainly right.
Full seldom doth a man repent, or use
Both grace and will to pick the vicious quitch
Of blood and custom wholly out of him,
And make all clean, and plant himself afresh.
Edyrn has done it weeding all his heart
As I will weed this land before I go.
I, therefore, made him of our Table Round,
Not rashly, but have proved him every way
One of our noblest, our most valorous,
Sanest and most obedient; and indeed
This work of Edyrn, wrought upon himself
After a life of violence, seems to me
A thousand-fold more great and wonderful
Than if some knight of mine, risking his life,
My subject with my subjects under him,
Should make an onslaught single on a realm
Of robbers, tho' he slew them one by one,
And were himself nigh wounded to the death."

So spake the King; low bow'd the prince, and felt
His work was neither great nor wonderful,
And past to Enid's tent; and thither came
The King's own leech to look into his hurt;
And Enid tended on him there; and there
Her constant motion round him, and the breath
Of her sweet tendance hovering over him,

Fill'd all the genial courses of his blood
With deeper and with ever deeper love,
As the Southwest that blowing Bala lake
Fills all the sacred Dee. So past the days.

But while Geraint lay healing of his hurt,
The blameless King went forth and cast his eyes
On each of all whom Uther left in charge
Long since, to guard the justice of the King.
He look'd and found them wanting; and as now
Men weed the White Horse on the Berkshire hills,
To keep him bright and clean as heretofore,
He rooted out the slothful officer
Or guilty, which for bribe had wink'd at wrong,
And in their chairs set up a stronger race
With hearts and hands, and sent a thousand men
To till the wastes, and moving everywhere
Clear'd the dark places and let in the law,
And broke the bandit holds and cleansed the land.

Then, when Geraint was whole again, they past
With Arthur to Caerleon upon Usk.
There the great Queen once more embraced her friend,
And clothed her in apparel like the day.
And tho' Geraint could never take again
That comfort from their converse which he took
Before the Queen's fair name was breathed upon,
He rested well content that all was well.
Thence after tarrying for a space they rode,
And fifty knights rode with them to the shores
Of Severn, and they past to their own land.
And there he kept the justice of the King
So vigorously yet mildly that all hearts
Applauded, and the spiteful whisper died;
And being ever foremost in the chase,
And victor at the tilt and tournament,
They call'd him the great prince and man of men.
But Enid, whom her ladies loved to call
Enid the Fair, a grateful people named
Enid the Good; and in their halls arose
The cry of children, Enids and Geraints
Of times to be; nor did he doubt her more,
But rested in her fealty till he crown'd
A happy life with a fair death, and fell
Against the heathen of the Northern Sea
In battle, fighting for the blameless King.

✠✠✠✠✠✠✠ BALIN AND BALAN ✠✠✠✠✠✠✠

PELLAM the king, who held and lost with Lot
In that first war, and had his realm restored
But render'd tributary, fail'd of late
To send his tribute; wherefore Arthur call'd
His treasurer, one of many years, and spake:
"Go thou with him and him and bring it to us,
Lest we should set one truer on his throne.
Man's world is God in man."

　　　　　　　　　　His baron said:
"We go, but harken: there be two strange knights
Who sit near Camelot at a fountain-side
A mile beneath the forest, challenging
And overthrowing every knight who comes.
Wilt thou I undertake them as we pass,
And send them to thee?"

　　　　　　　　　　Arthur laugh'd upon him:
"Old friend, too old to be so young, depart,
Delay not thou for aught, but let them sit,
Until they find a lustier than themselves."

So these departed. Early, one fair dawn,
The light-wing'd spirit of his youth return'd
On Arthur's heart; he arm'd himself and went,
So coming to the fountain-side beheld
Balin and Balan sitting statue-like,
Brethren, to right and left the spring, that down,
From underneath a plume of lady-fern,
Sang, and the sand danced at the bottom of it.
And on the right of Balin Balin's horse
Was fast beside an alder, on the left
Of Balan Balan's near a poplar-tree.
"Fair sirs," said Arthur, "wherefore sit ye here?"
Balin and Balan answer'd: "For the sake
Of glory; we be mightier men than all
In Arthur's court; that also have we proved,
For whatsoever knight against us came
Or I or he have easily overthrown."

"I too," said Arthur, "am of Arthur's hall,
But rather proven in his Paynim wars
Than famous jousts; but see, or proven or not,
Whether me likewise ye can overthrow."
And Arthur lightly smote the brethren down,
And lightly so return'd, and no man knew.

Then Balin rose, and Balan, and beside
The carolling water set themselves again,
And spake no word until the shadow turn'd;
When from the fringe of coppice round them burst
A spangled pursuivant, and crying, "Sirs,
Rise, follow! ye be sent for by the King,"
They follow'd; whom when Arthur seeing ask'd,
"Tell me your names; why sat ye by the well?"
Balin the stillness of a minute broke
Saying, "An unmelodious name to thee,
Balin, 'the Savage'—that addition thine—
My brother and my better, this man here,
Balan. I smote upon the naked skull
A thrall of thine in open hall; my hand
Was gauntleted, half slew him, for I heard
He had spoken evil of me; thy just wrath
Sent me a three-years' exile from thine eyes.
I have not lived my life delightsomely;
For I that did that violence to thy thrall,
Had often wrought some fury on myself,
Saving for Balan. Those three kingless years
Have past—were wormwood-bitter to me. King,
Methought that if we sat beside the well,
And hurl'd to ground what knight soever spurr'd
Against us, thou would'st take me gladlier back,
And make, as ten times worthier to be thine
Than twenty Balins, Balan knight. I have said.
Not so—not all. A man of thine today
Abash'd us both, and brake my boast. Thy will?"
Said Arthur: "Thou hast ever spoken truth;
Thy too fierce manhood would not let thee lie.
Rise, my true knight. As children learn, be thou
Wiser for falling! walk with me, and move
To music with thine Order and the King.
Thy chair, a grief to all the brethren, stands
Vacant, but thou retake it, mine again!"

Thereafter, when Sir Balin enter'd hall,
The lost one found was greeted as in heaven
With joy that blazed itself in woodland wealth

Of leaf, and gayest garlandage of flowers,
Along the walls and down the board; they sat,
And cup clash'd cup; they drank, and someone sang,
Sweet-voiced, a song of welcome, whereupon
Their common shout in chorus, mounting, made
Those banners of twelve battles overhead
Stir as they stirr'd of old, when Arthur's host
Proclaim'd him victor and the day was won.

Then Balan added to their Order lived
A wealthier life than heretofore with these
And Balin, till their embassage return'd.

"Sir King," they brought report, "we hardly found,
So bush'd about it is with gloom, the hall
Of him to whom ye sent us, Pellam, once
A Christless foe of thine as ever dash'd
Horse against horse; but seeing that thy realm
Hath prosper'd in the name of Christ, the King
Took, as in rival heat, to holy things,
And finds himself descended from the Saint
Arimathæan Joseph, him who first
Brought the great faith to Britain over seas.
He boasts his life as purer than thine own;
Eats scarce enow to keep his pulse a-beat;
Hath push'd aside his faithful wife, nor lets
Or dame or damsel enter at his gates
Lest he should be polluted. This gray king
Show'd us a shrine wherein were wonders—yea,
Rich arks with priceless bones of martyrdom,
Thorns of the crown and shivers of the cross,
And therewithal,—for thus he told us,—brought
By Holy Joseph hither, that same spear
Wherewith the Roman pierced the side of Christ.
He much amazed us; after, when we sought
The tribute, answer'd, 'I have quite foregone
All matters of this world. Garlon, mine heir,
Of him demand it,' which this Garlon gave
With much ado, railing at thine and thee.

"But when we left, in those deep woods we found
A knight of thine spear-stricken from behind,
Dead, whom we buried; more than one of us
Cried out on Garlon, but a woodman there
Reported of some demon in the woods
Was once a man, who, driven by evil tongues
From all his fellows, lived alone, and came

To learn black magic, and to hate his kind
With such a hate that when he died his soul
Became a fiend, which, as the man in life
Was wounded by blind tongues he saw not whence,
Strikes from behind. This woodman show'd the cave
From which he sallies and wherein he dwelt.
We saw the hoof-print of a horse, no more."

Then Arthur, "Let who goes before me see
He do not fall behind me. Foully slain
And villainously! who will hunt for me
This demon of the woods?" Said Balan, "I!"
So claim'd the quest and rode away, but first,
Embracing Balin: "Good my brother, hear!
Let not thy moods prevail when I am gone
Who used to lay them! hold them outer fiends,
Who leap at thee to tear thee; shake them aside,
Dreams ruling when wit sleeps! yea, but to dream
That any of these would wrong thee wrongs thyself.
Witness their flowery welcome. Bound are they
To speak no evil. Truly, save for fears,
My fears for thee, so rich a fellowship
Would make me wholly blest; thou one of them,
Be one indeed. Consider them, and all
Their bearing in their common bond of love,
No more of hatred than in heaven itself,
No more of jealousy than in Paradise."

So Balan warn'd, and went; Balin remain'd,
Who—for but three brief moons had glanced away
From being knighted till he smote the thrall,
And faded from the presence into years
Of exile—now would strictlier set himself
To learn what Arthur meant by courtesy,
Manhood, and knighthood; wherefore hover'd round
Lancelot, but when he mark'd his high sweet smile
In passing, and a transitory word
Make knight or churl or child or damsel seem
From being smiled at happier in themselves—
Sigh'd, as a boy, lame-born beneath a height
That glooms his valley, sighs to see the peak
Sun-flush'd or touch at night the northern star;
For one from out his village lately climb'd
And brought report of azure lands and fair,
Far seen to left and right; and he himself
Hath hardly scaled with help a hundred feet
Up from the base. So Balin, marvelling oft

How far beyond him Lancelot seem'd to move,
Groan'd, and at times would mutter: "These be gifts,
Born with the blood, not learnable, divine,
Beyond my reach. Well had I foughten—well—
In those fierce wars, struck hard—and had I crown'd
With my slain self the heaps of whom I slew—
So—better!—But this worship of the Queen,
That honor too wherein she holds him—this,
This was the sunshine that hath given the man
A growth, a name that branches o'er the rest,
And strength against all odds, and what the King
So prizes—overprizes—gentleness.
Her likewise would I worship an I might.
I never can be close with her, as he
That brought her hither. Shall I pray the King
To let me bear some token of his Queen
Whereon to gaze, remembering her—forget
My heats and violences? live afresh?
What if the Queen disdain'd to grant it! nay,
Being so stately-gentle, would she make
My darkness blackness? and with how sweet grace
She greeted my return! Bold will I be—
Some goodly cognizance of Guinevere,
In lieu of this rough beast upon my shield,
Langued gules, and tooth'd with grinning savagery."

    And Arthur, when Sir Balin sought him, said,
"What wilt thou bear?" Balin was bold, and ask'd
To bear her own crown-royal upon shield,
Whereat she smiled and turn'd her to the King,
Who answer'd: "Thou shalt put the crown to use.
The crown is but the shadow of the king,
And this a shadow's shadow, let him have it,
So this will help him of his violences!"
"No shadow," said Sir Balin, "O my Queen,
But light to me! no shadow, O my King,
But golden earnest of a gentler life!"

    So Balin bare the crown, and all the knights
Approved him, and the Queen; and all the world
Made music, and he felt his being move
In music with his Order and the King.

    The nightingale, full-toned in middle May,
Hath ever and anon a note so thin
It seems another voice in other groves;

Thus, after some quick burst of sudden wrath,
The music in him seem'd to change and grow
Faint and far-off.

                                And once he saw the thrall
His passion half had gauntleted to death,
That causer of his banishment and shame,
Smile at him, as he deem'd, presumptuously.
His arm half rose to strike again, but fell;
The memory of that cognizance on shield
Weighted it down, but in himself he moan'd:

"Too high this mount of Camelot for me;
These high-set courtesies are not for me.
Shall I not rather prove the worse for these?
Fierier and stormier from restraining, break
Into some madness even before the Queen?"

Thus, as a hearth lit in a mountain home,
And glancing on the window, when the gloom
Of twilight deepens round it, seems a flame
That rages in the woodland far below,
So when his moods were darken'd, court and king
And all the kindly warmth of Arthur's hall
Shadow'd an angry distance; yet he strove
To learn the graces of their Table, fought
Hard with himself, and seem'd at length in peace.

Then chanced, one morning, that Sir Balin sat
Close-bower'd in that garden nigh the hall.
A walk of roses ran from door to door,
A walk of lilies crost it to the bower;
And down that range of roses the great Queen
Came with slow steps, the morning on her face;
And all in shadow from the counter door
Sir Lancelot as to meet her, then at once,
As if he saw not, glanced aside, and paced
The long white walk of lilies toward the bower.
Follow'd the Queen; Sir Balin heard her "Prince,
Art thou so little loyal to thy Queen
As pass without good morrow to thy Queen?"
To whom Sir Lancelot with his eyes on earth,
"Fain would I still be loyal to the Queen."
"Yea, so," she said; "but so to pass me by—
So loyal scarce is loyal to thyself,
Whom all men rate the king of courtesy.
Let be; ye stand, fair lord, as in a dream."

Then Lancelot with his hand among the flowers:
"Yea—for a dream. Last night methought I saw
That maiden Saint who stands with lily in hand
In yonder shrine. All round her prest the dark,
And all the light upon her silver face
Flow'd from the spiritual lily that she held.
Lo! these her emblems drew mine eyes—away;
For see, how perfect-pure! As light a flush
As hardly tints the blossom of the quince
Would mar their charm of stainless maidenhood."

"Sweeter to me," she said, "this garden rose
Deep-hued and many-folded! sweeter still
The wild-wood hyacinth and the bloom of May!
Prince, we have ridden before among the flowers
In those fair days—not all as cool as these,
Tho' season-earlier. Art thou sad? or sick?
Our noble King will send thee his own leech—
Sick? or for any matter anger'd at me?"

Then Lancelot lifted his large eyes; they dwelt
Deep-tranced on hers, and could not fall. Her hue
Changed at his gaze; so turning side by side
They past, and Balin started from his bower.

"Queen? subject? but I see not what I see.
Damsel and lover? hear not what I hear.
My father hath begotten me in his wrath.
I suffer from the things before me, know,
Learn nothing; am not worthy to be knight—
A churl, a clown!" and in him gloom on gloom
Deepen'd; he sharply caught his lance and shield,
Nor stay'd to crave permission of the King,
But mad for strange adventure, dash'd away.

He took the selfsame track as Balan, saw
The fountain where they sat together, sigh'd,
"Was I not better there with him?" and rode
The skyless woods, but under open blue
Came on the hoar-head woodman at a bough
Wearily hewing. "Churl, thine axe!" he cried,
Descended, and disjointed it at a blow;
To whom the woodman utter'd wonderingly,
"Lord, thou couldst lay the devil of these woods
If arm of flesh could lay him!" Balin cried,
"Him, or the viler devil who plays his part;
To lay that devil would lay the devil in me."

"Nay," said the churl, "our devil is a truth,
I saw the flash of him but yester-even.
And some do say that our Sir Garlon too
Hath learn'd black magic, and to ride unseen.
Look to the cave." But Balin answer'd him,
"Old fabler, these be fancies of the churl;
Look to thy woodcraft," and so leaving him,
Now with slack rein and careless of himself,
Now with dug spur and raving at himself,
Now with droopt brow down the long glades he rode;
So mark'd not on his right a cavern-chasm
Yawn over darkness, where, nor far within,
The whole day died, but, dying, gleam'd on rocks
Roof-pendent, sharp; and others from the floor,
Tusklike, arising, made that mouth of night
Whereout the demon issued up from hell.
He mark'd not this, but, blind and deaf to all
Save that chain'd rage which ever yelpt within,
Past eastward from the falling sun. At once
He felt the hollow-beaten mosses thud
And tremble, and then the shadow of a spear,
Shot from behind him, ran along the ground.
Sideways he started from the path, and saw,
With pointed lance as if to pierce, a shape,
A light of armor by him flash, and pass
And vanish in the woods; and follow'd this,
But all so blind in rage that unawares
He burst his lance against a forest bough,
Dishorsed himself, and rose again, and fled
Far, till the castle of a king, the hall
Of Pellam, lichen-bearded, grayly draped
With streaming grass, appear'd, low-built but strong;
The ruinous donjon as a knoll of moss,
The battlement overtopt with ivy-tods.
A home of bats, in every tower an owl.

Then spake the men of Pellam crying, "Lord,
Why wear ye this crown-royal upon shield?"
Said Balin, "For the fairest and the best
Of ladies living gave me this to bear."
So stall'd his horse, and strode across the court,
But found the greetings both of knight and king
Faint in the low dark hall of banquet. Leaves
Laid their green faces flat against the panes,
Sprays grated, and the canker'd boughs without
Whined in the wood; for all was hush'd within,

Till when at feast Sir Garlon likewise ask'd,
"Why wear ye that crown-royal?" Balin said,
"The Queen we worship, Lancelot, I, and all,
As fairest, best, and purest, granted me
To bear it!" Such a sound—for Arthur's knights
Were hated strangers in the hall—as makes
The white swan-mother, sitting, when she hears
A strange knee rustle thro' her secret reeds,
Made Garlon, hissing; then he sourly smiled:
"Fairest I grant her—I have seen; but best,
Best, purest? *thou* from Arthur's hall, and yet
So simple! hast thou eyes, or if, are these
So far besotted that they fail to see
This fair wife-worship cloaks a secret shame?
Truly, ye men of Arthur be but babes."

A goblet on the board by Balin, boss'd
With holy Joseph's legend, on his right
Stood, all of massiest bronze. One side had sea
And ship and sail and angels blowing on it;
And one was rough with wattling, and the walls
Of that low church he built at Glastonbury.
This Balin graspt, but while in act to hurl,
Thro' memory of that token on the shield
Relax'd his hold. "I will be gentle," he thought,
"And passing gentle;" caught his hand away,
Then fiercely to Sir Garlon: "Eyes have I
That saw to-day the shadow of a spear,
Shot from behind me, run along the ground;
Eyes too that long have watch'd how Lancelot draws
From homage to the best and purest, might,
Name, manhood, and a grace, but scantly thine
Who, sitting in thine own hall, canst endure
To mouth so huge a foulness—to thy guest,
Me, me of Arthur's Table. Felon talk!
Let be! no more!"

But not the less by night
The scorn of Garlon, poisoning all his rest,
Stung him in dreams. At length, and dim thro' leaves
Blinkt the white morn, sprays grated, and old boughs
Whined in the wood. He rose, descended, met
The scorner in the castle court, and fain,
For hate and loathing, would have past him by;
But when Sir Garlon utter'd mocking-wise,
"What, wear ye still that same crown-scandalous?"

His countenance blacken'd, and his forehead veins
Bloated and branch'd; and tearing out of sheath
The brand, Sir Balin with a fiery, "Ha!
So thou be shadow, here I make thee ghost,"
Hard upon helm smote him, and the blade flew
Splintering in six, and clinkt upon the stones.
Then Garlon, reeling slowly backward, fell,
And Balin by the banneret of his helm
Dragg'd him, and struck, but from the castle a cry
Sounded across the court, and—men-at-arms,
A score with pointed lances, making at him—
He dash'd the pummel at the foremost face,
Beneath a low door dipt, and made his feet
Wings thro' a glimmering gallery, till he mark'd
The portal of King Pellam's chapel wide
And inward to the wall; he stept behind;
Thence in a moment heard them pass like wolves
Howling; but while he stared about the shrine,
In which he scarce could spy the Christ for Saints,
Beheld before a golden altar lie
The longest lance his eyes had ever seen,
Point-painted red; and seizing thereupon
Push'd thro' an open casement down, lean'd on it,
Leapt in a semicircle, and lit on earth;
Then hand at ear, and harkening from what side
The blindfold rummage buried in the walls
Might echo, ran the counter path, and found
His charger, mounted on him and away.
An arrow whizz'd to the right, one to the left,
One overhead; and Pellam's feeble cry,
"Stay, stay him! he defileth heavenly things
With earthly uses!" made him quickly dive
Beneath the boughs, and race thro' many a mile
Of dense and open, till his goodly horse,
Arising wearily at a fallen oak,
Stumbled headlong, and cast him face to ground.

Half-wroth he had not ended, but all glad,
Knightlike, to find his charger yet unlamed,
Sir Balin drew the shield from off his neck,
Stared at the priceless cognizance, and thought,
"I have shamed thee so that now thou shamest me,
Thee will I bear no more," high on a branch
Hung it, and turn'd aside into the woods,
And there in gloom cast himself all along,
Moaning, "My violences, my violences!"

But now the wholesome music of the wood
Was dumb'd by one from out the hall of Mark,
A damsel-errant, warbling, as she rode
The woodland alleys, Vivien, with her squire.

"The fire of heaven has kill'd the barren cold,
And kindled all the plain and all the wold.
The new leaf ever pushes off the old.
The fire of heaven is not the flame of hell.

"Old priest, who mumble worship in your quire—
Old monk and nun, ye scorn the world's desire,
Yet in your frosty cells ye feel the fire!
The fire of heaven is not the flame of hell.

"The fire of heaven is on the dusty ways.
The wayside blossoms open to the blaze.
The whole wood-world is one full peal of praise.
The fire of heaven is not the flame of hell.

"The fire of heaven is lord of all things good,
And starve not thou this fire within thy blood,
But follow Vivien thro' the fiery flood!
The fire of heaven is not the flame of hell!"

Then turning to her squire, "This fire of heaven,
This old sun-worship, boy, will rise again,
And beat the Cross to earth, and break the King
And all his Table."

              Then they reach'd a glade,
Where under one long lane of cloudless air
Before another wood, the roya crown
Sparkled, and swaying upon a restless elm
Drew the vague glance of Vivien and her squire.
Amazed were these; "Lo there," she cried—"a crown—
Borne by some high lord-prince of Arthur's hall,
And there a horse! the rider? where is he?
See, yonder lies one dead within the wood.
Not dead; he stirs!—but sleeping. I will speak.
Hail, royal knight, we break on thy sweet rest,
Not, doubtless, all unearn'd by noble deeds.
But bounden art thou, if from Arthur's hall,
To help the weak. Behold, I fly from shame,
A lustful king, who sought to win my love
Thro' evil ways. The knight with whom I rode
Hath suffer'd misadventure, and my squire
Hath in him small defence; but thou, Sir Prince,
Wilt surely guide me to the warrior King,

Arthur the blameless, pure as any maid,
To get me shelter for my maidenhood.
I charge thee by that crown upon thy shield,
And by the great Queen's name, arise and hence."

And Balin rose: "Thither no more! nor prince
Nor knight am I, but one that hath defamed
The cognizance she gave me. Here I dwell
Savage among the savage woods, here die—
Die—let the wolves' black maws ensepulchre
Their brother beast, whose anger was his lord!
O me, that such a name as Guinevere's,
Which our high Lancelot hath so lifted up,
And been thereby uplifted, should thro' me,
My violence, and my villainy, come to shame!"

Thereat she suddenly laugh'd and shrill, anon
Sigh'd all as suddenly. Said Balin to her:
"Is this thy courtesy—to mock me, ha?
Hence, for I will not with thee." Again she sigh'd:
"Pardon, sweet lord! we maidens often laugh
When sick at heart, when rather we should weep.
I knew thee wrong'd. I brake upon thy rest,
And now full loth am I to break thy dream,
But thou art man, and canst abide a truth,
Tho' bitter. Hither, boy—and mark me well.
Dost thou remember at Caerleon once—
A year ago—nay, then I love thee not—
Ay, thou rememberest well—one summer dawn—
By the great tower—Caerleon upon Usk—
Nay, truly we were hidden—this fair lord,
The flower of all their vestal knighthood, knelt
In amorous homage—knelt—what else?—O, ay,
Knelt, and drew down from out his nightblack hair
And mumbled that white hand whose ring'd caress
Had wander'd from her own King's golden head,
And lost itself in darkness, till she cried—
I thought the great tower would crash down on both—
'Rise, my sweet King, and kiss me on the lips,
Thou art my King.' This lad, whose lightest word
Is mere white truth in simple nakedness,
Saw them embrace; he reddens, cannot speak,
So bashful, he! but all the maiden Saints,
The deathless mother-maidenhood of heaven,
Cry out upon her. Up then, ride with me!
Talk not of shame! thou canst not, an thou wouldst,
Do these more shame than these have done themselves."

She lied with ease; but horror-stricken he,
Remembering that dark bower at Camelot,
Breathed in a dismal whisper, "It is truth."

Sunnily she smiled: "And even in this lone wood,
Sweet lord, ye do right well to whisper this.
Fools prate, and perish traitors. Woods have tongues,
As walls have ears; but thou shalt go with me,
And we will speak at first exceeding low.
Meet is it the good King be not deceived.
See now, I set thee high on vantage ground,
From whence to watch the time, and eagle-like
Stoop at thy will on Lancelot and the Queen."

She ceased; his evil spirit upon him leapt,
He ground his teeth together, sprang with a yell,
Tore from the branch and cast on earth the shield,
Drove his mail'd heel athwart the royal crown,
Stampt all into defacement, hurl'd it from him
Among the forest weeds, and cursed the tale,
The told-of, and the teller.

                            That weird yell,
Unearthlier than all shriek of bird or beast,
Thrill'd thro' the woods; and Balin lurking there—
His quest was unaccomplish'd—heard and thought
"The scream of that wood-devil I came to quell!"
Then nearing: "Lo! he hath slain some brother-knight,
And tramples on the goodly shield to show
His loathing of our Order and the Queen.
My quest, meseems, is here. Or devil or man,
Guard thou thine head." Sir Balin spake not a word,
But snatch'd a sudden buckler from the squire,
And vaulted on his horse, and so they crash'd
In onset, and King Pellam's holy spear,
Reputed to be red with sinless blood,
Redden'd at once with sinful, for the point
Across the maiden shield of Balin prick'd
The hauberk to the flesh; and Balin's horse
Was wearied to the death, and when they clash'd,
Rolling back upon Balin, crush'd the man
Inward, and either fell and swoon'd away.

Then to her squire mutter'd the damsel: "Fools!
This fellow hath wrought some foulness with his Queen;
Else never had he borne her crown, nor raved
And thus foam'd over at a rival name.

But thou, Sir Chick, that scarce hast broken shell,
Art yet half-yolk, not even come to down—
Who never sawest Caerleon upon Usk—
And yet hast often pleaded for my love—
See what I see, be thou where I have been,
Or else, Sir Chick—dismount and loose their casques;
I fain would know what manner of men they be."
And when the squire had loosed them, "Goodly!—look!
They might have cropt the myriad flower of May,
And butt each other here, like brainless bulls,
Dead for one heifer!"

Then the gentle squire:
"I hold them happy, so they died for love;
And, Vivien, tho' ye beat me like your dog,
I too could die, as now I live, for thee."

"Live on, Sir Boy," she cried; "I better prize
The living dog than the dead lion. Away!
I cannot brook to gaze upon the dead."
Then leapt her palfrey o'er the fallen oak,
And bounding forward, "Leave them to the wolves."

But when their foreheads felt the cooling air,
Balin first woke, and seeing that true face,
Familiar up from cradle-time, so wan,
Crawl'd slowly with low moans to where he lay,
And on his dying brother cast himself
Dying; and he lifted faint eyes; he felt
One near him; all at once they found the world,
Staring wild-wide, then with a childlike wail,
And drawing down the dim disastrous brow
That o'er him hung, he kiss'd it, moan'd, and spake:

"O Balin, Balin, I that fain had died
To save thy life, have brought thee to thy death.
Why had ye not the shield I knew? and why
Trampled ye thus on that which bare the crown?"

Then Balin told him brokenly and in gasps
All that had chanced, and Balan moan'd again:

"Brother, I dwelt a day in Pellam's hall;
This Garlon mock'd me, but I heeded not.
And one said, 'Eat in peace! a liar is he,
And hates thee for the tribute!' This good knight
Told me that twice a wanton damsel came,
And sought for Garlon at the castle-gates,

Whom Pellam drove away with holy heat.
I well believe this damsel, and the one
Who stood beside thee even now, the same.
'She dwells among the woods,' he said, 'and meets
And dallies with him in the Mouth of Hell.'
Foul are their lives, foul are their lips; they lied.
Pure as our own true mother is our Queen."

"O brother," answer'd Balin, "woe is me!
My madness all thy life has been thy doom,
Thy curse, and darken'd all thy day; and now
The night has come. I scarce can see thee now.
Good night! for we shall never bid again
Good morrow—Dark my doom was here, and dark
It will be there. I see thee now no more.
I would not mine again should darken thine;
Good night, true brother."

                Balan answer'd low,
"Good night, true brother, here! good morrow there!
We two were born together, and we die
Together by one doom:" and while he spoke
Closed his death-drowsing eyes, and slept the sleep
With Balin, either lock'd in either's arm.

✠✠✠✠✠ MERLIN AND VIVIEN ✠✠✠✠✠

A STORM was coming, but the winds were still,
And in the wild woods of Broceliande,
Before an oak, so hollow, huge, and old
It look'd a tower of ivied masonwork,
At Merlin's feet the wily Vivien lay.

For he that always bare in bitter grudge
The slights of Arthur and his Table, Mark
The Cornish King, had heard a wandering voice,
A minstrel of Caerleon by strong storm
Blown into shelter at Tintagil, say
That out of naked knight-like purity
Sir Lancelot worshipt no unmarried girl,
But the great Queen herself, fought in her name,
Sware by her—vows like theirs that high in heaven

Love most, but neither marry nor are given
In marriage, angels of our Lord's report.

He ceased, and then—for Vivien sweetly said—
She sat beside the banquet nearest Mark,—
"And is the fair example follow'd, sir,
In Arthur's household?"—answer'd innocently:—

"Ay, by some few—ay, truly—youths that hold
It more beseems the perfect virgin knight
To worship woman as true wife beyond
All hopes of gaining, than as maiden girl.
They place their pride in Lancelot and the Queen.
So passionate for an utter purity
Beyond the limit of their bond are these,
For Arthur bound them not to singleness.
Brave hearts and clean! and yet—God guide them!—young."

Then Mark was half in heart to hurl his cup
Straight at the speaker, but forbore. He rose
To leave the hall, and, Vivien following him,
Turn'd to her: "Here are snakes within the grass;
And you methinks, O Vivien, save ye fear
The monkish manhood, and the mask of pure
Worn by this court, can stir them till they sting."

And Vivien answer'd, smiling scornfully:
"Why fear? because that foster'd at thy court
I savor of thy—virtues? fear them? no,
As love, if love be perfect, casts out fear,
So hate, if hate be perfect, casts out fear.
My father died in battle against the King,
My mother on his corpse in open field;
She bore me there, for born from death was I
Among the dead and sown upon the wind—
And then on thee! and shown the truth betimes,
That old true filth, and bottom of the well,
Where Truth is hidden. Gracious lessons thine,
And maxims of the mud! 'This Arthur pure!
Great Nature thro' the flesh herself hath made
Gives him the lie! There is no being pure,
My cherub; saith not Holy Writ the same?'—
If I were Arthur, I would have thy blood.
Thy blessing, stainless King! I bring thee back,
When I have ferreted out their burrowings,
The hearts of all this Order in mine hand—
Ay—so that fate and craft and folly close,

Perchance, one curl of Arthur's golden beard.
To me this narrow grizzled fork of thine
Is cleaner-fashion'd—Well, I loved thee first;
That warps the wit."

Loud laugh'd the graceless Mark.
But Vivien, into Camelot stealing, lodged
Low in the city, and on a festal day
When Guinevere was crossing the great hall
Cast herself down, knelt to the Queen, and wail'd.

"Why kneel ye there? What evil have ye wrought?
Rise!" and the damsel bidden rise arose
And stood with folded hands and downward eyes
Of glancing corner and all meekly said:
"None wrought, but suffer'd much, an orphan maid!
My father died in battle for thy King,
My mother on his corpse—in open field,
The sad sea-sounding wastes of Lyonnesse—
Poor wretch—no friend!—and now by Mark the King,
For that small charm of feature mine, pursued—
If any such be mine—I fly to thee.
Save, save me thou! Woman of women—thine
The wreath of beauty, thine the crown of power,
Be thine the balm of pity, O heaven's own white
Earth-angel, stainless bride of stainless King—
Help, for he follows! take me to thyself!
O yield me shelter for mine innocency
Among thy maidens!"

Here her slow sweet eyes
Fear-tremulous, but humbly hopeful, rose
Fixt on her hearer's, while the Queen who stood
All glittering like May sunshine on May leaves
In green and gold, and plumed with green, replied:
"Peace, child! of overpraise and over-blame.
We choose the last. Our noble Arthur, him
Ye scarce can overpraise, will hear and know.
Nay—we believe all evil of thy Mark—
Well, we shall test thee farther; but this hour
We ride a-hawking with Sir Lancelot.
He hath given us a fair falcon which he train'd;
We go to prove it. Bide ye here the while."

She past; and Vivien murmur'd after, "Go!
I bide the while." Then thro' the portal-arch
Peering askance, and muttering broken-wise,

As one that labors with an evil dream,
Beheld the Queen and Lancelot get to horse.

"Is that the Lancelot? goodly—ay, but gaunt;
Courteous—amends for gauntness—takes her hand—
That glance of theirs, but for the street, had been
A clinging kiss—how hand lingers in hand!
Let go at last!—they ride away—to hawk
For waterfowl. Royaller game is mine.
For such a supersensual sensual bond
As that gray cricket chirpt of at our hearth—
Touch flax with flame—a glance will serve—the liars!
Ah little rat that borest in the dyke
Thy hole by night to let the boundless deep
Down upon far-off cities while they dance—
Or dream—of thee they dream'd not—nor of me
These—ay, but each of either; ride, and dream
The mortal dream that never yet was mine —
Ride, ride and dream until ye wake—to me!
Then, narrow court and lubber King, farewell!
For Lancelot will be gracious to the rat,
And our wise Queen, if knowing that I know,
Will hate, loathe, fear—but honor me the more."

Yet while they rode together down the plain,
Their talk was all of training, terms of art,
Diet and seeling, jesses, leash and lure.
"She is too noble," he said, "to check at pies,
Nor will she rake: there is no baseness in her."
Here when the Queen demanded as by chance,
"Know ye the stranger woman?" "Let her be,"
Said Lancelot, and unhooded casting off
The goodly falcon free; she tower'd; her bells,
Tone under tone, shrill'd; and they lifted up
Their eager faces, wondering at the strength,
Boldness, and royal knighthood of the bird,
Who pounced her quarry and slew it. Many a time
As once—of old—among the flowers—they rode.

But Vivien half-forgotten of the Queen
Among her damsels broidering sat, heard, watch'd,
And whisper'd. Thro' the peaceful court she crept
And whisper'd; then, as Arthur in the highest
Leaven'd the world, so Vivien in the lowest,
Arriving at a time of golden rest,
And sowing one ill hint from ear to ear,
While all the heathen lay at Arthur's feet,

And no quest came, but all was joust and play,
Leaven'd his hall. They heard and let her be.

    Thereafter, as an enemy that has left
Death in the living waters and withdrawn,
The wily Vivien stole from Arthur's court.

    She hated all the knights, and heard in thought
Their lavish comment when her name was named.
For once, when Arthur walking all alone,
Vext at a rumor issued from herself
Of some corruption crept among his knights,
Had met her, Vivien, being greeted fair,
Would fain have wrought upon his cloudy mood
With reverent eyes mock-loyal, shaken voice,
And flutter'd adoration, and at last
With dark sweet hints of some who prized him more
Than who should prize him most; at which the King
Had gazed upon her blankly and gone by.
But one had watch'd, and had not held his peace;
It made the laughter of an afternoon
That Vivien should attempt the blameless King.
And after that, she set herself to gain
Him, the most famous man of all those times,
Merlin, who knew the range of all their arts,
Had built the King his havens, ships, and halls,
Was also bard, and knew the starry heavens;
The people call'd him wizard; whom at first
She play'd about with slight and sprightly talk,
And vivid smiles, and faintly-venom'd points
Of slander, glancing here and grazing there;
And yielding to his kindlier moods, the seer
Would watch her at her petulance and play,
Even when they seem'd unlovable, and laugh
As those that watch a kitten. Thus he grew
Tolerant of what he half disdain'd, and she,
Perceiving that she was but half disdain'd,
Began to break her sports with graver fits,
Turn red or pale, would often when they met
Sigh fully, or all-silent gaze upon him
With such a fixt devotion that the old man,
Tho' doubtful, felt the flattery, and at times
Would flatter his own wish in age for love,
And half believe her true; for thus at times
He waver'd, but that other clung to him,
Fixt in her will, and so the seasons went.

Then fell on Merlin a great melancholy;
He walk'd with dreams and darkness, and he found
A doom that ever poised itself to fall,
An ever-moaning battle in the mist,
World-war of dying flesh against the life,
Death in all life and lying in all love,
The meanest having power upon the highest,
And the high purpose broken by the worm.

So leaving Arthur's court he gain'd the beach,
There found a little boat and stept into it;
And Vivien follow'd but he mark'd her not.
She took the helm and he the sail; the boat
Drave with a sudden wind across the deeps,
And, touching Breton sands, they disembark'd.
And then she follow'd Merlin all the way,
Even to the wild woods of Broceliande.
For Merlin once had told her of a charm,
The which if any wrought on any one
With woven paces and with waving arms,
The man so wrought on ever seem'd to lie
Closed in the four walls of a hollow tower,
From which was no escape for evermore;
And none could find that man for evermore,
Nor could he see but him who wrought the charm
Coming and going, and he lay as dead
And lost to life and use and name and fame.
And Vivien ever sought to work the charm
Upon the great enchanter of the time,
As fancying that her glory would be great
According to his greatness whom she quench'd.

There lay she all her length and kiss'd his feet,
As if in deepest reverence and in love.
A twist of gold was round her hair; a robe
Of samite without price, that more exprest
Than hid her, clung about her lissome limbs,
In color like the satin-shining palm
On sallows in the windy gleams of March.
And while she kiss'd them, crying, "Trample me,
Dear feet, that I have follow'd thro' the world,
And I will pay you worship; tread me down
And I will kiss you for it;" he was mute.
So dark a forethought roll'd about his brain,
As on a dull day in an ocean cave
The blind wave feeling round his long sea-hall

In silence; wherefore, when she lifted up
A face of sad appeal, and spake and said,
"O Merlin, do ye love me?" and again,
"O Merlin, do ye love me?" and once more,
"Great Master, do ye love me?" he was mute.
And lissome Vivien, holding by his heel,
Writhed toward him, slided up his knee and sat,
Behind his ankle twined her hollow feet
Together, curved an arm about his neck,
Clung like a snake; and letting her left hand
Droop from his mighty shoulder, as a leaf,
Made with her right a comb of pearl to part
The lists of such a beard as youth gone out
Had left in ashes. Then he spoke and said,
Not looking at her, "Who are wise in love
Love most, say least," and Vivien answer'd quick:
"I saw the little elf-god eyeless once
In Arthur's arras hall at Camelot;
But neither eyes nor tongue—O stupid child!
Yet you are wise who say it; let me think
Silence is wisdom. I am silent then,
And ask no kiss;" then adding all at once,
"And lo, I clothe myself with wisdom," drew
The vast and shaggy mantle of his beard
Across her neck and bosom to her knee,
And call'd herself a gilded summer fly
Caught in a great old tyrant spider's web,
Who meant to eat her up in that wild wood
Without one word. So Vivien call'd herself,
But rather seem'd a lovely baleful star
Veil'd in gray vapor; till he sadly smiled:
"To what request for what strange boon," he said,
"Are these your pretty tricks and fooleries,
O Vivien, the preamble? yet my thanks,
For these have broken up my melancholy."

And Vivien answer'd smiling saucily:
"What, O my Master, have ye found your voice?
I bid the stranger welcome. Thanks at last!
But yesterday you never open'd lip,
Except indeed to drink. No cup had we;
In mine own lady palms I cull'd the spring
That gather'd trickling dropwise from the cleft,
And made a pretty cup of both my hands
And offer'd you it kneeling. Then you drank
And knew no more, nor gave me one poor word;

O, no more thanks than might a goat have given
With no more sign of reverence than a beard.
And when we halted at that other well,
And I was faint to swooning, and you lay
Foot-gilt with all the blossom-dust of those
Deep meadows we had traversed, did you know
That Vivien bathed your feet before her own?
And yet no thanks; and all thro' this wild wood
And all this morning when I fondled you.
Boon, ay, there was a boon, one not so strange—
How had I wrong'd you? surely ye are wise,
But such a silence is more wise than kind."

And Merlin lock'd his hand in hers and said:
"O, did ye never lie upon the shore,
And watch the curl'd white of the coming wave
Glass'd in the slippery sand before it breaks?
Even such a wave, but not so pleasurable,
Dark in the glass of some presageful mood,
Had I for three days seen, ready to fall.
And then I rose and fled from Arthur's court
To break the mood. You follow'd me unask'd;
And when I look'd, and saw you following still,
My mind involved yourself the nearest thing
In that mind-mist—for shall I tell you truth?
You seem'd that wave about to break upon me
And sweep me from my hold upon the world,
My use and name and fame. Your pardon, child.
Your pretty sports have brighten'd all again.
And ask your boon, for boon I owe you thrice,
Once for wrong done you by confusion, next
For thanks it seems till now neglected, last
For these your dainty gambols; wherefore ask,
And take this boon so strange and not so strange."

And Vivien answer'd smiling mournfully:
"O, not so strange as my long asking it,
Not yet so strange as you yourself are strange,
Nor half so strange as that dark mood of yours.
I ever fear'd ye were not wholly mine;
And see, yourself have own'd ye did me wrong.
The people call you prophet; let it be;
But not of those that can expound themselves.
Take Vivien for expounder; she will call
That three-days-long presageful gloom of yours
No presage, but the same mistrustful mood

That makes you seem less noble than yourself,
Whenever I have ask'd this very boon,
Now ask'd again; for see you not, dear love,
That such a mood as that which lately gloom'd
Your fancy when ye saw me following you
Must make me fear still more you are not mine,
Must make me yearn still more to prove you mine,
And make me wish still more to learn this charm
Of woven paces and of waving hands,
As proof of trust. O Merlin, teach it me!
The charm so taught will charm us both to rest.
For, grant me some slight power upon your fate,
I, feeling that you felt me worthy trust,
Should rest and let you rest, knowing you mine.
And therefore be as great as ye are named,
Not muffled round with selfish reticence.
How hard you look and how denyingly!
O, if you think this wickedness in me,
That I should prove it on you unawares,
That makes me passing wrathful; then our bond
Had best be loosed for ever; but think or not,
By Heaven that hears, I tell you the clean truth,
As clean as blood of babes, as white as milk!
O Merlin, may this earth, if ever I,
If these unwitty wandering wits of mine,
Even in the jumbled rubbish of a dream,
Have tript on such conjectural treachery—
May this hard earth cleave to the nadir hell
Down, down, and close again and nip me flat,
If I be such a traitress! Yield my boon,
Till which I scarce can yield you all I am;
And grant my re-reiterated wish,
The great proof of your love; because I think,
However wise, ye hardly know me yet."

And Merlin loosed his hand from hers and said:
"I never was less wise, however wise,
Too curious Vivien, tho' you talk of trust,
Than when I told you first of such a charm.
Yea, if ye talk of trust I tell you this,
Too much I trusted when I told you that,
And stirr'd this vice in you which ruin'd man
Thro' woman the first hour; for howsoe'er
In children a great curiousness be well,
Who have to learn themselves and all the world,
In you, that are no child, for still I find

Your face is practised when I spell the lines,
I call it,—well, I will not call it vice;
But since you name yourself the summer fly,
I well could wish a cobweb for the gnat
That settles beaten back, and beaten back
Settles, till one could yield for weariness.
But since I will not yield to give you power
Upon my life and use and name and fame,
Why will ye never ask some other boon?
Yea, by God's rood, I trusted you too much!"

And Vivien, like the tenderest-hearted maid
That ever bided tryst at village stile,
Made answer, either eyelid wet with tears:
"Nay, Master, be not wrathful with your maid;
Caress her, let her feel herself forgiven
Who feels no heart to ask another boon.
I think ye hardly know the tender rhyme
Of 'trust me not at all or all in all.'
I heard the great Sir Lancelot sing it once
And it shall answer for me. Listen to it.

" 'In love, if love be love, if love be ours,
Faith and unfaith can ne'er be equal powers:
Unfaith in aught is want of faith in all.

" 'It is the little rift within the lute,
That by and by will make the music mute,
And ever widening slowly silence all.

" 'The little rift within the lover's lute,
Or little pitted speck in garner'd fruit,
That rotting inward slowly moulders all.

" 'It is not worth the keeping; let it go:
But shall it? answer, darling, answer, no.
And trust me not at all or all in all.'

"O master, do ye love my tender rhyme?"

And Merlin look'd and half believed her true,
So tender was her voice, so fair her face,
So sweetly gleam'd her eyes behind her tears
Like sunlight on the plain behind a shower;
And yet he answer'd half indignantly:

"Far other was the song that once I heard
By this huge oak, sung nearly where we sit;
For here we met, some ten or twelve of us,
To chase a creature that was current then

In these wild woods, the hart with golden horns.
It was the time when first the question rose
About the founding of a Table Round,
That was to be, for love of God and men
And noble deeds, the flower of all the world;
And each incited each to noble deeds.
And while we waited, one, the youngest of us,
We could not keep him silent, out he flash'd,
And into such a song, such fire for fame,
Such trumpet-blowings in it, coming down
To such a stern and iron-clashing close,
That when he stopt we long'd to hurl together,
And should have done it, but the beauteous beast
Scared by the noise upstarted at our feet,
And like a silver shadow slipt away
Thro' the dim land. And all day long we rode
Thro' the dim land against a rushing wind,
That glorious roundel echoing in our ears,
And chased the flashes of his golden horns
Until they vanish'd by the fairy well
That laughs at iron—as our warriors did—
Where children cast their pins and nails, and cry
'Laugh, little well!' but touch it with a sword,
It buzzes fiercely round the point; and there
We lost him—such a noble song was that.
But, Vivien, when you sang me that sweet rhyme,
I felt as tho' you knew this cursed charm,
Were proving it on me, and that I lay
And felt them slowly ebbing, name and fame."

And Viven answer'd smiling mournfully:
"O, mine have ebb'd away for evermore,
And all thro' following you to this wild wood,
Because I saw you sad, to comfort you.
Lo now, what hearts have men! they never mount
As high as woman in her selfless mood.
And touching fame, howe'er ye scorn my song,
Take one verse more—the lady speaks it—this:

    " 'My name, once mine, now thine, is closelier mine,
For fame, could fame be mine, that fame were thine,
And, shame, could shame be thine, that shame were mine.
So trust me not at all or all in all.'

    "Says she not well? and there is more—this rhyme
Is like the fair pearl-necklace of the Queen,
That burst in dancing and the pearls were spilt;

Some lost, some stolen, some as relics kept;
But nevermore the same two sister pearls
Ran down the silken thread to kiss each other
On her white neck—so is it with this rhyme.
It lives dispersedly in many hands,
And every minstrel sings it differently;
Yet is there one true line, the pearl of pearls:
'Man dreams of fame while woman wakes to love.'
Yea! love, tho' love were of the grossest, carves
A portion from the solid present, eats
And uses, careless of the rest; but fame,
The fame that follows death is nothing to us;
And what is fame in life but half-disfame
And counterchanged with darkness? ye yourself
Know well that envy calls you devil's son,
And since ye seem the master of all art,
They fain would make you master of all vice."

And Merlin lock'd his hand in hers and said:
"I once was looking for a magic weed,
And found a fair young squire who sat alone,
Had carved himself a knightly shield of wood,
And then was painting on it fancied arms,
Azure, an eagle rising or, the sun
In dexter chief; the scroll, 'I follow fame.'
And speaking not, but leaning over him,
I took his brush and blotted out the bird,
And made a gardener putting in a graff,
With this for motto, 'Rather use than fame.'
You should have seen him blush; but afterwards
He made a stalwart knight. O Vivien,
For you, methinks you think you love me well;
For me, I love you somewhat. Rest; and Love
Should have some rest and pleasure in himself,
Not ever be too curious for a boon,
Too prurient for a proof against the grain
Of him ye say ye love. But Fame with men,
Being but ampler means to serve mankind,
Should have small rest or pleasure in herself,
But work as vassal to the larger love
That dwarfs the petty love of one to one.
Use gave me fame at first, and fame again
Increasing gave me use. Lo, there my boon!
What other? for men sought to prove me vile,
Because I fain had given them greater wits;
And then did envy call me devil's son.

The sick weak beast, seeking to help herself
By striking at her better, miss'd, and brought
Her own claw back and wounded her own heart.
Sweet were the days when I was all unknown,
But when my name was lifted up the storm
Brake on the mountain and I cared not for it.
Right well know I that fame is half-disfame,
Yet needs must work my work. That other fame,
To one at least who hath not children, vague,
The cackle of the unborn about the grave,
I cared not for it. A single misty star,
Which is the second in line of stars
That seem a sword beneath a belt of three,
I never gazed upon it but I dreamt
Of some vast charm concluded in that star
To make fame nothing. Wherefore, if I fear,
Giving you power upon me thro' this charm,
That you might play me falsely, having power,
However well ye think ye love me now—
As sons of kings loving in pupilage
Have turn'd to tyrants when they came to power—
I rather dread the loss of use than fame;
If you—and not so much from wickedness,
As some wild turn of anger, or a mood
Of overstrain'd affection, it may be,
To keep me all to your own self,—or else
A sudden spurt of woman's jealousy,—
Should try this charm on whom ye say ye love."

And Vivien answer'd smiling as in wrath:
"Have I not sworn? I am not trusted. Good!
Well, hide it, hide it; I shall find it out,
And being found take heed of Vivien.
A woman and not trusted, doubtless I
Might feel some sudden turn of anger born
Of your misfaith; and your fine epithet
Is accurate too, for this full love of mine
Without the full heart back may merit well
Your term of overstrain'd. So used as I,
My daily wonder is, I love at all.
And as to woman's jealousy, O, why not?
O, to what end, except a jealous one,
And one to make me jealous if I love,
Was this fair charm invented by yourself?
I well believe that all about this world
Ye cage a buxom captive here and there,

Closed in the four walls of a hollow tower
From which is no escape for evermore."

Then the great master merrily answer'd her:
"Full many a love in loving youth was mine;
I needed then no charm to keep them mine
But youth and love; and that full heart of yours
Whereof ye prattle, may now assure you mine;
So live uncharm'd. For those who wrought it first,
The wrist is parted from the hand that waved,
The feet unmortised from their ankle-bones
Who paced it, ages back—but will ye hear
The legend as in guerdon for your rhyme?

"There lived a king in the most eastern East,
Less old than I, yet older, for my blood
Hath earnest in it of far springs to be.
A tawny pirate anchor'd in his port,
Whose bark had plunder'd twenty nameless isles;
And passing one, at the high peep of dawn,
He saw two cities in a thousand boats
All fighting for a woman on the sea.
And pushing his black craft among them all
He lightly scatter'd theirs and brought her off,
With loss of half his people arrow-slain;
A maid so smooth, so white, so wonderful,
They said a light came from her when she moved.
And since the pirate would not yield her up,
The king impaled him for his piracy,
Then made her queen. But those isle-nurtured eyes
Waged such unwilling tho' successful war
On all the youth, they sicken'd; councils thinn'd,
And armies waned, for magnet-like she drew
The rustiest iron of old fighters' hearts;
And beasts themselves would worship; camels knelt
Unbidden, and the brutes of mountain back
That carry kings in castles bow'd black knees
Of homage, ringing with their serpent hands,
To make her smile, her golden ankle-bells.
What wonder, being jealous, that he sent
His horns of proclamation out thro' all
The hundred under-kingdoms that he sway'd
To find a wizard who might teach the King
Some charm which, being wrought upon the Queen,
Might keep her all his own. To such a one
He promised more than ever king has given,
A league of mountain full of golden mines,

A province with a hundred miles of coast,
A palace and a princess, all for him;
But on all those who tried and fail'd the king
Pronounced a dismal sentence, meaning by it
To keep the list low and pretenders back,
Or, like a king, not to be trifled with—
Their heads should moulder on the city gates.
And many tried and fail'd, because the charm
Of nature in her overbore their own;
And many a wizard brow bleach'd on the walls,
And many weeks a troop of carrion crows
Hung like a cloud above the gateway towers."

    And Vivien breaking in upon him said:
"I sit and gather honey; yet, methinks,
Thy tongue has tript a little; ask thyself.
The lady never made unwilling war
With those fine eyes; she had her pleasure in it,
And made her good man jealous with good cause.
And lived there neither dame nor damsel then
Wroth at a lover's loss? were all as tame,
I mean, as noble, as their queen was fair?
Not one to flirt a venom at her eyes,
Or pinch a murderous dust into her drink,
Or make her paler with a poison'd rose?
Well, those were not our days—but did they find
A wizard? Tell me, was he like to thee?"

    She ceased, and made her lithe arm round his neck
Tighten, and then drew back, and let her eyes
Speak for her, glowing on him, like a bride's
On her new lord, her own, the first of men.

    He answer'd laughing: "Nay, not like to me.
At last they found—his foragers for charms—
A little glassy-headed hairless man,
Who lived alone in a great wild on grass,
Read but one book, and ever reading grew
So grated down and filed away with thought,
So lean his eyes were monstrous; while the skin
Clung but to crate and basket, ribs and spine.
And since he kept his mind on one sole aim,
Nor ever touch'd fierce wine, nor tasted flesh,
Nor own'd a sensual wish, to him the wall
That sunders ghosts and shadow-casting men
Became a crystal, and he saw them thro' it,
And heard their voices talk behind the wall,

And learnt their elemental secrets, powers
And forces; often o'er the sun's bright eye
Drew the vast eyelid of an inky cloud,
And lash'd it at the base with slanting storm;
Or in the noon of mist and driving rain,
When the lake whiten'd and the pinewood roar'd,
And the cairn'd mountain was a shadow, sunn'd
The world to peace again. Here was the man;
And so by force they dragg'd him to the King.
And then he taught the King to charm the Queen
In such-wise that no man could see her more,
Nor saw she save the King, who wrought the charm,
Coming and going, and she lay as dead,
And lost all use of life. But when the King
Made proffer of the league of golden mines,
The province with a hundred miles of coast,
The palace and the princess, that old man
Went back to his old wild, and lived on grass,
And vanish'd, and his book came down to me."

And Vivien answer'd smiling saucily:
"Ye have the book; the charm is written in it.
Good! take my counsel, let me know it at once;
For keep it like a puzzle chest in chest,
With each chest lock'd and padlock'd thirty-fold,
And whelm all this beneath as vast a mound
As after furious battle turfs the slain
On some wild down above the windy deep,
I yet should strike upon a sudden means
To dig, pick, open, find and read the charm;
Then, if I tried it, who should blame me then?"

And smiling as a master smiles at one
That is not of his school, nor any school
But that where blind and naked Ignorance
Delivers brawling judgments, unashamed,
On all things all day long, he answer'd her:

"Thou read the book, my pretty Vivien!
O, ay, it is but twenty pages long,
But every page having an ample marge,
And every marge enclosing in the midst
A square of text that looks a little blot,
The text no larger than the limbs of fleas;
And every square of text an awful charm,
Writ in a language that has long gone by,
So long that mountains have arisen since

With cities on their flanks—thou read the book!
And every margin scribbled, crost, and cramm'd
With comment, densest condensation, hard
To mind and eye; but the long sleepless nights
Of my long life have made it easy to me.
And none can read the text, not even I;
And none can read the comment but myself;
And in the comment did I find the charm.
O, the results are simple; a mere child
Might use it to the harm of any one,
And never could undo it. Ask no more;
For tho' you should not prove it upon me,
But keep that oath ye sware, ye might, perchance,
Assay it on some one of the Table Round,
And all because ye dream they babble of you."

And Vivien, frowning in true anger, said:
"What dare the full-fed liars say of me?
They ride abroad redressing human wrongs!
They sit with knife in meat and wine in horn.
They bound to holy vows of chastity!
Were I not woman, I could tell a tale.
But you are man, you well can understand
The shame that cannot be explain'd for shame.
Not one of all the drove should touch me—swine!"

Then answer'd Merlin careless of her words:
"You breathe but accusation vast and vague,
Spleen-born, I think, and proofless. If ye know,
Set up the charge ye know, to stand or fall!"

And Vivien answer'd frowning wrathfully:
"O, ay, what say ye to Sir Valence, him
Whose kinsman left him watcher o'er his wife
And two fair babes, and went to distant lands,
Was one year gone, and on returning found
Not two but three? there lay the reckling, one
But one hour old! What said the happy sire?
A seven-months' babe had been a truer gift.
Those twelve sweet moons confused his fatherhood."

Then answer'd Merlin: "Nay, I know the tale.
Sir Valence wedded with an outland dame;
Some cause had kept him sunder'd from his wife.
One child they had; it lived with her; she died.
His kinsman travelling on his own affair
Was charged by Valence to bring home the child.
He brought, not found it therefore; take the truth."

"O, ay," said Vivien, "over-true a tale!
What say ye then to sweet Sir Sagramore,
That ardent man? 'To pluck the flower in season,'
So says the song, 'I trow it is no treason.'
O Master, shall we call him over-quick
To crop his own sweet rose before the hour?"

And Merlin answer'd, "Over-quick art thou
To catch a loathly plume fallen from the wing
Of that foul bird of rapine whose whole prey
Is man's good name. He never wrong'd his bride.
I know the tale. An angry gust of wind
Puff'd out his torch among the myriad-room'd
And many-corridor'd complexities
Of Arthur's palace. Then he found a door,
And darkling felt the sculptured ornament
That wreathen round it made it seem his own,
And wearied out made for the couch and slept,
A stainless man beside a stainless maid;
And either slept, nor knew of other there,
Till the high dawn piercing the royal rose
In Arthur's casement glimmer'd chastely down,
Blushing upon them blushing, and at once
He rose without a word and parted from her.
But when the thing was blazed about the court,
The brute world howling forced them into bonds,
And as it chanced they are happy, being pure."

"Oh, ay," said Vivien, "that were likely too!
What say we then to fair Sir Percivale
And of the horrid foulness that he wrought,
The saintly youth, the spotless lamb of Christ,
Or some black wether of Saint Satan's fold?
What, in the precincts of the chapel-yard,
Among the knightly brasses of the graves,
And by the cold Hic Jacets of the dead!"

And Merlin answer'd careless of her charge:
"A sober man is Percivale and pure,
But once in life was fluster'd with new wine,
Then paced for coolness in the chapel-yard,
Where one of Satan's shepherdesses caught
And meant to stamp him with her master's mark.
And that he sinn'd is not believable;
For, look upon his face!—but if he sinn'd,
The sin that practice burns into the blood,
And not the one dark hour which brings remorse,

Will brand us, after, of whose fold we be;
Or else were he, the holy king whose hymns
Are chanted in the minster, worse than all.
But is your spleen froth'd out, or have ye more?"

And Vivien answer'd frowning yet in wrath:
"O, ay; what say ye to Sir Lancelot, friend,
Traitor or true? that commerce with the Queen,
I ask you, is it clamor'd by the child,
Or whisper'd in the corner? do ye know it?"

To which he answer'd sadly: "Yea, I know it.
Sir Lancelot went ambassador, at first,
To fetch her, and she watch'd him from her walls.
A rumor runs, she took him for the King,
So fixt her fancy on him; let them be.
But have ye no one word of loyal praise
For Arthur, blameless king and stainless man?"

She answer'd with a low and chuckling laugh:
"Man! is he man at all, who knows and winks?
Sees what his fair bride is and does, and winks?
By which the good King means to blind himself,
And blinds himself and all the Table Round
To all the foulness that they work. Myself
Could call him—were it not for womanhood—
The pretty, popular name such manhood earns,
Could call him the main cause of all their crime,
Yea, were he not crown'd king, coward and fool."

Then Merlin to his own heart, loathing, said:
"O true and tender! O my liege and King!
O selfless man and stainless gentleman,
Who would'st against thine own eyewitness fain
Have all men true and leal, all women pure!
How, in the mouths of base interpreters,
From over-fineness not intelligible
To things with every sense as false and foul
As the poach'd filth that floods the middle street,
Is thy white blamelessness accounted blame!"

But Vivien, deeming Merlin overborne
By instance, recommenced, and let her tongue
Rage like a fire among the noblest names,
Polluting, and imputing her whole self,
Defaming and defacing, till she left
Not even Lancelot brave nor Galahad clean.

Her words had issue other than she will'd.
He dragg'd his eyebrow bushes down, and made
A snowy pent-house for his hollow eyes,
And mutter'd in himself: "Tell *her* the charm!
So, if she had it, would she rail on me
To snare the next, and if she have it not
So will she rail. What did the wanton say?
'Not mount as high!' we scarce can sink as low;
For men at most differ as heaven and earth,
But women, worst and best, as heaven and hell.
I know the Table Round, my friends of old;
All brave, and many generous, and some chaste.
She cloaks the scar of some repulse with lies.
I well believe she tempted them and fail'd,
Being so bitter; for fine plots may fail,
Tho' harlots paint their talk as well as face
With colors of the heart that are not theirs.
I will not let her know; nine tithes of times
Face-flatterer and backbiter are the same.
And they, sweet soul, that most impute a crime
Are pronest to it, and impute themselves,
Wanting the mental range, or low desire
Not to feel lowest makes them level all;
Yea, they would pare the mountain to the plain,
To leave an equal baseness; and in this
Are harlots like the crowd that if they find
Some stain or blemish in a name of note,
Not grieving that their greatest are so small,
Inflate themselves with some insane delight,
And judge all nature from her feet of clay,
Without the will to lift their eyes, and see
Her godlike head crown'd with spiritual fire,
And touching other worlds. I am weary of her."

He spoke in words part heard, in whispers part,
Half-suffocated in the hoary fell
And many-winter'd fleece of throat and chin.
But Vivien, gathering somewhat of his mood,
And hearing 'harlot' mutter'd twice or thrice,
Leapt from her session on his lap, and stood
Stiff as a viper frozen; loathsome sight,
How from the rosy lips of life and love
Flash'd the bare-grinning skeleton of death!
White was her cheek; sharp breaths of anger puff'd
Her fairy nostril out; her hand half-clench'd
Went faltering sideways downward to her belt,

And feeling. Had she found a dagger there—
For in a wink the false love turns to hate—
She would have stabb'd him; but she found it not.
His eye was calm, and suddenly she took
To bitter weeping like a beaten child,
A long, long weeping, not consolable.
Then her false voice made way, broken with sobs:

"O crueller than was ever told in tale
Or sung in song! O vainly lavish'd love!
O cruel, there was nothing wild or strange,
Or seeming shameful—for what shame in love,
So love be true, and not as yours is?—nothing
Poor Vivien had not done to win his trust
Who call'd her what he call'd her—all her crime,
All—all—the wish to prove him wholly hers."

She mused a little, and then clapt her hands
Together with a wailing shriek, and said:
"Stabb'd through the heart's affections to the heart!
Seethed like the kid in its own mother's milk!
Kill'd with a word worse than a life of blows!
I thought that he was gentle, being great;
O God, that I had loved a smaller man!
I should have found in him a greater heart.
O, I, that flattering my true passion, saw
The knights, the court, the King, dark in your light,
Who loved to make men darker than they are,
Because of that high pleasure which I had
To seat you sole upon my pedestal
Of worship—I am answer'd, and henceforth
The course of life that seem'd so flowery to me
With you for guide and master, only you,
Becomes the sea-cliff pathway broken short,
And ending in a ruin—nothing left
But into some low cave to crawl, and there,
If the wolf spare me, weep my life away,
Kill'd with inutterable unkindliness."

She paused, she turn'd away, she hung her head,
The snake of gold slid from her hair, the braid
Slipt and uncoil'd itself, she wept afresh,
And the dark wood grew darker toward the storm
In silence, while his anger slowly died
Within him, till he let his wisdom go
For ease of heart, and half believed her true;
Call'd her to shelter in the hollow oak,

"Come from the storm," and having no reply,
Gazed at the heaving shoulder and the face
Hand-hidden, as for utmost grief or shame;
Then thrice essay'd, by tenderest-touching terms,
To sleek her ruffled peace of mind, in vain.
At last she let herself be conquer'd by him,
And as the cageling newly flown returns,
The seeming-injured simple-hearted thing
Came to her old perch back, and settled there.
There while she sat, half-falling from his knees,
Half-nestled at his heart, and since he saw
The slow tear creep from her closed eyelid yet,
About her, more in kindness than in love,
The gentle wizard cast a shielding arm.
But she dislink'd herself at once and rose,
Her arms upon her breast across, and stood,
A virtuous gentlewoman deeply wrong'd,
Upright and flush'd before him; then she said:

"There must be now no passages of love
Betwixt us twain henceforward evermore;
Since, if I be what I am grossly call'd,
What should be granted which your own gross heart
Would reckon worth the taking? I will go.
In truth, but one thing now—better have died
Thrice than have ask'd it once—could make me stay—
That proof of trust—so often ask'd in vain!
How justly, after that vile term of yours,
I find with grief! I might believe you then,
Who knows? once more. Lo! what was once to me
Mere matter of the fancy, now hath grown
The vast necessity of heart and life.
Farewell; think gently of me, for I fear
My fate or folly, passing gayer youth
For one so old, must be to love thee still.
But ere I leave thee let me swear once more
That if I schemed against thy peace in this,
May yon just heaven, that darkens o'er me, send
One flash that, missing all things else, may make
My scheming brain a cinder, if I lie."

Scarce had she ceased, when out of heaven a bolt—
For now the storm was close above them—struck,
Furrowing a giant oak, and javelining
With darted spikes and splinters of the wood
The dark earth round. He raised his eyes and saw
The tree that shone white-listed thro' the gloom.

But Vivien, fearing heaven had heard her oath,
And dazzled by the livid-flickering fork,
And deafen'd with the stammering cracks and claps
That follow'd, flying back and crying out,
"O Merlin, tho' you do not love me, save,
Yet save me!" clung to him and hugg'd him close;
And call'd him dear protector in her fright,
Nor yet forgot her practice in her fright,
But wrought upon his mood and hugg'd him close.
The pale blood of the wizard at her touch
Took gayer colors, like an opal warm'd.
She blamed herself for telling hearsay tales;
She shook from fear, and for her fault she wept
Of petulancy; she call'd him lord and liege,
Her seer, her bard, her silver star of eve,
Her God, her Merlin, the one passionate love
Of her whole life; and ever overhead
Bellow'd the tempest, and the rotten branch
Snapt in the rushing of the river-rain
Above them; and in change of glare and gloom
Her eyes and neck glittering went and came;
Till now the storm, its burst of passion spent,
Moaning and calling out of other lands,
Had left the ravaged woodland yet once more
To peace; and what should not have been had been,
For Merlin, overtalk'd and overworn,
Had yielded, told her all the charm, and slept.

　　Then, in one moment, she put forth the charm
Of woven paces and of waving hands,
And in the hollow oak he lay as dead,
And lost to life and use and name and fame.

　　Then crying, "I have made his glory mine,"
And shrieking out, "O fool!" the harlot leapt
Adown the forest, and the thicket closed
Behind her, and the forest echo'd "fool."

⊹⊹⊹⊹ LANCELOT AND ELAINE ⊹⊹⊹⊹

ELAINE the fair, Elaine the lovable,
Elaine, the lily maid of Astolat,
High in her chamber up a tower to the east
Guarded the sacred shield of Lancelot;

Which first she placed where morning's earliest ray
Might strike it, and awake her with the gleam;
Then fearing rust or soilure fashion'd for it
A case of silk, and braided thereupon
All the devices blazon'd on the shield
In their own tinct, and added, of her wit,
A border fantasy of branch and flower,
And yellow-throated nestling in the nest.
Nor rested thus content, but day by day,
Leaving her household and good father, climb'd
That eastern tower, and entering barr'd her door,
Stript off the case, and read the naked shield,
Now guess'd a hidden meaning in his arms,
Now made a pretty history to herself
Of every dint a sword had beaten in it,
And every scratch a lance had made upon it,
Conjecturing when and where: this cut is fresh,
That ten years back; this dealt him at Caerlyle,
That at Caerleon—this at Camelot—
And ah, God's mercy, what a stroke was there!
And here a thrust that might have kill'd, but God
Broke the strong lance, and roll'd his enemy down,
And saved him: so she lived in fantasy.

How came the lily maid by that good shield
Of Lancelot, she that knew not even his name?
He left it with her, when he rode to tilt
For the great diamond in the diamond jousts,
Which Arthur had ordain'd, and by that name
Had named them, since a diamond was the prize.

For Arthur, long before they crown'd him king,
Roving the trackless realms of Lyonnesse,
Had found a glen, gray boulder and black tarn.
A horror lived about the tarn, and clave
Like its own mists to all the mountain side;
For here two brothers, one a king, had met
And fought together, but their names were lost;
And each had slain his brother at a blow;
And down they fell and made the glen abhorr'd.
And there they lay till all their bones were bleach'd,
And lichen'd into color with the crags.
And he that once was king had on a crown
Of diamonds, one in front and four aside.
And Arthur came, and laboring up the pass,
All in a misty moonshine, unawares

Had trodden that crown'd skeleton, and the skull
Brake from the nape, and from the skull the crown
Roll'd into light, and turning on its rims
Fled like a glittering rivulet to the tarn.
And down the shingly scaur he plunged, and caught,
And set it on his head, and in his heart
Heard murmurs, "Lo, thou likewise shalt be king."

Thereafter, when a king, he had the gems
Pluck'd from the crown, and show'd them to his knights
Saying: "These jewels, whereupon I chanced
Divinely, are the kingdom's, not the King's—
For public use. Henceforward let there be,
Once every year, a joust for one of these;
For so by nine years' proof we needs must learn
Which is our mightiest, and ourselves shall grow
In use of arms and manhood, till we drive
The heathen, who, some say, shall rule the land
Hereafter, which God hinder!" Thus he spoke.
And eight years past, eight jousts had been, and still
Had Lancelot won the diamond of the year,
With purpose to present them to the Queen
When all were won; but, meaning all at once
To snare her royal fancy with a boon
Worth half her realm, had never spoken word.

Now for the central diamond and the last
And largest, Arthur, holding then his court
Hard on the river nigh the place which now
Is this world's hugest, let proclaim a joust
At Camelot, and when the time drew nigh
Spake—for she had been sick—to Guinevere:
"Are you so sick, my Queen, you cannot move
To these fair jousts?" "Yea, lord," she said, "ye know it."
"Then will ye miss," he answer'd, "the great deeds
Of Lancelot, and his prowess in the lists,
A sight ye love to look on." And the Queen
Lifted her eyes, and they dwelt languidly
On Lancelot, where he stood beside the King.
He, thinking that he read her meaning there,
"Stay with me, I am sick; my love is more
Than many diamonds," yielded; and a heart
Love-loyal to the least wish of the Queen—
However much he yearn'd to make complete
The tale of diamonds for his destined boon—
Urged him to speak against the truth, and say,
"Sir King, mine ancient wound is hardly whole,

And lets me from the saddle;" and the King
Glanced first at him, then her, and went his way.
No sooner gone than suddenly she began:

"To blame, my lord Sir Lancelot, much to blame!
Why go ye not to these fair jousts? the knights
Are half of them our enemies, and the crowd
Will murmur, 'Lo the shameless ones, who take
Their pastime now the trustful King is gone!'"
Then Lancelot, vext at having lied in vain:
"Are ye so wise? ye were not once so wise,
My Queen, that summer when ye loved me first.
Then of the crowd ye took no more account
Than of the myriad cricket of the mead,
When its own voice clings to each blade of grass,
And every voice is nothing. As to knights,
Them surely can I silence with all ease.
But now my loyal worship is allow'd
Of all men; many a bard, without offence,
Has link'd our names together in his lay,
Lancelot, the flower of bravery, Guinevere,
The pearl of beauty; and our knights at feast
Have pledged us in this union, while the King
Would listen smiling. How then? is there more?
Has Arthur spoken aught? or would yourself,
Now weary of my service and devoir,
Henceforth be truer to your faultless lord?"

She broke into a little scornful laugh:
"Arthur, my lord, Arthur, the faultless King,
That passionate perfection, my good lord—
But who can gaze upon the sun in heaven?
He never spake word of reproach to me,
He never had a glimpse of mine untruth,
He cares not for me. Only here today
There gleamed a vague suspicion in his eyes;
Some meddling rogue has tamper'd with him—else
Rapt in this fancy of his Table Round,
And swearing men to vows impossible,
To make them like himself; but, friend, to me
He is all fault who hath no fault at all.
For who loves me must have a touch of earth;
The low sun makes the color. I am yours,
Not Arthur's, as ye know, save by the bond.
And therefore hear my words: go to the jousts;
The tiny-trumpeting gnat can break our dream

When sweetest; and the vermin voices here
May buzz so loud—we scorn them, but they sting."

 Then answer'd Lancelot, the chief of knights:
"And with what face, after my pretext made,
Shall I appear, O Queen, at Camelot, I
Before a king who honors his own word
As if it were his God's?"

    "Yea," said the Queen,
"A moral child without the craft to rule,
Else had he not lost me; but listen to me,
If I must find you wit. We hear it said
That men go down before your spear at a touch,
But knowing you are Lancelot; your great name,
This conquers. Hide it therefore; go unknown.
Win! by this kiss you will; and our true King
Will then allow your pretext, O my knight,
As all for glory; for to speak him true,
Ye know right well, how meek soe'er he seem,
No keener hunter after glory breathes.
He loves it in his knights more than himself;
They prove to him his work. Win and return."

 Then got Sir Lancelot suddenly to horse,
Wroth at himself. Not willing to be known,
He left the barren-beaten thoroughfare,
Chose the green path that show'd the rarer foot,
And there among the solitary downs,
Full often lost in fancy, lost his way;
Till as he traced a faintly-shadow'd track,
That all in loops and links among the dales
Ran to the Castle of Astolat, he saw
Fired from the west, far on a hill, the towers.
Thither he made, and blew the gateway horn.
Then came an old, dumb, myriad-wrinkled man,
Who let him into lodging and disarm'd.
And Lancelot marvell'd at the wordless man;
And issuing found the Lord of Astolat
With two strong sons, Sir Torre and Sir Lavaine,
Moving to meet him in the castle court;
And close behind them stept the lily maid
Elaine, his daughter; mother of the house
There was not. Some light jest among them rose
With laughter dying down as the great knight
Approach'd them; then the Lord of Astolat:
"Whence comest thou, my guest, and by what name
Livest between the lips? for by thy state

And presence I might guess thee chief of those,
After the King, who eat in Arthur's halls.
Him have I seen; the rest, his Table Round,
Known as they are, to me they are unknown."

Then answer'd Lancelot, the chief of knights:
"Known am I, and of Arthur's hall, and known,
What I by mere mischance have brought, my shield.
But since I go to joust as one unknown
At Camelot for the diamond, ask me not;
Hereafter ye shall know me—and the shield—
I pray you lend me one, if such you have,
Blank, or at least with some device not mine."

Then said the Lord of Astolat: "Here is Torre's:
Hurt in his first tilt was my son, Sir Torre,
And so, God wot, his shield is blank as may be.
His ye can have." Then added plain Sir Torre,
"Yea, since I cannot use it, ye may have it."
Here laugh'd the father saying: "Fie, Sir Churl,
Is that an answer for a noble knight?
Allow him! but Lavaine, my younger here,
He is so full of lustihood, he will ride,
Joust for it, and win, and bring it in an hour,
And set it in this damsel's golden hair,
To make her thrice as wilful as before."

"Nay, father, nay, good father, shame me not
Before this noble knight," said young Lavaine,
"For nothing. Surely I but play'd on Torre,
He seem'd so sullen, vext he could not go;
A jest, no more! for, knight, the maiden dreamt
That some one put this diamond in her hand,
And that it was too slippery to be held,
And slipt and fell into some pool or stream,
The castle-well, belike; and then I said
That if I went and if I fought and won it—
But all was jest and joke among ourselves—
Then must she keep it safelier. All was jest.
But, father, give me leave, an if he will,
To ride to Camelot with this noble knight.
Win shall I not, but do my best to win;
Young as I am, yet would I do my best."

"So ye will grace me," answer'd Lancelot,
Smiling a moment, "with your fellowship
O'er these waste downs whereon I lost myself,
Then were I glad of you as guide and friend:

And you shall win this diamond,—as I hear,
It is a fair large diamond,—if ye may,
And yield it to this maiden, if ye will."
"A fair large diamond," added plain Sir Torre,
"Such be for queens, and not for simple maids."
Then she, who held her eyes upon the ground,
Elaine, and heard her name so tost about,
Flush'd slightly at the slight disparagement
Before the stranger knight, who, looking at her,
Full courtly, yet not falsely, thus return'd:
"If what is fair be but for what is fair,
And only queens are to be counted so,
Rash were my judgment then, who deem this maid
Might wear as fair a jewel as is on earth,
Not violating the bond of like to like."

He spoke and ceased; the lily maid Elaine,
Won by the mellow voice before she look'd,
Lifted her eyes and read his lineaments.
The great and guilty love he bare the Queen,
In battle with the love he bare his lord,
Had marr'd his face, and mark'd it ere his time.
Another sinning on such heights with one,
The flower of all the west and all the world,
Had been the sleeker for it; but in him
His mood was often like a fiend, and rose
And drove him into wastes and solitudes
For agony, who was yet a living soul.
Marr'd as he was, he seem'd the goodliest man
That ever among ladies ate in hall,
And noblest, when she lifted up her eyes.
However marr'd, of more than twice her years,
Seam'd with an ancient sword-cut on the cheek,
And bruised and bronzed, she lifted up her eyes
And loved him, with that love which was her doom.

Then the great knight, the darling of the court,
Loved of the loveliest, into that rude hall
Stept with all grace, and not with half disdain
Hid under grace, as in a smaller time,
But kindly man moving among his kind;
Whom they with meats and vintage of their best
And talk and minstrel melody entertain'd.
And much they ask'd of court and Table Round,
And ever well and readily answer'd he;
But Lancelot, when they glanced at Guinevere,
Suddenly speaking of the wordless man,

Heard from the baron that, ten years before,
The heathen caught and reft him of his tongue.
"He learnt and warn'd me of their fierce design
Against my house, and him they caught and maim'd;
But I, my sons, and little daughter fled
From bonds or death, and dwelt among the woods
By the great river in a boatman's hut.
Dull days were those, till our good Arthur broke
The Pagan yet once more on Badon hill."

"O, there, great lord, doubtless," Lavaine said, rapt
By all the sweet and sudden passion of youth
Toward greatness in its elder, "you have fought.
O, tell us—for we live apart—you know
Of Arthur's glorious wars." And Lancelot spoke
And answer'd him at full, as having been
With Arthur in the fight which all day long
Rang by the white mouth of the violent Glem;
And in the four loud battles by the shore
Of Duglas; that on Bassa; then the war
That thunder'd in and out the gloomy skirts
Of Celidon the forest; and again
By Castle Gurnion, where the glorious King
Had on his cuirass worn our Lady's Head,
Carved of one emerald centred in a sun
Of silver rays, that lighten'd as he breathed;
And at Caerleon had he help'd his lord,
When the strong neighings of the wild White Horse
Set every gilded parapet shuddering;
And up in Agned-Cathregonion too,
And down the waste sand-shores of Trath Treroit,
Where many a heathen fell, "and on the mount
Of Badon I myself beheld the King
Charge at the head of all his Table Round,
And all his legions crying Christ and him,
And break them; and I saw him, after, stand
High on a heap of slain, from spur to plume
Red as the rising sun with heathen blood,
And seeing me, with a great voice he cried,
'They are broken, they are broken!' for the King,
However mild he seems at home, nor cares
For triumph in our mimic wars, the jousts—
For if his own knight casts him down, he laughs,
Saying his knights are better men than he—
Yet in this heathen war the fire of God

Fills him. I never saw his like; there lives
No greater leader."

                    While he utter'd this,
Low to her own heart said the lily maid,
"Save your great self, fair lord;" and when he fell
From talk of war to traits of pleasantry—
Being mirthful he, but in a stately kind—
She still took note that when the living smile
Died from his lips, across him came a cloud
Of melancholy severe, from which again,
Whenever in her hovering to and fro
The lily maid had striven to make him cheer,
There brake a sudden-beaming tenderness
Of manners and of nature; and she thought
That all was nature, all, perchance, for her.
And all night long his face before her lived,
As when a painter, poring on a face,
Divinely thro' all hindrance finds the man
Behind it, and so paints him that his face,
The shape and color of a mind and life,
Lives for his children, ever at its best
And fullest; so the face before her lived,
Dark-splendid, speaking in the silence, full
Of noble things, and held her from her sleep,
Till rathe she rose, half-cheated in the thought
She needs must bid farewell to sweet Lavaine.
First as in fear, step after step, she stole
Down the long tower-stairs, hesitating.
Anon, she heard Sir Lancelot cry in the court,
"This shield, my friend, where is it?" and Lavaine
Past inward, as she came from out the tower.
There to his proud horse Lancelot turn'd, and smooth'd
The glossy shoulder, humming to himself.
Half-envious of the flattering hand, she drew
Nearer and stood. He look'd, and, more amazed
Than if seven men had set upon him, saw
The maiden standing in the dewy light.
He had not dream'd she was so beautiful.
Then came on him a sort of sacred fear,
For silent, tho' he greeted her, she stood
Rapt on his face as if it were a god's.
Suddenly flash'd on her a wild desire
That he should wear her favor at the tilt.
She braved a riotous heart in asking for it.
"Fair lord, whose name I know not—noble it is,

I well believe, the noblest—will you wear
My favor at this tourney?" "Nay," said he,
"Fair lady, since I never yet have worn
Favor of any lady in the lists.
Such is my wont, as those who know me know."
"Yea, so," she answer'd; "then in wearing mine
Needs must be lesser likelihood, noble lord,
That those who know should know you." And he turn'd
Her counsel up and down within his mind,
And found it true, and answer'd: "True, my child.
Well, I will wear it; fetch it out to me.
What is it?" and she told him, "A red sleeve
Broider'd with pearls," and brought it. Then he bound
Her token on his helmet, with a smile
Saying, "I never yet have done so much
For any maiden living," and the blood
Sprang to her face and fill'd her with delight;
But left her all the paler when Lavaine
Returning brought the yet-unblazon'd shield,
His brother's, which he gave to Lancelot,
Who parted with his own to fair Elaine:
"Do me this grace, my child, to have my shield
In keeping till I come." "A grace to me,"
She answer'd, "twice to-day. I am your squire!"
Whereat Lavaine said laughing: "Lily maid,
For fear our people call you lily maid
In earnest, let me bring your color back;
Once, twice, and thrice. Now get you hence to bed;"
So kiss'd her, and Sir Lancelot his own hand,
And thus they moved away. She staid a minute,
Then made a sudden step to the gate, and there—
Her bright hair blown about the serious face
Yet rosy-kindled with her brother's kiss—
Paused by the gateway, standing near the shield
In silence, while she watch'd their arms far-off
Sparkle, until they dipt below the downs.
Then to her tower she climb'd, and took the shield,
There kept it, and so lived in fantasy.

Meanwhile the new companions past away
Far o'er the long backs of the bushless downs,
To where Sir Lancelot knew there lived a knight
Not far from Camelot, now for forty years
A hermit, who had pray'd, labor'd and pray'd,
And ever laboring had scoop'd himself
In the white rock a chapel and a hall

On massive columns, like a shore-cliff cave,
And cells and chambers. All were fair and dry;
The green light from the meadows underneath
Struck up and lived along the milky roofs;
And in the meadows tremulous aspen trees
And poplars made a noise of falling showers.
And thither wending there that night they bode.

But when the next day broke from underground,
And shot red fire and shadows thro' the cave,
They rose, heard mass, broke fast, and rode away.
Then Lancelot saying, "Hear, but hold my name
Hidden, you ride with Lancelot of the Lake,"
Abash'd Lavaine, whose instant reverence,
Dearer to true young hearts than their own praise,
But left him leave to stammer, "Is it indeed?"
And after muttering, "The great Lancelot,"
At last he got his breath and answer'd: "One,
One have I seen—that other, our liege lord,
The dread Pendragon, Britain's King of kings,
Of whom the people talk mysteriously,
He will be there—then were I stricken blind
That minute, I might say that I had seen."

So spake Lavaine, and when they reach'd the lists
By Camelot in the meadow, let his eyes
Run thro' the peopled gallery which half round
Lay like a rainbow fallen upon the grass,
Until they found the clear-faced King, who sat
Robed in red samite, easily to be known,
Since to his crown the golden dragon clung,
And down his robe the dragon writhed in gold,
And from the carven-work behind him crept
Two dragons gilded, sloping down to make
Arms for his chair, while all the rest of them
Thro' knots and loops and folds innumerable
Fled ever thro' the woodwork, till they found
The new design wherein they lost themselves,
Yet with all ease, so tender was the work;
And, in the costly canopy o'er him set,
Blazed the last diamond of the nameless king.

Then Lancelot answer'd young Lavaine and said:
"Me you call great; mine is the firmer seat,
The truer lance; but there is many a youth
Now crescent, who will come to all I am
And overcome it; and in me there dwells

No greatness, save it be some far-off touch
Of greatness to know well I am not great.
There is the man." And Lavaine gaped upon him
As on a thing miraculous, and anon
The trumpets blew; and then did either side,
They that assail'd, and they that held the lists,
Set lance in rest, strike spur, suddenly move,
Meet in the midst, and there so furiously
Shock that a man far-off might well perceive,
If any man that day were left afield,
The hard earth shake, and a low thunder of arms.
And Lancelot bode a little, till he saw
Which were the weaker; then he hurl'd into it
Against the stronger. Little need to speak
Of Lancelot in his glory! King, duke, earl,
Count, baron—whom he smote, he overthrew.

But in the field were Lancelot's kith and kin,
Ranged with the Table Round that held the lists,
Strong men, and wrathful that a stranger knight
Should do and almost overdo the deeds
Of Lancelot; and one said to the other, "Lo!
What is he? I do not mean the force alone—
The grace and versatility of the man!
Is it not Lancelot?" "When has Lancelot worn
Favor of any lady in the lists?
Not such his wont, as we that know him know."
"How then? who then?" a fury seized them all,
A fiery family passion for the name
Of Lancelot, and a glory one with theirs.
They couch'd their spears and prick'd their steeds, and thus,
Their plumes driven backward by the wind they made
In moving, all together down upon him
Bare, as a wild wave in the wide North Sea,
Green-glimmering toward the summit, bears, with all
Its stormy crests that smoke against the skies.
Down on a bark, and overbears the bark
And him that helms it; so they overbore
Sir Lancelot and his charger, and a spear
Down-glancing lamed the charger, and a spear
Prick'd sharply his own cuirass, and the head
Pierced thro' his side, and there snapt and remain'd.

Then Sir Lavaine did well and worshipfully;
He bore a knight of old repute to the earth,
And brought his horse to Lancelot where he lay.

He up the side, sweating with agony, got,
But thought to do while he might yet endure,
And being lustily holpen by the rest,
His party,—tho' it seem'd half-miracle
To those he fought with,—drave his kith and kin,
And all the Table Round that held the lists,
Back to the barrier; then the trumpets blew
Proclaiming his the prize who wore the sleeve
Of scarlet and the pearls; and all the knights,
His party, cried, "Advance and take thy prize
The diamond;" but he answer'd: "Diamond me
No diamonds! for God's love, a little air!
Prize me no prizes, for my prize is death!
Hence will I, and I charge you, follow me not."

He spoke, and vanish'd suddenly from the field
With young Lavaine into the poplar grove.
There from his charger down he slid, and sat,
Gasping to Sir Lavaine, "Draw the lance-head."
"Ah, my sweet lord Sir Lancelot," said Lavaine,
"I dread me, if I draw it, you will die."
But he, "I die already with it: draw—
Draw,"—and Lavaine drew, and Sir Lancelot gave
A marvellous great shriek and ghastly groan,
And half his blood burst forth, and down he sank
For the pure pain, and wholly swoon'd away.
Then came the hermit out and bare him in,
There stanch'd his wound; and there, in daily doubt
Whether to live or die, for many a week
Hid from the wild world's rumor by the grove
Of poplars with their noise of falling showers,
And ever-tremulous aspen-trees, he lay.

But on that day when Lancelot fled the lists,
His party, knights of utmost North and West,
Lords of waste marshes, kings of desolate isles,
Came round their great Pendragon, saying to him,
"Lo, Sire, our knight, thro' whom we won the day,
Hath gone sore wounded, and hath left his prize
Untaken, crying that his prize is death."
"Heaven hinder," said the King, "that such an one,
So great a knight as we have seen today—
He seem'd to me another Lancelot—
Yea, twenty times I thought him Lancelot—
He must not pass uncared for. Wherefore rise,
O Gawain, and ride forth and find the knight.

Wounded and wearied, needs must he be near.
I charge you that you get at once to horse.
And, knights and kings, there breathes not one of you
Will deem this prize of ours is rashly given;
His prowess was too wondrous. We will do him
No customary honor; since the knight
Came not to us, of us to claim the prize,
Ourselves will send it after. Rise and take
This diamond, and deliver it, and return,
And bring us where he is, and how he fares,
And cease not from your quest until ye find."

So saying, from the carven flower above,
To which it made a restless heart, he took
And gave the diamond. Then from where he sat
At Arthur's right, with smiling face arose,
With smiling face and frowning heart, a prince
In the mid might and flourish of his May,
Gawain, surnamed the Courteous, fair and strong,
And after Lancelot, Tristram, and Geraint,
And Gareth, a good knight, but therewithal
Sir Modred's brother, and the child of Lot,
Nor often loyal to his word, and now
Wroth that the King's command to sally forth
In quest of whom he knew not, made him leave
The banquet and concourse of knights and kings.

So all in wrath he got to horse and went;
While Arthur to the banquet, dark in mood,
Past, thinking, "Is it Lancelot who hath come
Despite the wound he spake of, all for gain
Of glory, and hath added wound to wound,
And ridden away to die?" So fear'd the King,
And, after two days' tarriance there, return'd.
Then when he saw the Queen, embracing ask'd,
"Love, are you yet so sick?" "Nay, lord," she said.
"And where is Lancelot?" Then the Queen amazed,
"Was he not with you? won he not your prize?"
"Nay, but one like him." "Why, that like was he."
And when the King demanded how she knew,
Said: "Lord, no sooner had ye parted from us
Than Lancelot told me of a common talk
That men went down before his spear at a touch,
But knowing he was Lancelot; his great name
Conquer'd; and therefore would he hide his name
From all men, even the King, and to this end

Had made the pretext of a hindering wound,
That he might joust unknown of all, and learn
If his old prowess were in aught decay'd;
And added, 'Our true Arthur, when he learns,
Will well allow my pretext, as for gain
Of purer glory.' "

        Then replied the King:
"Far lovelier in our Lancelot had it been,
In lieu of idly dallying with the truth,
To have trusted me as he hath trusted thee.
Surely his King and most familiar friend
Might well have kept his secret. True, indeed,
Albeit I know my knights fantastical,
So fine a fear in our large Lancelot
Must needs have moved my laughter; now remains
But little cause for laughter. His own kin—
Ill news, my Queen, for all who love him, this!—
His kith and kin, not knowing, set upon him;
So that he went sore wounded from the field.
Yet good news too; for goodly hopes are mine
That Lancelot is no more a lonely heart.
He wore, against his wont, upon his helm
A sleeve of scarlet, broider'd with great pearls,
Some gentle maiden's gift."

              "Yea, lord," she said,
"Thy hopes are mine," and saying that, she choked,
And sharply turn'd about to hide her face,
Past to her chamber, and there flung herself
Down on the great King's couch, and writhed upon it,
And clench'd her fingers till they bit the palm,
And shriek'd out "Traitor!" to the unhearing wall,
Then flash'd into wild tears, and rose again,
And moved about her palace, proud and pale.

  Gawain the while thro' all the region round
Rode with his diamond, wearied of the quest,
Touch'd at all points except the poplar grove,
And came at last, tho' late, to Astolat;
Whom glittering in enamell'd arms the maid
Glanced at, and cried, "What news from Camelot, lord?
What of the knight with the red sleeve?" "He won."
"I knew it," she said. "But parted from the jousts
Hurt in the side;" whereat she caught her breath.
Thro' her own side she felt the sharp lance go.
Thereon she smote her hand; well-nigh she swoon'd.

And, while he gazed wonderingly at her, came
The Lord of Astolat out, to whom the prince
Reported who he was, and on what quest
Sent, that he bore the prize and could not find
The victor, but had ridden a random round
To seek him, and had wearied of the search.
To whom the Lord of Astolat: "Bide with us,
And ride no more at random, noble prince!
Here was the knight, and here he left a shield;
This will he send or come for. Furthermore
Our son is with him; we shall hear anon,
Needs must we hear." To this the courteous prince
Accorded with his wonted courtesy,
Courtesy with a touch of traitor in it,
And stay'd; and cast his eyes on fair Elaine;
Where could be found face daintier? then her shape
From forehead down to foot, perfect—again
From foot to forehead exquisitely turn'd:
"Well—if I bide, lo! this wild flower for me!"
And oft they met among the garden yews,
And there he set himself to play upon her
With sallying wit, free flashes from a height
Above her, graces of the court, and songs,
Sighs, and low smiles, and golden eloquence
And amorous adulation, till the maid
Rebell'd against it, saying to him: "Prince,
O loyal nephew of our noble King,
Why ask you not to see the shield he left,
Whence you might learn his name? Why slight your King,
And lose the quest he sent you on, and prove
No surer than our falcon yesterday,
Who lost the hern we slipt her at, and went
To all the winds?" "Nay, by mine head," said he,
"I lose it, as we lose the lark in heaven,
O damsel, in the light of your blue eyes;
But an ye will it let me see the shield."
And when the shield was brought, and Gawain saw
Sir Lancelot's azure lions, crown'd with gold,
Ramp in the field, he smote his thigh, and mock'd:
"Right was the King! our Lancelot! that true man!"
"And right was I," she answer'd merrily, "I,
Who dream'd my knight the greatest knight of all."
"And if I dream'd," said Gawain, "that you love
This greatest knight, your pardon! lo, ye know it!
Speak therefore; shall I waste myself in vain?"

Full simple was her answer: "What know I?
My brethren have been all my fellowship;
And I, when often they have talk'd of love,
Wish'd it had been my mother, for they talk'd,
Meseem'd, of what they knew not; so myself—
I know not if I know what true love is,
But if I know, then, if I love not him,
I know there is none other I can love."
"Yea, by God's death," said he, "ye love him well,
But would not, knew ye what all others know,
And whom he loves." "So be it," cried Elaine,
And lifted her fair face and moved away;
But he pursued her, calling, "Stay a little!
One golden minute's grace! he wore your sleeve.
Would he break faith with one I may not name?
Must our true man change like a leaf at last?
Nay—like enow. Why then, far be it from me
To cross our mighty Lancelot in his loves!
And, damsel, for I deem you know full well
Where your great knight is hidden, let me leave
My quest with you; the diamond also—here!
For if you love, it will be sweet to give it;
And if he love, it will be sweet to have it
From your own hand; and whether he love or not,
A diamond is a diamond. Fare you well
A thousand times!—a thousand times farewell!
Yet, if he love, and his love hold, we two
May meet at court hereafter! there, I think,
So ye will learn the courtesies of the court,
We two shall know each other."

              Then he gave,
And slightly kiss'd the hand to which he gave,
The diamond, and all wearied of the quest
Leapt on his horse, and carolling as he went
A true-love ballad, lightly rode away.

    Thence to the court he past; there told the King
What the King knew, "Sir Lancelot is the knight."
And added, "Sire, my liege, so much I learnt,
But fail'd to find him, tho' I rode all round
The region; but I lighted on the maid
Whose sleeve he wore. She loves him; and to her,
Deeming our courtesy is the truest law,
I gave the diamond. She will render it;
For by mine head she knows his hiding-place."

The seldom-frowning King frown'd, and replied,
"Too courteous truly! ye shall go no more
On quest of mine, seeing that ye forget
Obedience is the courtesy due to kings."

He spake and parted. Wroth, but all in awe,
For twenty strokes of the blood, without a word,
Linger'd that other, staring after him;
Then shook his hair, strode off, and buzz'd abroad
About the maid of Astolat, and her love.
All ears were prick'd at once, all tongues were loosed:
"The maid of Astolat loves Sir Lancelot,
Sir Lancelot loves the maid of Astolat."
Some read the King's face, some the Queen's, and all
Had marvel what the maid might be, but most
Predoom'd her as unworthy. One old dame
Came suddenly on the Queen with the sharp news.
She, that had heard the noise of it before,
But sorrowing Lancelot should have stoop'd so low,
Marr'd her friend's aim with pale tranquillity.
So ran the tale like fire about the court,
Fire in dry stubble a nine-days' wonder flared;
Till even the knights at banquet twice or thrice
Forgot to drink to Lancelot and the Queen,
And pledging Lancelot and the lily maid
Smiled at each other, while the Queen, who sat
With lips severely placid, felt the knot
Climb in her throat, and with her feet unseen
Crush'd the wild passion out against the floor
Beneath the banquet, where the meats became
As wormwood and she hated all who pledged.

But far away the maid in Astolat,
Her guiltless rival, she that ever kept
The one-day-seen Sir Lancelot in her heart,
Crept to her father, while he mused alone,
Sat on his knee, stroked his gray face and said:
"Father, you call me wilful, and the fault
Is yours who let me have my will, and now,
Sweet father, will you let me lose my wits?"
"Nay," said he, "surely." "Wherefore, let me hence,"
She answer'd, "and find out our dear Lavaine."
"Ye will not lose your wits for dear Lavaine.
Bide," answer'd he: "we needs must hear anon
Of him, and of that other." "Ay," she said,
"And of that other, for I needs must hence

And find that other, wheresoe'er he be,
And with mine own hand give his diamond to him,
Lest I be found as faithless in the quest
As yon proud prince who left the quest to me.
Sweet father, I behold him in my dreams
Gaunt as it were the skeleton of himself,
Death-pale, for the lack of gentle maiden's aid.
The gentler-born the maiden, the more bound,
My father, to be sweet and serviceable
To noble knights in sickness, as ye know,
When these have worn their tokens. Let me hence,
I pray you." Then her father nodding said:
"Ay, ay, the diamond. Wit ye well, my child,
Right fain were I to learn this knight were whole,
Being our greatest. Yea, and you must give it—
And sure I think this fruit is hung too high
For any mouth to gape for save a queen's—
Nay, I mean nothing; so then, get you gone,
Being so very wilful you must go."

Lightly, her suit allow'd, she slipt away,
And while she made her ready for her ride
Her father's latest word humm'd in her ear,
"Being so very wilful you must go."
And changed itself and echo'd in her heart,
"Being so very wilful you must die."
But she was happy enough and shook it off,
As we shake off the bee that buzzes at us;
And in her heart she answer'd it and said,
"What matter, so I help him back to life?"
Then far away with good Sir Torre for guide
Rode o'er the long backs of the bushless downs
To Camelot, and before the city-gates
Came on her brother with a happy face
Making a roan horse caper and curvet
For pleasure all about a field of flowers;
Whom when she saw, "Lavaine," she cried, "Lavaine,
How fares my lord Sir Lancelot?" He amazed,
"Torre and Elaine! why here? Sir Lancelot!
How know ye my lord's name is Lancelot?"
But when the maid had told him all her tale,
Then turn'd Sir Torre, and being in his moods
Left them, and under the strange-statued gate,
Where Arthur's wars were render'd mystically,
Past up the still rich city to his kin,
His own far blood, which dwelt at Camelot;

And her, Lavaine across the poplar grove
Led to the caves. There first she saw the casque
Of Lancelot on the wall; her scarlet sleeve,
Tho' carved and cut, and half the pearls away,
Stream'd from it still; and in her heart she laugh'd,
Because he had not loosed it from his helm,
But meant once more perchance to tourney in it.
And when they gain'd the cell wherein he slept,
His battle-writhen arms and mighty hands
Lay naked on the wolf-skin, and a dream
Of dragging down his enemy made them move.
Then she that saw him lying unsleek, unshorn,
Gaunt as it were the skeleton of himself,
Utter'd a little tender dolorous cry.
The sound not wonted in a place so still
Woke the sick knight, and while he roll'd his eyes
Yet blank from sleep, she started to him, saying,
"Your prize the diamond sent you by the King."
His eyes glisten'd; she fancied, "Is it for me?"
And when the maid had told him all the tale
Of king and prince, the diamond sent, the quest
Assign'd to her not worthy of it, she knelt
Full lowly by the corners of his bed,
And laid the diamond in his open hand.
Her face was near, and as we kiss the child
That does the task assign'd, he kiss'd her face.
At once she slipt like water to the floor.
"Alas," he said, "your ride hath wearied you.
Rest must you have." "No rest for me," she said;
"Nay, for near you, fair lord, I am at rest."
What might she mean by that? his large black eyes,
Yet larger thro' his leanness, dwelt upon her,
Till all her heart's sad secret blazed itself
In the heart's colors on her simple face;
And Lancelot look'd and was perplext in mind,
And being weak in body said no more,
But did not love the color; woman's love,
Save one, he not regarded, and so turn'd
Sighing, and feign'd a sleep until he slept.

Then rose Elaine and glided thro' the fields,
And past beneath the weirdly-sculptured gates
Far up the dim rich city to her kin;
There bode the night, but woke with dawn, and past
Down thro' the dim rich city to the fields,
Thence to the cave. So day by day she past

In either twilight ghost-like to and fro
Gliding, and every day she tended him,
And likewise many a night; and Lancelot
Would, tho' he call'd his wound a little hurt
Whereof he should be quickly whole, at times
Brain-feverous in his heat and agony, seem
Uncourteous, even he. But the meek maid
Sweetly forbore him ever, being to him
Meeker than any child to a rough nurse,
Milder than any mother to a sick child,
And never woman yet, since man's first fall,
Did kindlier unto man, but her deep love
Upbore her; till the hermit, skill'd in all
The simples and the science of that time,
Told him that her fine care had saved his life.
And the sick man forgot her simple blush,
Would call her friend and sister, sweet Elaine,
Would listen for her coming and regret
Her parting step, and held her tenderly,
And loved her with all love except the love
Of man and woman when they love their best,
Closest and sweetest, and had died the death
In any knightly fashion for her sake.
And peradventure had he seen her first
She might have made this and that other world
Another world for the sick man; but now
The shackles of an old love straiten'd him,
His honor rooted in dishonor stood,
And faith unfaithful kept him falsely true.

Yet the great knight in his mid-sickness made
Full many a holy vow and pure resolve.
These, as but born of sickness, could not live;
For when the blood ran lustier in him again,
Full often the bright image of one face,
Making a treacherous quiet in his heart,
Dispersed his resolution like a cloud.
Then if the maiden, while that ghostly grace
Beam'd on his fancy, spoke, he answer'd not,
Or short and coldly, and she knew right well
What the rough sickness meant, but what this meant
She knew not, and the sorrow dimm'd her sight,
And drave her ere her time across the fields
Far into the rich city, where alone
She murmur'd, "Vain, in vain! it cannot be.
He will not love me. How then? must I die?"

Then as a little helpless innocent bird,
That has but one plain passage of few notes,
Will sing the simple passage o'er and o'er
For all an April morning, till the ear
Wearies to hear it, so the simple maid
Went half the night repeating, "Must I die?"
And now to right she turn'd, and now to left,
And found no ease in turning or in rest;
And "Him or death," she mutter'd, "death or him,"
Again and like a burthen, "Him or death."

But when Sir Lancelot's deadly hurt was whole,
To Astolat returning rode the three.
There morn by morn, arraying her sweet self
In that wherein she deem'd she look'd her best,
She came before Sir Lancelot, for she thought,
"If I be loved, these are my festal robes,
If not, the victim's flowers before he fall."
And Lancelot ever prest upon the maid
That she should ask some goodly gift of him
For her own self or hers: "and do not shun
To speak the wish most near to your true heart:
Such service have ye done me that I make
My will of yours, and prince and lord am I
In mine own land, and what I will I can."
Then like a ghost she lifted up her face,
But like a ghost without the power to speak.
And Lancelot saw that she withheld her wish,
And bode among them yet a little space
Till he should learn it; and one morn it chanced
He found her in among the garden yews,
And said, "Delay no longer, speak your wish,
Seeing I go to-day." Then out she brake:
"Going? and we shall never see you more.
And I must die for want of one bold word."
"Speak; that I live to hear," he said, "is yours."
Then suddenly and passionately she spoke:
"I have gone mad. I love you; let me die."
"Ah, sister," answer'd Lancelot, "what is this?"
And innocently extending her white arms,
"Your love," she said, "your love—to be your wife."
And Lancelot answer'd, "Had I chosen to wed,
I had been wedded earlier, sweet Elaine;
But now there never will be wife of mine."
"No, no," she cried, "I care not to be wife,
But to be with you still, to see your face,

To serve you, and to follow you thro' the world."
And Lancelot answer'd: "Nay, the world, the world,
All ear and eye, with such a stupid heart
To interpret ear and eye, and such a tongue
To blare its own interpretation—nay,
Full ill then should I quit your brother's love,
And your good father's kindness." And she said,
"Not to be with you, not to see your face—
Alas for me then, my good days are done!"
"Nay, noble maid," he answer'd, "ten times nay!
This is not love, but love's first flash in youth,
Most common; yea, I know it of mine own self,
And you yourself will smile at your own self
Hereafter, when you yield your flower of life
To one more fitly yours, not thrice your age.
And then will I, for true you are and sweet
Beyond mine old belief in womanhood,
More specially should your good knight be poor,
Endow you with broad land and territory
Even to the half my realm beyond the seas,
So that would make you happy; furthermore,
Even to the death, as tho' ye were my blood,
In all your quarrels will I be your knight.
This will I do, dear damsel, for your sake,
And more than this I cannot."

                While he spoke
She neither blush'd nor shook, but deathly-pale
Stood grasping what was nearest, then replied,
"Of all this will I nothing;" and so fell,
And thus they bore her swooning to her tower.

    Then spake, to whom thro' those black walls of yew
Their talk had pierced, her father: "Ay, a flash,
I fear me, that will strike my blossom dead.
Too courteous are ye, fair Lord Lancelot.
I pray you, use some rough discourtesy
To blunt or break her passion."

                Lancelot said,
"That were against me; what I can I will;"
And there that day remain'd, and toward even
Sent for his shield. Full meekly rose the maid,
Stript off the case, and gave the naked shield;
Then, when she heard his horse upon the stones,
Unclasping flung the casement back, and look'd
Down on his helm, from which her sleeve had gone.

And Lancelot knew the little clinking sound;
And she by tact of love was well aware
That Lancelot knew that she was looking at him.
And yet he glanced not up, nor waved his hand,
Nor bade farewell, but sadly rode away.
This was the one discourtesy that he used.

So in her tower alone the maiden sat.
His very shield was gone; only the case,
Her own poor work, her empty labor, left.
But still she heard him, still his picture form'd
And grew between her and the pictured wall.
Then came her father, saying in low tones,
"Have comfort," whom she greeted quietly.
Then came her brethren saying, "Peace to thee,
Sweet sister," whom she answer'd with all calm.
But when they left her to herself again,
Death, like a friend's voice from a distant field
Approaching thro' the darkness, call'd; the owls
Wailing had power upon her, and she mixt
Her fancies with the sallow-rifted glooms
Of evening and the moanings of the wind.

And in those days she made a little song,
And call'd her song "The Song of Love and Death,"
And sang it; sweetly could she make and sing.

"Sweet is true love tho' given in vain, in vain;
And sweet is death who puts an end to pain.
I know not which is sweeter, no, not I.

"Love, art thou sweet? then bitter death must be.
Love, thou art bitter; sweet is death to me.
O Love, if death be sweeter, let me die.

"Sweet love, that seems not made to fade away;
Sweet death, that seems to make us loveless clay;
I know not which is sweeter, no, not I.

"I fain would follow love, if that could be;
I needs must follow death, who calls for me;
Call and I follow, I follow! let me die."

High with the last line scaled her voice, and this,
All in a fiery dawning wild with wind
That shook her tower, the brothers heard, and thought
With shuddering, "Hark the Phantom of the house
That ever shrieks before a death," and call'd
The father, and all three in hurry and fear

Ran to her, and lo! the blood-red light of dawn
Flared on her face, she shrilling, "Let me die!"

　　As when we dwell upon a word we know,
Repeating, till the word we know so well
Becomes a wonder, and we know not why,
So dwelt the father on her face, and thought,
"Is this Elaine?" till back the maiden fell,
Then gave a languid hand to each, and lay,
Speaking a still good-morrow with her eyes.
At last she said: "Sweet brothers, yester-night
I seem'd a curious little maid again,
As happy as when we dwelt among the woods,
And when ye used to take me with the flood
Up the great river in the boatman's boat.
Only ye would not pass beyond the cape
That has the poplar on it; there ye fixt
Your limit, oft returning with the tide.
And yet I cried because ye would not pass
Beyond it, and far up the shining flood
Until we found the palace of the King.
And yet ye would not; but this night I dream'd
That I was all alone upon the flood,
And then I said, 'Now shall I have my will;'
And there I woke, but still the wish remain'd.
So let me hence that I may pass at last
Beyond the poplar and far up the flood,
Until I find the palace of the King.
There will I enter in among them all,
And no man there will dare to mock at me;
But there the fine Gawain will wonder at me,
And there the great Sir Lancelot muse at me;
Gawain, who bade a thousand farewells to me,
Lancelot, who coldly went, nor bade me one.
And there the King will know me and my love,
And there the Queen herself will pity me,
And all the gentle court will welcome me,
And after my long voyage I shall rest!"

　　"Peace," said her father, "O my child, ye seem
Light-headed, for what force is yours to go
So far, being sick? and wherefore would ye look
On this proud fellow again, who scorns us all?"

　　Then the rough Torre began to heave and move,
And bluster into stormy sobs and say:
"I never loved him; an I meet with him,

I care not howsoever great he be,
Then will I strike at him and strike him down.
Give me good fortune, I will strike him dead,
For this discomfort he hath done the house."

To whom the gentle sister made reply:
"Fret not yourself, dear brother, nor be wroth,
Seeing it is no more Sir Lancelot's fault
Not to love me than it is mine to love
Him of all men who seems to me the highest."

"Highest?" the father answer'd, echoing "highest?"—
He meant to break the passion in her—"nay,
Daughter, I know not what you call the highest;
But this I know, for all the people know it,
He loves the Queen, and in an open shame,
And she returns his love in open shame;
If this be high, what is it to be low?"

Then spake the lily maid of Astolat:
"Sweet father, all too faint and sick am I
For anger. These are slanders; never yet
Was noble man but made ignoble talk.
He makes no friend who never made a foe.
But now it is my glory to have loved
One peerless, without stain; so let me pass,
My father, howsoe'er I seem to you,
Not all unhappy, having loved God's best
And greatest, tho' my love had no return.
Yet, seeing you desire your child to live,
Thanks, but you work against your own desire,
For if I could believe the things you say
I should but die the sooner; wherefore cease,
Sweet father, and bid call the ghostly man
Hither, and let me shrive me clean and die."

So when the ghostly man had come and gone,
She, with a face bright as for sin forgiven,
Besought Lavaine to write as she devised
A letter, word for word; and when he ask'd,
"Is it for Lancelot, is it for my dear lord?
Then will I bear it gladly;" she replied,
"For Lancelot and the Queen and all the world,
But I myself must bear it." Then he wrote
The letter she devised; which being writ
And folded, "O sweet father, tender and true,
Deny me not," she said—"ye never yet

Denied my fancies—this, however strange,
My latest. Lay the letter in my hand
A little ere I die, and close the hand
Upon it; I shall guard it even in death.
And when the heat has gone from out my heart,
Then take the little bed on which I died
For Lancelot's love, and deck it like the Queen's
For richness, and me also like the Queen
In all I have of rich, and lay me on it.
And let there be prepared a chariot-bier
To take me to the river, and a barge
Be ready on the river, clothed in black.
I go in state to court, to meet the Queen.
There surely I shall speak for mine own self,
And none of you can speak for me so well.
And therefore let our dumb old man alone
Go with me; he can steer and row, and he
Will guide me to that palace, to the doors."

She ceased. Her father promised; whereupon
She grew so cheerful that they deem'd her death
Was rather in the fantasy than the blood.
But ten slow mornings past, and on the eleventh
Her father laid the letter in her hand,
And closed the hand upon it, and she died.
So that day there was dole in Astolat.

But when the next sun brake from underground,
Then, those two brethren slowly with bent brows
Accompanying, the sad chariot-bier
Past like a shadow thro' the field, that shone
Full-summer, to that stream whereon the barge,
Pall'd all its length in blackest samite, lay.
There sat the lifelong creature of the house,
Loyal, the dumb old servitor, on deck,
Winking his eyes, and twisted all his face.
So those two brethren from the chariot took
And on the black decks laid her in her bed,
Set in her hand a lily, o'er her hung
The silken case with braided blazonings,
And kiss'd her quiet brows, and saying to her,
"Sister, farewell forever," and again,
"Farewell, sweet sister," parted all in tears.
Then rose the dumb old servitor, and the dead,
Oar'd by the dumb, went upward with the flood—
In her right hand the lily, in her left
The letter—all her bright hair streaming down—

And all the coverlid was cloth of gold
Drawn to her waist, and she herself in white
All but her face, and that clear-featured face
Was lovely, for she did not seem as dead,
But fast asleep, and lay as tho' she smiled.

That day Sir Lancelot at the palace craved
Audience of Guinevere, to give at last
The price of half a realm, his costly gift,
Hard-won and hardly won with bruise and blow,
With deaths of others, and almost his own,
The nine-years-fought-for diamonds; for he saw
One of her house, and sent him to the Queen
Bearing his wish, whereto the Queen agreed
With such and so unmoved a majesty
She might have seem'd her statue, but that he,
Low-drooping till he wellnigh kiss'd her feet
For loyal awe, saw with a sidelong eye
The shadow of some piece of pointed lace,
In the Queen's shadow, vibrate on the walls,
And parted, laughing in his courtly heart.

All in an oriel on the summer side,
Vine-clad, of Arthur's palace toward the stream,
They met, and Lancelot kneeling utter'd: "Queen,
Lady, my liege, in whom I have my joy,
Take, what I had not won except for you,
These jewels, and make me happy, making them
An armlet for the roundest arm on earth,
Or necklace for a neck to which the swan's
Is tawnier than her cygnet's. These are words;
Your beauty is your beauty, and I sin
In speaking, yet O, grant my worship of it
Words, as we grant grief tears. Such sin in words
Perchance, we both can pardon; but, my Queen,
I hear of rumors flying thro' your court.
Our bond, as not the bond of man and wife,
Should have in it an absoluter trust
To make up that defect: let rumors be.
When did not rumors fly? these, as I trust
That you trust me in your own nobleness,
I may not well believe that you believe."

While thus he spoke, half turn'd away, the Queen
Brake from the vast oriel-embowering vine
Leaf after leaf, and tore, and cast them off,
Till all the place whereon she stood was green;

Then, when he ceased, in one cold passive hand
Received at once and laid aside the gems
There on a table near her, and replied:

"It may be I am quicker of belief
Than you believe me, Lancelot of the Lake.
Our bond is not the bond of man and wife.
This good is in it, whatsoe'er of ill,
It can be broken easier. I for you
This many a year have done despite and wrong
To one whom ever in my heart of hearts
I did acknowledge nobler. What are these?
Diamonds for me! they had been thrice their worth
Being your gift, had you not lost your own.
To loyal hearts the value of all gifts
Must vary as the giver's. Not for me!
For her! for your new fancy. Only this
Grant me, I pray you; have your joys apart.
I doubt not that, however changed, you keep
So much of what is graceful; and myself
Would shun to break those bounds of courtesy
In which as Arthur's Queen I move and rule,
So cannot speak my mind. An end to this!
A strange one! yet I take it with Amen.
So pray you, add my diamonds to her pearls;
Deck her with these; tell her, she shines me down:
An armlet for an arm to which the Queen's
Is haggard, or a necklace for a neck
O, as much fairer—as a faith once fair
Was richer than these diamonds—hers not mine—
Nay, by the mother of our Lord himself,
Or hers or mine, mine now to work my will—
She shall not have them."

                Saying which she seized,
And, thro' the casement standing wide for heat,
Flung them, and down they flash'd, and smote the stream.
Then from the smitten surface flash'd, as it were,
Diamonds to meet them, and they past away.
Then while Sir Lancelot leant, in half disdain
At love, life, all things, on the window ledge,
Close underneath his eyes, and right across
Where these had fallen, slowly past the barge
Whereon the lily maid of Astolat
Lay smiling, like a star in blackest night.

    But the wild Queen, who saw not, burst away
To weep and wail in secret; and the barge,

On to the palace-doorway sliding, paused.
There two stood arm'd, and kept the door; to whom,
All up the marble stair, tier over tier,
Were added mouths that gaped, and eyes that ask'd,
"What is it?" but that oarsman's haggard face,
As hard and still as is the face that men
Shape to their fancy's eye from broken rocks
On some cliff-side, appall'd them, and they said:
"He is enchanted, cannot speak—and she,
Look how she sleeps—the Fairy Queen, so fair!
Yea, but how pale! what are they? flesh and blood?
Or come to take the King to Fairyland?
For some do hold our Arthur cannot die,
But that he passes into Fairyland."

While thus they babbled of the King, the King
Came girt with knights. Then turn'd the tongueless man
From the half-face to the full eye, and rose
And pointed to the damsel and the doors.
So Arthur bade the meek Sir Percivale
And pure Sir Galahad to uplift the maid;
And reverently they bore her into hall.
Then came the fine Gawain and wonder'd at her.
And Lancelot later came and mused at her,
And last the Queen herself, and pitied her;
But Arthur spied the letter in her hand,
Stoopt, took, brake seal, and read it; this was all:

"Most noble lord, Sir Lancelot of the Lake,
I, sometimes call'd the maid of Astolat,
Come, for you left me taking no farewell,
Hither, to take my last farewell of you.
I loved you, and my love had no return,
And therefore my true love has been my death.
And therefore to our Lady Guinevere,
And to all other ladies, I make moan:
Pray for my soul, and yield me burial.
Pray for my soul thou too, Sir Lancelot,
As thou art a knight peerless."

Thus he read;
And ever in the reading lords and dames
Wept, looking often from his face who read
To hers which lay so silent, and at times,
So touch'd were they, half-thinking that her lips
Who had devised the letter moved again.

Then freely spoke Sir Lancelot to them all:
"My lord liege Arthur, and all ye that hear,
Know that for this most gentle maiden's death
Right heavy am I; for good she was and true,
But loved me with a love beyond all love
In women, whomsoever I have known.
Yet to be loved makes not to love again;
Not at my years, however it hold in youth.
I swear by truth and knighthood that I gave
No cause, not willingly, for such a love.
To this I call my friends in testimony,
Her brethren, and her father, who himself
Besought me to be plain and blunt, and use,
To break her passion, some discourtesy
Against my nature; what I could, I did.
I left her and I bade her no farewell;
Tho', had I dreamt the damsel would have died,
I might have put my wits to some rough use,
And help'd her from herself."

                 Then said the Queen—
Sea was her wrath, yet working after storm:
"Ye might at least have done her so much grace,
Fair lord, as would have help'd her from her death."
He raised his head, their eyes met and hers fell,
He adding: "Queen, she would not be content
Save that I wedded her, which could not be.
Then might she follow me thro' the world, she ask'd;
It could not be. I told her that her love
Was but the flash of youth, would darken down,
To rise hereafter in a stiller flame
Toward one more worthy of her—then would I,
More specially were he she wedded poor,
Estate them with large land and territory
In mine own realm beyond the narrow seas,
To keep them in all joyance. More than this
I could not; this she would not, and she died."

He pausing, Arthur answer'd: "O my knight,
It will be to thy worship, as my knight,
And mine, as head of all our Table Round,
To see that she be buried worshipfully."

So toward that shrine which then in all the realm
Was richest, Arthur leading, slowly went
The marshall'd Order of their Table Round,
And Lancelot sad beyond his wont, to see

The maiden buried, not as one unknown,
Nor meanly, but with gorgeous obsequies,
And mass, and rolling music, like a queen.
And when the knights had laid her comely head
Low in the dust of half-forgotten kings,
Then Arthur spake among them: "Let her tomb
Be costly, and her image thereupon,
And let the shield of Lancelot at her feet
Be carven, and her lily in her hand.
And let the story of her dolorous voyage
For all true hearts be blazon'd on her tomb
In letters gold and azure!" which was wrought
Thereafter; but when now the lords and dames
And people, from the high door streaming, brake
Disorderly, as homeward each, the Queen,
Who mark'd Sir Lancelot where he moved apart,
Drew near, and sigh'd in passing, "Lancelot,
Forgive me; mine was jealousy in love."
He answer'd with his eyes upon the ground,
"That is love's curse; pass on, my Queen, forgiven."
But Arthur, who beheld his cloudy brows,
Approach'd him, and with full affection said:

"Lancelot, my Lancelot, thou in whom I have
Most joy and most affiance, for I know
What thou hast been in battle by my side,
And many a time have watch'd thee at the tilt
Strike down the lusty and long practised knight
And let the younger and unskill'd go by
To win his honor and to make his name,
And loved thy courtesies and thee, a man
Made to be loved; but now I would to God,
Seeing the homeless trouble in thine eyes,
Thou couldst have loved this maiden, shaped, it seems,
By God for thee alone, and from her face,
If one may judge the living by the dead,
Delicately pure and marvellously fair,
Who might have brought thee, now a lonely man
Wifeless and heirless, noble issue, sons
Born to the glory of thy name and fame,
My knight, the great Sir Lancelot of the Lake."

Then answer'd Lancelot: "Fair she was, my King,
Pure, as you ever wish your knights to be.
To doubt her fairness were to want an eye,
To doubt her pureness were to want a heart—

Yea, to be loved, if what is worthy love
Could bind him, but free love will not be bound."

"Free love, so bound, were freest," said the King.
"Let love be free; free love is for the best.
And, after heaven, on our dull side of death,
What should be best, if not so pure a love
Clothed in so pure a loveliness? yet thee
She fail'd to bind, tho' being, as I think,
Unbound as yet, and gentle, as I know."

And Lancelot answer'd nothing, but he went,
And at the inrunning of a little brook
Sat by the river in a cove, and watch'd
The high reed wave, and lifted up his eyes
And saw the barge that brought her moving down,
Far-off, a blot upon the stream, and said
Low in himself: "Ah, simple heart and sweet,
Ye loved me, damsel, surely with a love
Far tenderer than my Queen's. Pray for thy soul?
Ay, that will I. Farewell too—now at last—
Farewell, fair lily. 'Jealousy in love'?
Not rather dead love's harsh heir, jealous pride?
Queen, if I grant the jealousy as of love,
May not your crescent fear for name and fame
Speak, as it waxes, of a love that wanes?
Why did the King dwell on my name to me?
Mine own name shames me, seeming a reproach,
Lancelot, whom the Lady of the Lake
Caught from his mother's arms—the wondrous one
Who passes thro' the vision of the night—
She chanted snatches of mysterious hymns
Heard on the winding waters, eve and morn
She kiss'd me, saying, 'Thou art fair, my child,
As a king's son,' and often in her arms
She bare me, pacing on the dusky mere.
Would she had drown'd me in it, where'er it be!
For what am I? what profits me my name
Of greatest knight? I fought for it, and have it.
Pleasure to have it, none; to lose it, pain;
Now grown a part of me; but what use in it?
To make men worse by making my sin known?
Or sin seem less, the sinner seeming great?
Alas for Arthur's greatest knight, a man
Not after Arthur's heart! I needs must break
These bonds that so defame me. Not without

She wills it—would I, if she will'd it? nay,
Who knows? but if I would not, then may God,
I pray him, send a sudden angel down
To seize me by the hair and bear me far,
And fling me deep in that forgotten mere,
Among the tumbled fragments of the hills."

So groan'd Sir Lancelot in remorseful pain,
Not knowing he should die a holy man.

✠✠✠✠✠ THE HOLY GRAIL ✠✠✠✠✠

FROM noiseful arms, and acts of prowess done
In tournament or tilt, Sir Percivale
Whom Arthur and his knighthood call'd the Pure,
Had past into the silent life of prayer,
Praise, fast, and alms; and leaving for the cowl
The helmet in an abbey far away
From Camelot, there, and not long after, died.

And one, a fellow-monk among the rest,
Ambrosius, loved him much beyond the rest,
And honor'd him, and wrought into his heart
A way by love that waken'd love within,
To answer that which came; and as they sat
Beneath a world-old yew-tree, darkening half
The cloisters, on a gustful April morn
That puff'd the swaying branches into smoke
Above them, ere the summer when he died,
The monk Ambrosius question'd Percivale:

"O brother, I have seen this yew-tree smoke,
Spring after spring, for half a hundred years;
For never have I known the world without,
Nor ever stray'd beyond the pale. But thee,
When first thou camest—such a courtesy
Spake thro' the limbs and in the voice—I knew
For one of those who eat in Arthur's hall;
For good ye are and bad, and like to coins,
Some true, some light, but every one of you
Stamp'd with the image of the King; and now
Tell me, what drove thee from the Table Round,
My brother? was it earthly passion crost?"

"Nay," said the knight; "for no such passion mine.
But the sweet vision of the Holy Grail
Drove me from all vainglories, rivalries,
And earthly heats that spring and sparkle out
Among us in the jousts, while women watch
Who wins, who falls, and waste the spiritual strength
Within us, better offer'd up to heaven."

To whom the monk: "The Holy Grail!—I trust
We are green in Heaven's eyes; but here too much
We moulder—as to things without I mean—
Yet one of your own knights, a guest of ours,
Told us of this in our refectory,
But spake with such a sadness and so low
We heard not half of what he said. What is it?
The phantom of a cup that comes and goes?"

"Nay, monk! what phantom?" answer'd Percivale.
"The cup, the cup itself, from which our Lord
Drank at the last sad supper with his own.
This, from the blessed land of Aromat—
After the day of darkness, when the dead
Went wandering o'er Moriah—the good saint
Arimathæan Joseph, journeying brought
To Glastonbury, where the winter thorn
Blossoms at Christmas, mindful of our Lord.
And there a while it bode; and if a man
Could touch or see it, he was heal'd at once,
By faith, of all his ills. But then the times
Grew to such evil that the holy cup
Was caught away to heaven, and disappear'd."

To whom the monk: "From our old books I know
That Joseph came of old to Glastonbury,
And there the heathen Prince, Arviragus,
Gave him an isle of marsh whereon to build;
And there he built with wattles from the marsh
A little lonely church in days of yore,
For so they say, these books of ours, but seem
Mute of this miracle, far as I have read.
But who first saw the holy thing to-day?"

"A woman," answer'd Percivale, "a nun,
And one no further off in blood from me
Than sister; and if ever holy maid
With knees of adoration wore the stone,
A holy maid; tho' never maiden glow'd,

But that was in her earlier maidenhood,
With such a fervent flame of human love,
Which, being rudely blunted, glanced and shot
Only to holy things; to prayer and praise
She gave herself, to fast and alms. And yet,
Nun as she was, the scandal of the Court,
Sin against Arthur and the Table Round.
And the strange sound of an adulterous race,
Across the iron grating of her cell
Beat, and she pray'd and fasted all the more.

"And he to whom she told her sins, or what
Her all but utter whiteness held for sin,
A man wellnigh a hundred winters old,
Spake often with her of the Holy Grail,
A legend handed down thro' five or six,
And each of these a hundred winters old,
From our Lord's time. And when King Arthur made
His Table Round, and all men's hearts became
Clean for a season, surely he had thought
That now the Holy Grail would come again;
But sin broke out. Ah, Christ, that it would come,
And heal the world of all their wickedness!
'O Father!' ask'd the maiden, 'might it come
To me by prayer and fasting?' 'Nay,' said he,
'I know not, for thy heart is pure as snow.'
And so she pray'd and fasted, till the sun
Shone, and the wind blew, thro' her, and I thought
She might have risen and floated when I saw her.

"For on a day she sent to speak with me.
And when she came to speak, behold her eyes
Beyond my knowing of them, beautiful.
Beyond all knowing of them, wonderful,
Beautiful in the light of holiness!
And 'O my brother Percivale,' she said,
'Sweet brother, I have seen the Holy Grail;
For, waked at dead of night, I heard a sound
As of a silver horn from o'er the hills
Blown, and I thought, "It is not Arthur's use
To hunt by moonlight." And the slender sound
As from a distance beyond distance grew
Coming upon me—O never harp nor horn,
Nor aught we blow with breath, or touch with hand,
Was like that music as it came; and then
Stream'd thro' my cell a cold and silver beam,

And down the long beam stole the Holy Grail,
Rose-red with beatings in it, as if alive,
Till all the white walls of my cell were dyed
With rosy colors leaping on the wall;
And then the music faded, and the Grail
Past, and the beam decay'd, and from the walls
The rosy quiverings died into the night.
So now the Holy Thing is here again
Among us, brother, fast thou too and pray,
And tell thy brother knights to fast and pray,
That so perchance the vision may be seen
By thee and those, and all the world be heal'd.'

"Then leaving the pale nun, I spake of this
To all men; and myself fasted and pray'd
Always, and many among us many a week
Fasted and pray'd even to the uttermost,
Expectant of the wonder that would be.

"And one there was among us, ever moved
Among us in white armor, Galahad.
'God make thee good as thou art beautiful!'
Said Arthur, when he dubb'd him knight, and none
In so young youth was ever made a knight
Till Galahad; and this Galahad, when he heard
My sister's vision, fill'd me with amaze;
His eyes became so like her own, they seem'd
Hers, and himself her brother more than I.

"Sister or brother none had he; but some
Call'd him a son of Lancelot, and some said
Begotten by enchantment—chatterers they,
Like birds of passage piping up and down,
That gape for flies—we know not whence they come;
For when was Lancelot wanderingly lewd?

"But she, the wan sweet maiden, shore away
Clean from her forehead all that wealth of hair
Which made a silken mat-work for her feet;
And out of this she plaited broad and long
A strong sword-belt, and wove with silver thread
And crimson in the belt a strange device,
A crimson grail within a silver beam;
And saw the bright boy-knight, and bound it on him,
Saying: 'My knight, my love, my knight of heaven,
O thou, my love, whose love is one with mine,
I, maiden, round thee, maiden, bind my belt.

Go forth, for thou shalt see what I have seen,
And break thro' all, till one will crown thee king
Far in the spiritual city;' and as she spake
She sent the deathless passion in her eyes
Thro' him, and made him hers, and laid her mind
On him, and he believed in her belief.

"Then came a year of miracle. O brother,
In our great hall there stood a vacant chair,
Fashion'd by Merlin ere he past away,
And carven with strange figures; and in and out
The figures, like a serpent, ran a scroll
Of letters in a tongue no man could read.
And Merlin call'd it 'the Siege Perilous,'
Perilous for good and ill; 'for there,' he said,
'No man could sit but he should lose himself.'
And once by misadvertence Merlin sat
In his own chair, and so was lost; but he,
Galahad, when he heard of Merlin's doom,
Cried, 'If I lose myself, I save myself!'

"Then on a summer night it came to pass,
While the great banquet lay along the hall.
That Galahad would sit down in Merlin's chair.

"And all at once, as there we sat, we heard
A cracking and a riving of the roofs,
And rending, and a blast, and overhead
Thunder, and in the thunder was a cry;
And in the blast there smote along the hall
A beam of light seven times more clear than day;
And down the long beam stole the Holy Grail
All over cover'd with a luminous cloud,
And none might see who bare it, and it past.
But every knight beheld his fellow's face
As in a glory, and all the knights arose,
And staring each at other like dumb men
Stood, till I found a voice and sware a vow.

"I sware a vow before them all, that I,
Because I had not seen the Grail, would ride
A twelvemonth and a day in quest of it,
Until I found and saw it, as the nun
My sister saw it; and Galahad sware the vow,
And good Sir Bors, our Lancelot's cousin, sware,
And Lancelot sware, and many among the knights,
And Gawain sware, and louder than the rest."

Then spake the monk Ambrosius, asking him,
"What said the King? Did Arthur take the vow?"

"Nay, for my lord," said Percivale, "the King,
Was not in hall; for early that same day,
Scaped thro' a cavern from a bandit bold,
An outraged maiden sprang into the hall
Crying on help; for all her shining hair
Was smear'd with earth, and either milky arm
Red-rent with hooks of bramble, and all she wore
Torn as a sail that leaves the rope is torn
In tempest. So the King arose and went
To smoke the scandalous hive of those wild bees
That made such honey in his realm. Howbeit
Some little of this marvel he too saw,
Returning o'er the plain that then began
To darken under Camelot; whence the King
Look'd up, calling aloud, 'Lo, there! the roofs
Of our great hall are roll'd in thunder-smoke!
Pray heaven, they be not smitten by the bolt!'
For dear to Arthur was that hall of ours,
As having there so oft with all his knights
Feasted, and as the stateliest under heaven.

"O brother, had you known our mighty hall,
Which Merlin built for Arthur long ago!
For all the sacred mount of Camelot,
And all the dim rich city, roof by roof,
Tower after tower, spire beyond spire,
By grove, and garden-lawn, and rushing brook,
Climbs to the mighty hall that Merlin built.
And four great zones of sculpture, set betwixt
With many a mystic symbol, gird the hall;
And in the lowest beasts are slaying men,
And in the second men are slaying beasts,
And on the third are warriors, perfect men,
And on the fourth are men with growing wings,
And over all one statue in the mould
Of Arthur, made by Merlin, with a crown,
And peak'd wings pointed to the Northern Star.
And eastward fronts the statue, and the crown
And both the wings are made of gold, and flame
At sunrise till the people in far fields,
Wasted so often by the heathen hordes,
Behold it, crying, 'We have still a king.'

"And, brother, had you known our hall within,
Broader and higher than any in all the lands!
Where twelve great windows blazon Arthur's wars,
And all the light that falls upon the board
Streams thro' the twelve great battles of our King.
Nay, one there is, and at the eastern end,
Wealthy with wandering lines of mount and mere,
Where Arthur finds the brand Excalibur.
And also one to the west, and counter to it,
And blank; and who shall blazon it? when and how?—
O, there, perchance, when all our wars are done,
The brand Excalibur will be cast away!

"So to this hall full quickly rode the King,
In horror lest the work by Merlin wrought,
Dreamlike, should on the sudden vanish, wrapt
In unremorseful folds of rolling fire.
And in he rode, and up I glanced, and saw
The golden dragon sparkling over all;
And many of those who burnt the hold, their arms
Hack'd, and their foreheads grimed with smoke and sear'd,
Follow'd, and in among bright faces, ours,
Full of the vision, prest; and then the King
Spake to me, being nearest, 'Percivale,'—
Because the hall was all in tumult—some
Vowing, and some protesting,—'What is this?'

"O brother, when I told him what had chanced,
My sister's vision and the rest, his face
Darken'd, as I have seen it more than once,
When some brave deed seem'd to be done in vain,
Darken; and 'Woe is me, my knights,' he cried,
'Had I been here, ye had not sworn the vow.'
Bold was mine answer, 'Had thyself been here,
My King, thou wouldst have sworn.' 'Yea, yea,' said he,
'Art thou so bold and hast not seen the Grail?'

" 'Nay, lord, I heard the sound, I saw the light,
But since I did not see the holy thing,
I sware a vow to follow it till I saw.'

"Then when he ask'd us, knight by knight, if any
Had seen it, all their answers were as one:
'Nay, lord, and therefore have we sworn our vows.'

" 'Lo, now,' said Arthur, 'have ye seen a cloud?
What go ye into the wilderness to see?'

"Then Galahad on the sudden, and in a voice
Shrilling along the hall to Arthur, call'd,
'But I, Sir Arthur, saw the Holy Grail,
I saw the Holy Grail and heard a cry—
"O Galahad, and O Galahad, follow me!"'

" 'Ah, Galahad, Galahad,' said the King, 'for such
As thou art is the vision, not for these.
Thy holy nun and thou have seen a sign—
Holier is none, my Percivale, than she—
A sign to maim this Order which I made.
But ye that follow but the leader's bell,'—
Brother, the King was hard upon his knights,—
'Taliessin is our fullest throat of song,
And one hath sung and all the dumb will sing.
Lancelot is Lancelot, and hath overborne
Five knights at once, and every younger knight,
Unproven, holds himself as Lancelot,
Till overborne by one, he learns—and ye,
What are ye? Galahads?—no, nor Percivales'—
For thus it pleased the King to range me close
After Sir Galahad;—'nay,' said he, 'but men
With strength and will to right the wrong'd, of power
To lay the sudden heads of violence flat,
Knights that in twelve great battles splash'd and dyed
The strong White Horse in his own heathen blood—
But one hath seen, and all the blind will see.
Go, since your vows are sacred, being made.
Yet—for ye know the cries of all my realm
Pass thro' this hall—how often, O my knights,
Your places being vacant at my side,
This chance of noble deeds will come and go
Unchallenged, while ye follow wandering fires
Lost in the quagmire! Many of you, yea most,
Return no more. Ye think I show myself
Too dark a prophet. Come now, let us meet
The morrow morn once more in one full field
Of gracious pastime, that once more the King,
Before ye leave him for this quest, may count
The yet-unbroken strength of all his knights,
Rejoicing in that Order which he made.'

"So when the sun broke next from underground,
All the great Table of our Arthur closed
And clash'd in such a tourney and so full,
So many lances broken—never yet

Had Camelot seen the like since Arthur came;
And I myself and Galahad, for a strength
Was in us from the vision, overthrew
So many knights that all the people cried,
And almost burst the barriers in their heat,
Shouting, 'Sir Galahad and Sir Percivale!'

"But when the next day brake from underground—
O brother, had you known our Camelot,
Built by old kings, age after age, so old
The King himself had fears that it would fall,
So strange, and rich, and dim; for where the roofs
Totter'd toward each other in the sky,
Met foreheads all along the street of those
Who watch'd us pass; and lower, and where the long
Rich galleries, lady-laden, weigh'd the necks
Of dragons clinging to the crazy walls,
Thicker than drops from thunder, showers of flowers
Fell as we past; and men and boys astride
On wyvern, lion, dragon, griffin, swan,
At all the corners, named us each by name,
Calling 'God speed!' but in the ways below
The knights and ladies wept, and rich and poor
Wept, and the King himself could hardly speak
For grief, and all in middle street the Queen,
Who rode by Lancelot, wail'd and shriek'd aloud,
'This madness has come on us for our sins.'
So to the Gate of the Three Queens we came,
Where Arthur's wars are render'd mystically,
And thence departed every one his way.

"And I was lifted up in heart, and thought
Of all my late-shown prowess in the lists,
How my strong lance had beaten down the knights,
So many and famous names; and never yet
Had heaven appear'd so blue, nor earth so green,
For all my blood danced in me, and I knew
That I should light upon the Holy Grail.

"Thereafter, the dark warning of our King,
That most of us would follow wandering fires,
Came like a driving gloom across my mind.
Then every evil word I had spoken once,
And every evil thought I had thought of old,
And every evil deed I ever did,
Awoke and cried, 'This quest is not for thee.

And lifting up mine eyes, I found myself
Alone, and in a land of sand and thorns,
And I was thirsty even unto death;
And I, too, cried, 'This quest is not for thee.'

   "And on I rode, and when I thought my thirst
Would slay me, saw deep lawns, and then a brook,
With one sharp rapid, where the crisping white
Play'd ever back upon the sloping wave
And took both ear and eye; and o'er the brook
Were apple-trees, and apples by the brook
Fallen, and on the lawns. 'I will rest here,'
I said, 'I am not worthy of the quest;'
But even while I drank the brook, and ate,
The goodly apples, all these things at once
Fell into dust, and I was left alone
And thirsting in a land of sand and thorns.

   "And then behold a woman at a door
Spinning; and fair the house whereby she sat,
And kind the woman's eyes and innocent,
And all her bearing gracious; and she rose
Opening her arms to meet me, as who should say,
'Rest here;' but when I touch'd her, lo! she, too,
Fell into dust and nothing, and the house
Became no better than a broken shed,
And in it a dead babe; and also this
Fell into dust, and I was left alone.

   "And on I rode, and greater was my thirst.
Then flash'd a yellow gleam across the world,
And where it smote the plowshare in the field
The plowman left his plowing and fell down
Before it; where it glitter'd on her pail
The milkmaid left her milking and fell down
Before it, and I knew not why, but thought
'The sun is rising,' tho' the sun had risen.
Then was I ware of one that on me moved
In golden armor with a crown of gold
About a casque all jewels, and his horse
In golden armor jewelled everywhere;
And on the splendor came, flashing me blind.
And seem'd to me the lord of all the world,
Being so huge. But when I thought he meant
To crush me, moving on me, lo! he, too,
Open'd his arms to embrace me as he came,

And up I went and touch'd him, and he, too,
Fell into dust, and I was left alone
And wearying in a land of sand and thorns.

"And I rode on and found a mighty hill,
And on the top a city wall'd; the spires
Prick'd with incredible pinnacles into heaven.
And by the gateway stirr'd a crowd; and these
Cried to me climbing, 'Welcome, Percivale!
Thou mightiest and thou purest among men!'
And glad was I and clomb, but found at top
No man, nor any voice. And thence I past
Far thro' a ruinous city, and I saw
That man had once dwelt there; but there I found
Only one man of an exceeding age.
'Where is that goodly company,' said I,
'That so cried out upon me?' and he had
Scarce any voice to answer, and yet gasp'd,
'Whence and what art thou?' and even as he spoke
Fell into dust and disappear'd, and I
Was left alone once more and cried in grief,
'Lo, if I find the Holy Grail itself
And touch it, it will crumble into dust!'

"And thence I dropt into a lowly vale,
Low as the hill was high, and where the vale
Was lowest found a chapel, and thereby
A holy hermit in a hermitage,
To whom I told my phantoms, and he said:

" 'O son, thou hast not true humility,
The highest virtue, mother of them all;
For when the Lord of all things made Himself
Naked of glory for His mortal change,
"Take thou my robe," she said, "for all is thine,"
And all her form shone forth with sudden light
So that the angels were amazed, and she
Follow'd Him down, and like a flying star
Led on the gray-hair'd wisdom of the east.
But her thou hast not known; for what is this
Thou thoughtest of thy prowess and thy sins?
Thou hast not lost thyself to save thyself
As Galahad.' When the hermit made an end,
In silver armor suddenly Galahad shone
Before us, and against the chapel door
Laid lance and enter'd, and we knelt in prayer.
And there the hermit slaked my burning thirst,

And at the sacring of the mass I saw
The holy elements alone: but he,
'Saw ye no more? I, Galahad, saw the Grail,
The Holy Grail, descend upon the shrine.
I saw the fiery face as of a child
That smote itself into the bread and went ;
And hither am I come; and never yet
Hath what thy sister taught me first to see.
This holy thing, fail'd from my side, nor come
Cover'd, but moving with me night and day,
Fainter by day, but always in the night
Blood-red, and sliding down the blacken'd marsh
Blood-red, and on the naked mountain top
Blood-red, and in the sleeping mere below
Blood-red. And in the strength of this I rode,
Shattering all evil customs everywhere,
And past thro' Pagan realms, and made them mine,
And clash'd with Pagan hordes, and bore them down,
And broke thro' all, and in the strength of this
Come victor. But my time is hard at hand,
And hence I go, and one will crown me king
Far in the spiritual city; and come thou, too,
For thou shalt see the vision when I go.'

  "While thus he spake, his eye, dwelling on mine,
Drew me, with power upon me, till I grew
One with him, to believe as he believed.
Then, when the day began to wane, we went.

  "There rose a hill that none but man could climb,
Scarr'd with a hundred wintry watercourses—
Storm at the top, and when we gain'd it, storm
Round us and death; for every moment glanced
His silver arms and gloom'd, so quick and thick
The lightnings here and there to left and right
Struck, till the dry old trunks about us, dead,
Yea, rotten with a hundred years of death,
Sprang into fire. And at the base we found
On either hand, as far as eye could see,
A great black swamp and of an evil smell,
Part black, part whiten'd with the bones of men,
Not to be crost, save that some ancient king
Had built a way, where, link'd with many a bridge,
A thousand piers ran into the great Sea.
And Galahad fled along them bridge by bridge,
And every bridge as quickly as he crost
Sprang into fire and vanish'd, tho' I yearn'd

To follow; and thrice above him all the heavens
Open'd and blazed with thunder such as seem'd
Shoutings of all the sons of God. And first
At once I saw him far on the great Sea,
In silver-shining armor starry-clear;
And o'er his head the Holy Vessel hung
Clothed in white samite or a luminous cloud.
And with exceeding swiftness ran the boat,
If boat it were—I saw not whence it came.
And when the heavens open'd and blazed again
Roaring, I saw him like a silver star—
And had he set the sail, or had the boat
Become a living creature clad with wings?
And o'er his head the Holy Vessel hung
Redder than any rose, a joy to me,
For now I knew the veil had been withdrawn.
Then in a moment when they blazed again
Opening, I saw the least of little stars
Down on the waste, and straight beyond the star
I saw the spiritual city and all her spires
And gateways in a glory like one pearl—
No larger, tho' the goal of all the saints—
Strike from the sea; and from the star there shot
A rose-red sparkle to the city, and there
Dwelt, and I knew it was the Holy Grail,
Which never eyes on earth again shall see.
Then fell the floods of heaven drowning the deep,
And how my feet recrost the deathful ridge
No memory in me lives; but that I touch'd
The chapel-doors at dawn I know, and thence
Taking my war-horse from the holy man,
Glad that no phantom vext me more, return'd
To whence I came, the gate of Arthur's wars."

"O brother," ask'd Ambrosius,—"for in sooth
These ancient books—and they would win thee—teem,
Only I find not there this Holy Grail,
With miracles and marvels like to these,
Not all unlike; which oftentime I read,
Who read but on my breviary with ease,
Till my head swims, and then go forth and pass
Down to the little thorpe that lies so close,
And almost plaster'd like a martin's nest
To these old walls—and mingle with our folk;
And knowing every honest face of theirs
As well as ever shepherd knew his sheep,

And every homely secret in their hearts,
Delight myself with gossip and old wives,
And ills and aches, and teethings, lyings-in,
And mirthful sayings, children of the place,
That have no meaning half a league away;
Or lulling random squabbles when they rise,
Chafferings and chatterings at the market-cross,
Rejoice, small man, in this small world of mine,
Yea, even in their hens and in their eggs—
O brother, saving this Sir Galahad,
Came ye on none but phantoms in your quest,
No man, no woman?"

Then Sir Percivale:
"All men, to one so bound by such a vow,
And women were as phantoms. O, my brother,
Why wilt thou shame me to confess to thee
How far I falter'd from my quest and vow?
For after I had lain so many nights,
A bed-mate of the snail and eft and snake,
In grass and burdock, I was changed to wan
And meagre, and the vision had not come;
And then I chanced upon a goodly town
With one great dwelling in the middle of it.
Thither I made, and there was I disarm'd
By maidens each as fair as any flower;
But when they led me into hall, behold,
The princess of that castle was the one,
Brother, and that one only, who had ever
Made my heart leap; for when I moved of old
A slender page about her father's hall,
And she a slender maiden, all my heart
Went after her with longing, yet we twain
Had never kiss'd a kiss or vow'd a vow.
And now I came upon her once again,
And one had wedded her, and he was dead,
And all his land and wealth and state were hers.
And while I tarried, every day she set
A banquet richer than the day before
By me, for all her longing and her will
Was toward me as of old; till one fair morn,
I walking to and fro beside a stream
That flash'd across her orchard underneath
Her castle-walls, she stole upon my walk,
And calling me the greatest of all knights,
Embraced me, and so kiss'd me the first time,

And gave herself and all her wealth to me.
Then I remember'd Arthur's warning word,
That most of us would follow wandering fires,
And the quest faded in my heart. Anon,
The heads of all her people drew to me,
With supplication both of knees and tongue:
'We have heard of thee; thou art our greatest knight,
Our Lady says it, and we well believe.
Wed thou our Lady, and rule over us,
And thou shalt be as Arthur in our land.'
O me, my brother! but one night my vow
Burnt me within, so that I rose and fled,
But wail'd and wept, and hated mine own self,
And even the holy quest, and all but her;
Then after I was join'd with Galahad
Cared not for her nor anything upon earth."

Then said the monk: "Poor men, when yule is cold,
Must be content to sit by little fires.
And this am I, so that ye care for me
Ever so little; yea, and blest be heaven
That brought thee here to this poor house of ours
Where all the brethren are so hard, to warm
My cold heart with a friend; but O the pity
To find thine own first love once more—to hold,
Hold her a wealthy bride within thine arms.
Or all but hold, and then—cast her aside,
Foregoing all her sweetness, like a weed!
For we that want the warmth of double life,
We that are plagued with dreams of something sweet
Beyond all sweetness in a life so rich,—
Ah, blessed Lord, I speak too earthly-wise,
Seeing I never stray'd beyond the cell,
But live like an old badger in his earth,
With earth about him everywhere, despite
All fast and penance. Saw ye none beside,
None of your knights?"

"Yea, so," said Percivale:
"One night my pathway swerving east, I saw
The pelican on the casque of our Sir Bors
All in the middle of the rising moon,
And toward him spurr'd, and hail'd him, and he me,
And each made joy of either. Then he ask'd:
'Where is he? hast thou seen him—Lancelot?—Once,'
Said good Sir Bors, 'he dash'd across me—mad,
And maddening what he rode; and when I cried,

"Ridest thou then so hotly on a quest
So holy?" Lancelot shouted, "Stay me not!
I have been the sluggard, and I ride apace,
For now there is a lion in the way!"
So vanish'd.'

    "Then Sir Bors had ridden on
Softly, and sorrowing for our Lancelot,
Because his former madness, once the talk
And scandal of our table, had return'd;
For Lancelot's kith and kin so worship him
That ill to him is ill to them, to Bors
Beyond the rest. He well had been content
Not to have seen, so Lancelot might have seen,
The Holy Cup of healing; and, indeed,
Being so clouded with his grief and love,
Small heart was his after the holy quest.
If God would send the vision, well; if not,
The quest and he were in the hands of Heaven.

    "And then, with small adventure met, Sir Bors
Rode to the lonest tract of all the realm,
And found a people there among their crags,
Our race and blood, a remnant that were left
Paynim amid their circles, and the stones
They pitch up straight to heaven; and their wise men
Were strong in that old magic which can trace
The wandering of the stars, and scoff'd at him
And this high quest as at a simple thing,
Told him he follow'd—almost Arthur's words—
A mocking fire: 'what other fire than he
Whereby the blood beats, and the blossom blows,
And the sea rolls, and all the world is warm'd?'
And when his answer chafed them, the rough crowd,
Hearing he had a difference with their priests,
Seized him, and bound and plunged him into a cell
Of great piled stones; and lying bounden there
In darkness thro' innumerable hours
He heard the hollow-ringing heavens sweep
Over him till by miracle—what else?—
Heavy as it was, a great stone slipt and fell,
Such as no wind could move; and thro' the gap
Glimmer'd the streaming scud. Then came a night
Still as the day was loud, and thro' the gap
The seven clear stars of Arthur's Table Round—
For, brother, so one night, because they roll

Thro' such a round in heaven, we named the stars,
Rejoicing in ourselves and in our King—
And these, like bright eyes of familiar friends,
In on him shone: 'And then to me, to me,'
Said good Sir Bors, 'beyond all hopes of mine,
Who scarce had pray'd or ask'd it for myself—
Across the seven clear stars—O grace to me!—
In color like the fingers of a hand
Before a burning taper, the sweet Grail
Glided and past, and close upon it peal'd
A sharp quick thunder.' Afterwards, a maid,
Who kept our holy faith among her kin
In secret, entering, loosed and let him go."

To whom the monk: "And I remember now
That pelican on the casque. Sir Bors it was
Who spake so low and sadly at our board,
And mighty reverent at our grace was he;
A square-set man and honest, and his eyes,
An outdoor sign of all the warmth within,
Smiled with his lips—a smile beneath a cloud.
But heaven had meant it for a sunny one.
Ay, ay, Sir Bors, who else? But when ye reach'd
The city, found ye all your knights return'd,
Or was there sooth in Arthur's prophecy,
Tell me, and what said each, and what the King?"

Then answer'd Percivale: "And that can I,
Brother, and truly; since the living words
Of so great men as Lancelot and our King
Pass not from door to door and out again,
But sit within the house. O, when we reach'd
The city, our horses stumbling as they trode
On heaps of ruin, hornless unicorns.
Crack'd basilisks, and splinter'd cockatrices,
And shatter'd talbots, which had left the stones
Raw that they fell from, brought us to the hall.

"And there sat Arthur on the dais-throne,
And those that had gone out upon the quest,
Wasted and worn, and but a tithe of them,
And those that had not, stood before the King,
Who, when he saw me, rose and bade me hail,
Saying: 'A welfare in thine eyes reproves
Our fear of some disastrous chance for thee
On hill or plain, at sea or flooding ford.
So fierce a gale made havoc here of late

Among the strange devices of our kings,
Yea, shook this newer, stronger hall of ours,
And from the statue Merlin moulded for us
Half-wrench'd a golden wing; but now—the quest,
This vision—hast thou seen the Holy Cup
That Joseph brought of old to Glastonbury?'

"So when I told him all thyself hast heard,
Ambrosius, and my fresh but fixt resolve
To pass away into the quiet life,
He answered not, but, sharply turning, ask'd
Of Gawain, 'Gawain, was this quest for thee?'

" 'Nay, lord,' said Gawain, 'not for such as I.
Therefore I communed with a saintly man,
Who made me sure the quest was not for me;
For I was much a-wearied of the quest,
But found a silk pavilion in a field,
And merry maidens in it; and then this gale
Tore my pavilion from the tenting-pin,
And blew my merry maidens all about
With all discomfort; yea, and but for this,
My twelvemonth and a day were pleasant to me.'

"He ceased; and Arthur turn'd to whom at first
He saw not, for Sir Bors, on entering, push'd
Athwart the throng to Lancelot, caught his hand,
Held it, and there, half-hidden by him, stood,
Until the King espied him, saying to him,
'Hail, Bors! if ever loyal man and true
Could see it, thou hast seen the Grail;' and Bors,
'Ask me not, for I may not speak of it;
I saw it;' and the tears were in his eyes.

"Then there remain'd but Lancelot, for the rest
Spake but of sundry perils in the storm.
Perhaps, like him of Cana in Holy Writ,
Our Arthur kept his best until the last;
'Thou, too, my Lancelot,' ask'd the King, 'my friend,
Our mightiest, hath this quest avail'd for thee?'

" 'Our mightiest!' answer'd Lancelot, with a groan;
'O King!'—and when he paused methought I spied
A dying fire of madness in his eyes—
'O King, my friend, if friend of thine I be,
Happier are those that welter in their sin,
Swine in the mud, that cannot see for slime,
Slime of the ditch; but in me lived a sin

So strange, of such a kind, that all of pure,
Noble, and knightly in me twined and clung
Round that one sin, until the wholesome flower
And poisonous grew together, each as each,
Not to be pluck'd asunder; and when thy knights
Sware, I sware with them only in the hope
That could I touch or see the Holy Grail
They might be pluck'd asunder. Then I spake
To one most holy saint, who wept and said
That, save they could be pluck'd asunder, all
My quest were but in vain; to whom I vow'd
That I would work according as he will'd.
And forth I went, and while I yearn'd and strove
To tear the twain asunder in my heart,
My madness came upon me as of old,
And whipt me into waste fields far away.
There was I beaten down by little men,
Mean knights, to whom the moving of my sword
And shadow of my spear had been enow
To scare them from me once; and then I came
All in my folly to the naked shore,
Wide flats, where nothing but coarse grasses grew;
But such a blast, my King, began to blow,
So loud a blast along the shore and sea,
Ye could not hear the waters for the blast,
Tho' heapt in mounds and ridges all the sea
Drove like a cataract, and all the sand
Swept like a river, and the clouded heavens
Were shaken with the motion and the sound.
And blackening in the sea-foam sway'd a boat,
Half-swallow'd in it, anchor'd with a chain;
And in my madness to myself I said,
"I will embark and I will lose myself,
And in the great sea wash away my sin."
I burst the chain, I sprang into the boat.
Seven days I drove along the dreary deep,
And with me drove the moon and all the stars;
And the wind fell, and on the seventh night
I heard the shingle grinding in the surge,
And felt the boat shock earth, and looking up,
Behold, the enchanted towers of Carbonek,
A castle like a rock upon a rock,
With chasm-like portals open to the sea,
And steps that met the breaker! There was none
Stood near it but a lion on each side
That kept the entry, and the moon was full.

Then from the boat I leapt, and up the stairs,
There drew my sword. With sudden-flaring manes
Those two great beasts rose upright like a man,
Each gript a shoulder, and I stood between,
And, when I would have smitten them, heard a voice,
"Doubt not, go forward; if thou doubt, the beasts
Will tear thee piecemeal." Then with violence
The sword was dash'd from out my hand, and fell.
And up into the sounding hall I past;
But nothing in the sounding hall I saw,
No bench nor table, painting on the wall
Or shield of knight, only the rounded moon
Thro' the tall oriel on the rolling sea.
But always in the quiet house I heard,
Clear as a lark, high o'er me as a lark,
A sweet voice singing in the topmost tower
To the eastward. Up I climb'd a thousand steps
With pain; as in a dream I seem'd to climb
For ever; at the last I reach'd a door,
A light was in the crannies, and I heard,
"Glory and joy and honor to our Lord
And to the Holy Vessel of the Grail!"
Then in my madness I essay'd the door;
It gave, and thro' a stormy glare, a heat
As from a seven-times-heated furnace, I,
Blasted and burnt, and blinded as I was,
With such a fierceness that I swoon'd away—
O, yet methought I saw the Holy Grail,
All pall'd in crimson samite, and around
Great angels, awful shapes, and wings and eyes!
And but for all my madness and my sin,
And then my swooning, I had sworn I saw
That which I saw; but what I saw was veil'd
And cover'd, and this quest was not for me.'

   "So speaking, and here ceasing, Lancelot left
The hall long silent, till Sir Gawain—nay,
Brother, I need not tell thee foolish words,—
A reckless and irreverent knight was he,
Now bolden'd by the silence of his King,—
Well, I will tell thee: 'O King, my liege,' he said,
'Hath Gawain fail'd in any quest of thine?
When have I stinted stroke in foughten field?
But as for thine, my good friend Percivale,
Thy holy nun and thou have driven men mad,
Yea, made our mightiest madder than our least.

But by mine eyes and by mine ears swear,
I will be deafer than the blue-eyed cat,
And thrice as blind as any noonday owl,
To holy virgins in their ecstasies,
Henceforward.'

    " 'Deafer,' said the blameless King,
'Gawain, and blinder unto holy things,
Hope not to make thyself by idle vows,
Being too blind to have desire to see.
But if indeed there came a sign from heaven,
Blessed are Bors, Lancelot, and Percivale,
For these have seen according to their sight.
For every fiery prophet in old times,
And all the sacred madness of the bard,
When God made music thro' them, could but speak
His music by the framework and the chord;
And as ye saw it ye have spoken truth.

    " 'Nay—but thou errest, Lancelot; never yet
Could all of true and noble in knight and man
Twine round one sin, whatever it might be,
With such a closeness but apart there grew,
Save that he were the swine thou spakest of,
Some root of knighthood and pure nobleness;
Whereto see thou, that it may bear its flower.

    " 'And spake I not too truly, O my knights?
Was I too dark a prophet when I said
To those who went upon the Holy Quest,
That most of them would follow wandering fires,
Lost in the quagmire?—lost to me and gone,
And left me gazing at a barren board,
And a lean Order—scarce return'd a tithe—
And out of those to whom the vision came
My greatest hardly will believe he saw.
Another hath beheld it afar off,
And, leaving human wrongs to right themselves,
Cares but to pass into the silent life.
And one hath had the vision face to face,
And now his chair desires him here in vain,
However they may crown him otherwhere.

    " 'And some among you held that if the King
Had seen the sight he would have sworn the vow.
Not easily, seeing that the King must guard
That which he rules, and is but as the hind

To whom a space of land is given to plow,
Who may not wander from the allotted field
Before his work be done, but, being done,
Let visions of the night or of the day
Come as they will; and many a time they come,
Until this earth he walks on seems not earth,
This light that strikes his eyeball is not light,
This air that smites his forehead is not air
But vision—yea, his very hand and foot—
In moments when he feels he cannot die,
And knows himself no vision to himself,
Nor the high God a vision, nor that One
Who rose again. Ye have seen what ye have seen.'

   "So spake the King; I knew not all he meant."

✠✠✠✠ PELLEAS AND ETTARRE ✠✠✠✠

KING ARTHUR made new knights to fill the gap
Left by the Holy Quest; and as he sat
In hall at old Caerleon, the high doors
Were softly sunder'd, and thro' these a youth,
Pelleas, and the sweet smell of the fields
Past, and the sunshine came along with him.

   "Make me thy knight, because I know, Sir King,
All that belongs to knighthood, and I love."
Such was his cry; for having heard the King
Had let proclaim a tournament—the prize
A golden circlet and a knightly sword,
Full fain had Pelleas for his lady won
The golden circlet, for himself the sword.
And there were those who knew him near the King,
And promised for him; and Arthur made him knight.

   And this new knight, Sir Pelleas of the Isles—
But lately come to his inheritance,
And lord of many a barren isle was he—
Riding at noon, a day or twain before,
Across the forest call'd of Dean, to find
Caerleon and the King, had felt the sun
Beat like a strong knight on his helm and reel'd

Almost to falling from his horse, but saw
Near him a mound of even-sloping side
Whereon a hundred stately beeches grew,
And here and there great hollies under them;
But for a mile all round was open space
And fern and heath. And slowly Pelleas drew
To that dim day, then, binding his good horse
To a tree, cast himself down; and as he lay
At random looking over the brown earth
Thro' that green-glooming twilight of the grove,
It seem'd to Pelleas that the fern without
Burnt as a living fire of emeralds,
So that his eyes were dazzled looking at it.
Then o'er it crost the dimness of a cloud
Floating, and once the shadow of a bird
Flying, and then a fawn; and his eyes closed.
And since he loved all maidens, but no maid
In-special, half-awake he whisper'd: "Where?
O, where? I love thee, tho' I know thee not.
For fair thou art and pure as Guinevere,
And I will make thee with my spear and sword
As famous—O my Queen, my Guinevere,
For I will be thine Arthur when we meet."

Suddenly waken'd with a sound of talk
And laughter at the limit of the wood,
And glancing thro' the hoary boles, he saw,
Strange as to some old prophet might have seem'd
A vision hovering on a sea of fire,
Damsels in divers colors like the cloud
Of sunset and sunrise, and all of them
On horses, and the horses richly trapt
Breast-high in that bright line of bracken stood;
And all the damsels talk'd confusedly,
And one was pointing this way and one that,
Because the way was lost.

                              And Pelleas rose,
And loosed his horse, and led him to the light.
There she that seem'd the chief among them said:
"In happy time behold our pilot-star!
Youth, we are damsels-errant, and we ride,
Arm'd as ye see, to tilt against the knights
There at Caerleon, but have lost our way.
To right? to left? straight forward? back again?
Which? tell us quickly."

Pelleas gazing thought,
"Is Guinevere herself so beautiful?"
For large her violet eyes look'd, and her bloom
A rosy dawn kindled in stainless heavens,
And round her limbs, mature in womanhood;
And slender was her hand and small her shape;
And but for those large eyes, the haunts of scorn,
She might have seem'd a toy to trifle with,
And pass and care no more. But while he gazed
The beauty of her flesh abash'd the boy,
As tho' it were the beauty of her soul;
For as the base man, judging of the good,
Puts his own baseness in him by default
Of will and nature, so did Pelleas lend
All the young beauty of his own soul to hers,
Believing her, and when she spake to him
Stammer'd, and could not make a reply.
For out of the waste islands had he come,
Where saving his own sisters he had known
Scarce any but the women of his isles,
Rough wives, that laugh'd and scream'd against the gulls,
Makers of nets, and living from the sea.

Then with a slow smile turn'd the lady round
And look'd upon her people; and, as when
A stone is flung into some sleeping tarn
The circle widens till it lip the marge,
Spread the slow smile thro' all her company.
Three knights were thereamong, and they too smiled,
Scorning him; for the lady was Ettarre,
And she was a great lady in her land.

Again she said: "O wild and of the woods,
Knowest thou not the fashion of our speech?
Or have the Heavens but given thee a fair face,
Lacking a tongue?"

"O damsel," answer'd he,
"I woke from dreams, and coming out of gloom
Was dazzled by the sudden light, and crave
Pardon; but will ye to Caerleon? I
Go likewise; shall I lead you to the King?"

"Lead then," she said; and thro' the woods they went.
And while they rode, the meaning in his eyes,
His tenderness of manner, and chaste awe,
His broken utterances and bashfulness,
Were all a burthen to her, and in her heart

She mutter'd, "I have lighted on a fool,
Raw, yet so stale!" But since her mind was bent
On hearing, after trumpet blown, her name
And title, "Queen of Beauty," in the lists
Cried—and beholding him so strong she thought
That peradventure he will fight for me,
And win the circlet—therefore flatter'd him,
Being so gracious that he wellnight deem'd
His wish by hers was echo'd; and her knights
And all her damsels too were gracious to him,
For she was a great lady.

          And when they reach'd
Caerleon, ere they past to lodging, she,
Taking his hand, "O the strong hand," she said,
"See! look at mine! but wilt thou fight for me,
And win me this fine circlet, Pelleas,
That I may love thee?"

          Then his helpless heart
Leapt, and he cried, "Ay! wilt thou if I win?"
"Ay, that will I," she answer'd, and she laugh'd,
And straitly nipt the hand, and flung it from her;
Then glanced askew at those three knights of hers,
Till all her ladies laugh'd along with her.

"O happy world," thought Pelleas, "all, meseems,
Are happy; I the happiest of them all!"
Nor slept that night for pleasure in his blood,
And green wood-ways, and eyes among the leaves;
Then being on the morrow knighted, sware
To love one only. And as he came away,
The men who met him rounded on their heels
And wonder'd after him, because his face
Shone like the countenance of a priest of old
Against the flame about a sacrifice
Kindled by fire from heaven; so glad was he.

Then Arthur made vast banquets, and strange knights
From the four winds came in; and each one sat,
Tho' served with choice from air, land, stream, and sea,
Oft in mid-banquet measuring with his eyes
His neighbor's make and might; and Pelleas look'd
Noble among the noble, for he dream'd
His lady loved him, and he knew himself
Loved of the King; and him his new-made knight

Worshipt, whose lightest whisper moved him more
Than all the ranged reasons of the world.

Then blush'd and brake the morning of the jousts,
And this was call'd "The Tournament of Youth;"
For Arthur, loving his young knight, withheld
His older and his mightier from the lists,
That Pelleas might obtain his lady's love,
According to her promise, and remain
Lord of the tourney. And Arthur had the jousts
Down in the flat field by the shore of Usk
Holden; the gilded parapets were crown'd
With faces, and the great tower fill'd with eyes
Up to the summit, and the trumpets blew.
There all day long Sir Pelleas kept the field
With honor; so by that strong hand of his
The sword and golden circlet were achieved.

Then rang the shout his lady loved; the heat
Of pride and glory fired her face, her eye
Sparkled; she caught the circlet from his lance,
And there before the people crown'd herself.
So for the last time she was gracious to him.

Then at Caerleon for a space—her look
Bright for all others, cloudier on her knight—
Linger'd Ettarre; and, seeing Pelleas droop
Said Guinevere, "We marvel at thee much,
O damsel, wearing this unsunny face
To him who won thee glory!" And she said,
"Had ye not held your Lancelot in your bower,
My Queen, he had not won." Whereat the Queen,
As one whose foot is bitten by an ant,
Glanced down upon her, turn'd and went her way.

But after, when her damsels, and herself,
And those three knights all set their faces home,
Sir Pelleas follow'd. She that saw him cried:
"Damsels—and yet I should be shamed to say it—
I cannot bide Sir Baby. Keep him back
Among yourselves. Would rather that we had
Some rough old knight who knew the worldly way,
Albeit grizzlier than a bear, to ride
And jest with! Take him to you, keep him off,
And pamper him with papmeat, if ye will,
Old milky fables of the wolf and sheep,
Such as the wholesome mothers tell their boys.

Nay, should ye try him with a merry one
To find his mettle, good; and if he fly us,
Small matter! let him." This her damsels heard,
And, mindful of her small and cruel hand,
They, closing round him thro' the journey home,
Acted her hest, and always from her side
Restrain'd him with all manner of device,
So that he could not come to speech with her.
And when she gain'd her castle, upsprang the bridge,
Down rang the grate of iron thro' the groove,
And he was left alone in open field.

"These be the ways of ladies," Pelleas thought,
"To those who love them, trials of our faith.
Yea, let her prove me to the uttermost,
For loyal to the uttermost am I."
So made his moan, and, darkness falling, sought
A priory not far off, there lodged, but rose
With morning every day, and, moist or dry,
Full-arm'd upon his charger all day long
Sat by the walls, and no one open'd to him.

And this persistence turn'd her scorn to wrath.
Then, calling her three knights, she charged them, "Out!
And drive him from the walls." And out they came,
But Pelleas overthrew them as they dash'd
Against him one by one; and these return'd,
But still he kept his watch beneath the wall.

Thereon her wrath became a hate; and once,
A week beyond, while walking on the walls
With her three knights, she pointed downward, "Look,
He haunts me—I cannot breathe—besieges me!
Down! strike him! put my hate into your strokes,
And drive him from my walls." And down they went,
And Pelleas overthrew them one by one;
And from the tower above him cried Ettarre,
"Bind him, and bring him in."

                              He heard her voice;
Then let the strong hand, which had overthrown
Her minion-knights, by those he overthrew
Be bounden straight, and so they brought him in.

Then when he came before Ettarre, the sight
Of her rich beauty made him at one glance
More bondsman in his heart than in his bonds.
Yet with good cheer he spake: "Behold me, lady,

A prisoner, and the vassal of thy will;
And if thou keep me in thy donjon here,
Content am I so that I see thy face
But once a day; for I have sworn my vows,
And thou hast given thy promise, and I know
That all these pains are trials of my faith,
And that thyself, when thou hast seen me strain'd
And sifted to the utmost, wilt at length
Yield me thy love and know me for thy knight."

Then she began to rail so bitterly,
With all her damsels, he was stricken mute,
But, when she mock'd his vows and the great King,
Lighted on words: "For pity of thine own self,
Peace, lady, peace; is he not thine and mine?"
"Thou fool," she said, "I never heard his voice
But long'd to break away. Unbind him now,
And thrust him out of doors; for save he be
Fool to the midmost marrow of his bones,
He will return no more." And those, her three,
Laugh'd, and unbound, and thrust him from the gate.

And after this, a week beyond, again
She call'd them, saying: "There he watches yet,
There like a dog before his master's door!
Kick'd, he returns; do ye not hate him, ye?
Ye know yourselves; how can ye bide at peace,
Affronted with his fulsome innocence?
Are ye but creatures of the board and bed,
No men to strike? Fall on him all at once,
And if ye slay him I reck not; if ye fail,
Give ye the slave mine order to be bound,
Bind him as heretofore, and bring him in.
It may be ye shall slay him in his bonds."

She spake, and at her will they couch'd their spears,
Three against one; and Gawain passing by,
Bound upon solitary adventure, saw
Low down beneath the shadow of those towers
A villainy, three to one; and thro' his heart
The fire of honor and all noble deeds
Flash'd, and he call'd, "I strike upon thy side—
The caitiffs!" "Nay," said Pelleas, "but forbear;
He needs no aid who doth his lady's will."

So Gawain, looking at the villainy done,
Forbore, but in his heat and eagerness

Trembled and quiver'd, as the dog, withheld
A moment from the vermin that he sees
Before him, shivers ere he springs and kills.

And Pelleas overthrew them, one to three;
And they rose up, and bound, and brought him in.
Then first her anger, leaving Pelleas, burn'd
Full on her knights in many an evil name
Of craven, weakling, and thrice-beaten hound:
"Yet, take him, ye that scarce are fit to touch,
Far less to bind, your victor, and thrust him out,
And let who will release him from his bonds.
And if he comes again"—there she brake short;
And Pelleas answer'd: "Lady, for indeed
I loved you and I deem'd you beautiful,
I cannot brook to see your beauty marr'd
Thro' evil spite; and ye love me not,
I cannot bear to dream you so forsworn:
I had liefer ye were worthy of my love
Than to be loved again of you—farewell.
And tho' ye kill my hope, not yet my love,
Vex not yourself; ye will not see me more."

While thus he spake, she gazed upon the man
Of princely bearing, tho' in bonds, and thought:
"Why have I push'd him from me? this man loves,
If love there be; yet him I loved not. Why?
I deem'd him fool? yea, so? or that in him
A something—was it nobler than myself?—
Seem'd my reproach? He is not of my kind.
He could not love me, did he know me well.
Nay, let him go—and quickly." And her knights
Laugh'd not, but thrust him bounden out of door.

Forth sprang Gawain, and loosed him from his bonds,
And flung them o'er the walls; and afterward,
Shaking his hands, as from a lazar's rag,
"Faith of my body," he said, "and art thou not—
Yea thou art he, whom late our Arthur made
Knight of his table; yea, and he that won
The circlet? wherefore hast thou so defamed
Thy brotherhood in me and all the rest
As let these caitiffs on thee work their will?"

And Pelleas answer'd: "O, their wills are hers
For whom I won the circlet; and mine, hers,
Thus to be bounden, so to see her face,

Marr'd tho' it be with spite and mockery now,
Other than when I found her in the woods.
And tho' she hath me bounden but in spite,
And all to flout me, when they bring me in,
Let me be bounden, I shall see her face;
Else must I die thro' mine unhappiness."

And Gawain answer'd kindly tho' in scorn:
"Why, let my lady bind me if she will,
And let my lady beat me if she will;
But an she send her delegate to thrall
These fighting hands of mine—Christ kill me then
But I will slice him handless by the wrist,
And let my lady sear the stump for him,
Howl as he may! But hold me for your friend.
Come, ye know nothing; here I pledge my troth,
Yea, by the honor of the Table Round
I will be leal to thee and work thy work,
And tame thy jailing princess to thine hand.
Lend me thine horse and arms, and I will say
That I have slain thee. She will let me in
To hear the manner of thy fight and fall;
Then, when I come within her counsels, then
From prime to vespers will I chant thy praise
As prowest knight and truest lover, more
Than any have sung thee living, till she long
To have thee back in lusty life again,
Not to be bound, save by white bonds and warm,
Dearer than freedom. Wherefore now thy horse
And armor; let me go; be comforted.
Give me three days to melt her fancy, and hope
The third night hence will bring thee news of gold."

Then Pelleas lent his horse and all his arms,
Saving the goodly sword, his prize, and took
Gawain's and said, "Betray me not but help—
Art thou not he whom men call light-of-love?"

"Ay," said Gawain, "for women be so light;"
Then bounded forward to the castle walls,
And raised a bugle hanging from his neck,
And winded it, and that so musically
That all the old echoes hidden in the wall
Rang out like hollow woods at hunting-tide.

Up ran a score of damsels to the tower;
"Avaunt," they cried, "our lady loves thee not!"

But Gawain lifting up his visor said:
"Gawain am I, Gawain of Arthur's court,
And I have slain this Pelleas whom ye hate.
Behold his horse and armor. Open gate,
And I will make you merry."

                              And down they ran,
Her damsels, crying to their lady, "Lo!
Pelleas is dead—he told us—he that hath
His horse and armor; will ye let him in?
He slew him! Gawain, Gawain of the court,
Sir Gawain—there he waits below the wall,
Blowing his bugle as who should say him nay."

And so, leave given, straight on thro' open door
Rode Gawain, whom she greeted courteously.
"Dead, is it so?" she ask'd. "Ay, ay," said he,
"And oft in dying cried upon your name."
"Pity on him," she answer'd, "a good knight,
But never let me bide one hour at peace."
"Ay," thought Gawain, "and you be fair enow;
But I to your dead man have given my troth,
That whom ye loathe, him will I make you love."

So those three days, aimless about the land,
Lost in doubt, Pelleas wandering
Waited, until the third night brought a moon
With promise of large light on woods and ways.

Hot was the night and silent; but a sound
Of Gawain ever coming, and this lay—
Which Pelleas had heard sung before the Queen,
And seen her sadden listening—vext his heart,
And marr'd his rest—"A worm within the rose."

"A rose, but one, none other rose had I,
A rose, one rose, and this was wondrous fair,
One rose, a rose that gladden'd earth and sky,
One rose, my rose, that sweeten'd all mine air—
I cared not for the thorns; the thorns were there.

"One rose, a rose to gather by and by,
One rose, a rose, to gather and to wear,
No rose but one—what other rose had I?
One rose, my rose; a rose that will not die,—
He dies who loves it,—if the worm be there."

This tender rhyme, and evermore the doubt,
"Why lingers Gawain with his golden news?"

So shook him that he could not rest, but rode
Ere midnight to her walls, and bound his horse
Hard by the gates. Wide open were the gates,
And no watch kept; and in thro' these he past,
And heard but his own steps, and his own heart
Beating, for nothing moved but his own self
And his own shadow. Then he crost the court,
And spied not any light in hall or bower,
But saw the postern portal also wide
Yawning; and up a slope of garden, all
Of roses white and red, and brambles mixt
And overgrowing them, went on, and found,
Here too, all hush'd below the mellow moon,
Save that one rivulet from a tiny cave
Came lightening downward, and so spilt itself
Among the roses and was lost again.

Then was he ware of three pavilions rear'd
Above the bushes, gilden-peakt. In one,
Red after revel, droned her lurdane knights
Slumbering, and their three squires across their feet;
In one, their malice on the placid lip
Frozen by sweet sleep, four of her damsels lay;
And in the third, the circlet of the jousts
Bound on her brow, were Gawain and Ettarre.

Back, as a hand that pushes thro' the leaf
To find a nest and feels a snake, he drew;
Back, as a coward slinks from what he fears
To cope with, or a traitor proven, or hound
Beaten, did Pelleas in an utter shame
Creep with his shadow thro' the court again,
Fingering at his sword-handle until he stood
There on the castle-bridge once more, and thought,
"I will go back, and slay them where they lie."

And so went back, and seeing them yet in sleep
Said, "Ye, that so dishallow the holy sleep,
Your sleep is death," and drew the sword and thought,
"What! slay a sleeping knight? the King hath bound
And sworn me to this brotherhood;" again,
"Alas that ever a knight should be so false!"
Then turn'd, and so return'd, and groaning laid
The naked sword athwart their naked throats,
There left it, and them sleeping; and she lay,
The circlet of the tourney round her brows,
And the sword of the tourney across her throat.

And forth he past, and mounting on his horse
Stared at her towers that, larger than themselves
In their own darkness, throng'd into the moon:
Then crush'd the saddle with his thighs, and clench'd
His hands, and madden'd with himself and moan'd:

"Would they have risen against me in their blood
At the last day? I might have answer'd them
Even before high God. O towers so strong,
Huge, solid, would that even while I gaze
The crack of earthquake shivering to your base
Split you, and hell burst up your harlot roofs
Bellowing, and charr'd you thro' and thro' within,
Black as the harlot's heart—hollow as a skull!
Let the fierce east scream thro' your eyelet-holes,
And whirl the dust of harlots round and round
In dung and nettles! hiss, snake—I saw him there—
Let the fox bark, let the wolf yell! Who yells
Here in the still sweet summer night but I—
I, the poor Pelleas whom she call'd her fool?
Fool, beast—he, she, or I? myself most fool;
Beast too, as lacking human wit—disgraced,
Dishonor'd all for trial of true love—
Love?—we be all alike; only the King
Hath made us fools and liars. O noble vows!
O great and sane and simple race of brutes
That own no lust because they have no law!
For why should I have loved her to my shame?
I loathe her, as I loved her to my shame.
I never loved her, I but lusted for her—
Away!"—

He dash'd the rowel into his horse,
And bounded forth and vanish'd thro' the night.

Then she, that felt the cold touch on her throat,
Awaking knew the sword, and turn'd herself
To Gawain: "Liar, for thou hast not slain
This Pelleas! here he stood, and might have slain
Me and thyself." And he that tells the tale
Says that her ever-veering fancy turn'd
To Pelleas, as the one true knight on earth
And only lover; and thro' her love her life
Wasted and pined, desiring him in vain.

But he by wild and way, for half the night,
And over hard and soft, striking the sod

From out the soft, the spark from off the hard,
Rode till the star above the wakening sun,
Beside that tower where Percivale was cowl'd,
Glanced from the rosy forehead of the dawn.
For so the words were flash'd into his heart
He knew not whence or wherefore: "O sweet star,
Pure on the virgin forehead of the dawn!"
And there he would have wept, but felt his eyes
Harder and drier than a fountain bed
In summer. Thither came the village girls
And linger'd talking, and they come no more
Till the sweet heavens have fill'd it from the heights
Again with living waters in the change
Of seasons. Hard his eyes, harder his heart
Seem'd; but so weary were his limbs that he,
Gasping, "Of Arthur's hall am I, but here,
Here let me rest and die," cast himself down,
And gulf'd his griefs in inmost sleep; so lay,
Till shaken by a dream, that Gawain fired
The hall of Merlin, and the morning star
Reel'd in the smoke, brake into flame, and fell.

He woke, and being ware of some one nigh,
Sent hands upon him, as to tear him, crying,
"False! and I held thee pure as Guinevere."

But Percivale stood near him and replied,
"Am I but false as Guinevere is pure?
Or art thou mazed with dreams? or being one
Of our free-spoken Table hast not heard
That Lancelot"——there he check'd himself and paused.

Then fared it with Sir Pelleas as with one
Who gets a wound in battle, and the sword
That made it plunges thro' the wound again,
And pricks it deeper; and he shrank and wail'd,
"Is the Queen false?" and Percivale was mute.
"Have any of our Round Table held their vows?"
And Percivale made answer not a word.
"Is the King true?" "The King!" said Percivale.
"Why, then let men couple at once with wolves.
What! art thou mad?"

But Pelleas, leaping up,
Ran thro' the doors and vaulted on his horse
And fled. Small pity upon his horse had he,

Or on himself, or any, and when he met
A cripple, one that held a hand for alms—
Hunch'd as he was, and like an old dwarf-elm
That turns its back on the salt blast, the boy
Paused not, but overrode him, shouting, "False,
And false with Gawain!" and so left him bruised
And batter'd, and fled on, and hill and wood
Went ever streaming by him till the gloom
That follows on the turning of the world
Darken'd the common path. He twitch'd the reins,
And made his beast, that better knew it, swerve
Now off it and now on; but when he saw
High up in heaven the hall that Merlin built,
Blackening against the dead-green stripes of even,
"Black nest of rats," he groan'd, "ye build too high."

Not long thereafter from the city gates
Issued Sir Lancelot riding airily,
Warm with a gracious parting from the Queen,
Peace at his heart, and gazing at a star
And marvelling what it was; on whom the boy,
Across the silent seeded meadow-grass
Borne, clash'd; and Lancelot, saying, "What name hast thou
That ridest here so blindly and so hard?"
"No name, no name," he shouted, "a scourge am I
To lash the treasons of the Table Round."
"Yea, but thy name?" "I have many names," he cried:
"I am wrath and shame and hate and evil fame,
And like a poisonous wind I pass to blast
And blaze the crime of Lancelot and the Queen."
"First over me," said Lancelot, "shalt thou pass."
"Fight therefore," yell'd the youth, and either knight
Drew back a space, and when they closed, at once
The weary steed of Pelleas floundering flung
His rider, who call'd out from the dark field,
"Thou art false as hell; slay me, I have no sword."
Then Lancelot, "Yea, between thy lips—and sharp;
But here will I disedge it by thy death."
"Slay then," he shriek'd, "my will is to be slain,"
And Lancelot, with his heel upon the fallen,
Rolling his eyes, a moment stood, then spake:
"Rise, weakling; I am Lancelot; say thy say."

And Lancelot slowly rode his warhorse back
To Camelot, and Sir Pelleas in brief while

Caught his unbroken limbs from the dark field,
And follow'd to the city. It chanced that both
Brake into hall together, worn and pale.
There with her knights and dames was Guinevere.
Full wonderingly she gazed on Lancelot
So soon return'd, and then on Pelleas, him
Who had not greeted her, but cast himself
Down on a bench, hard-breathing. "Have ye fought?"
She ask'd of Lancelot. "Ay, my Queen," he said.
"And thou hast overthrown him?" "Ay, my Queen."
Then she, turning to Pelleas, "O young knight,
Hath the great heart of knighthood in thee fail'd
So far thou canst not bide, unfrowardly,
A fall from *him*?" Then, for he answer'd not,
"Or hast thou other griefs? If I, the Queen,
May help them, loose thy tongue, and let me know."
But Pelleas lifted up an eye so fierce
She quail'd; and he, hissing "I have no sword,"
Sprang from the door into the dark. The Queen
Look'd hard upon her lover, he on her,
And each foresaw the dolorous day to be;
And all talk died, as in a grove all song
Beneath the shadow of some bird of prey.
Then a long silence came upon the hall,
And Modred thought, "The time is hard at hand."

✠✠✠✠ THE LAST TOURNAMENT ✠✠✠✠

DAGONET, the fool, whom Gawain in his mood
Had made mock-knight of Arthur's Table Round,
At Camelot, high above the yellowing woods,
Danced like a wither'd leaf before the hall.
And toward him from the hall, with harp in hand,
And from the crown thereof a carcanet
Of ruby swaying to and fro, the prize
Of Tristram in the jousts of yesterday,
Came Tristram, saying, "Why skip ye so, Sir Fool?"

  For Arthur and Sir Lancelot riding once
Far down beneath a winding wall of rock

Heard a child wail. A stump of oak half-dead,
From roots like some black coil of carven snakes,
Clutch'd at the crag, and started thro' mid air
Bearing an eagle's nest; and thro' the tree
Rush'd ever a rainy wind, and thro' the wind
Pierced ever a child's cry; and crag and tree
Scaling, Sir Lancelot from the perilous nest,
This ruby necklace thrice around her neck,
And all unscarr'd from beak or talon, brought
A maiden babe, which Arthur pitying took,
Then gave it to his Queen to rear. The Queen
But coldly acquiescing, in her white arms
Received, and after loved it tenderly,
And named it Nestling; so forgot herself
A moment, and her cares; till that young life
Being smitten in mid heaven with mortal cold
Past from her, and in time the carcanet
Vext her with plaintive memories of the child.
So she, delivering it to Arthur, said,
"Take thou the jewels of this dead innocence,
And make them, an thou wilt, a tourney-prize."

To whom the King: "Peace to thine eagle-borne
Dead nestling, and this honor after death,
Following thy will! but, O my Queen, I muse
Why ye not wear on arm, or neck, or zone
Those diamonds that I rescued from the tarn,
And Lancelot won, methought, for thee to wear."

"Would rather you had let them fall," she cried,
"Plunge and be lost—ill-fated as they were,
A bitterness to me!—ye look amazed,
Not knowing they were lost as soon as given—
Slid from my hands when I was leaning out
Above the river—that unhappy child
Past in her barge; but rosier luck will go
With these rich jewels, seeing that they came
Not from the skeleton of a brother-slayer,
But the sweet body of a maiden babe.
Perchance—who knows?—the purest of thy knights
May win them for the purest of my maids."

She ended, and the cry of a great jousts
With trumpet-blowings ran on all the ways
From Camelot in among the faded fields
To furthest towers; and everywhere the knights
Arm'd for a day of glory before the King.

But on the hither side of that loud morn
Into the hall stagger'd, his visage ribb'd
From ear to ear with dogwhip-weals, his nose
Bridge-broken, one eye out, and one hand off,
And one with shatter'd fingers dangling lame,
A churl, to whom indignantly the King:

"My churl, for whom Christ died, what evil beast
Hath drawn his claws athwart thy face? or fiend?
Man was it who marr'd heaven's image in thee thus?"

Then, sputtering thro' the hedge of splinter'd teeth,
Yet strangers to the tongue, and with blunt stump
Pitch-blacken'd sawing the air, said the maim'd churl:

"He took them and he drave them to his tower—
Some hold he was a table-knight of thine—
A hundred goodly ones—the Red Knight, he—
Lord, I was tending swine, and the Red Knight
Brake in upon me and drave them to his tower;
And when I call'd upon thy name as one
That doest right by gentle and by churl,
Maim'd me and maul'd, and would outright have slain,
Save that he sware me to a message, saying:
'Tell thou the King and all his liars that I
Have founded my Round Table in the North,
And whatsoever his own knights have sworn
My knights have sworn the counter to it—and say
My tower is full of harlots, like his court,
But mine are worthier, seeing they profess
To be none other than themselves—and say
My knights are all adulterers like his own,
But mine are truer, seeing they profess
To be none other: and say his hour is come,
The heathen are upon him, his long lance
Broken, and his Excalibur a straw.'"

Then Arthur turn'd to Kay the seneschal.
"Take thou my churl, and tend him curiously
Like a king's heir, till all his hurts be whole.
The heathen—but that ever-climbing wave,
Hurl'd back again so often in empty foam,
Hath lain for years at rest—and renegades,
Thieves, bandits, leavings of confusion, whom
The wholesome realm is purged of otherwhere,

Friends, thro' your manhood and your fealty,—now
Make their last head like Satan in the North.
My younger knights, new-made, in whom your flower
Waits to be solid fruit of golden deeds,
Move with me toward their quelling, which achieved,
The loneliest ways are safe from shore to shore.
But thou, Sir Lancelot, sitting in my place
Enchair'd to-morrow, arbitrate the field;
For wherefore shouldst thou care to mingle with it,
Only to yield my Queen her own again?
Speak, Lancelot, thou art silent; is it well?"

    Thereto Sir Lancelot answer'd: "It is well;
Yet better if the King abide, and leave
The leading of his younger knights to me.
Else, for the King has will'd it, it is well."

    Then Arthur rose and Lancelot follow'd him,
And while they stood without the doors, the King
Turn'd to him, saying: "Is it then so well?
Or mine the blame that oft I seem as he
Of whom was written, 'A sound is in his ears'?
The foot that loiters, bidden go,—the glance
That only seems half-loyal to command,—
A manner somewhat fallen from reverence—
Or have I dream'd the bearing of our knights
Tells of a manhood ever less and lower?
Or whence the fear lest this my realm, uprear'd,
By noble deeds at one with noble vows,
From flat confusion and brute violences,
Reel back into the beast, and be no more?"

    He spoke, and taking all his younger knights,
Down the slope city rode, and sharply turn'd
North by the gate. In her high bower the Queen,
Working a tapestry, lifted up her head,
Watch'd her lord pass, and knew not that she sigh'd.
Then ran across her memory the strange rhyme
Of bygone Merlin, "Where is he who knows?
From the great deep to the great deep he goes."

    But when the morning of a tournament,
By these in earnest those in mockery call'd
The Tournament of the Dead Innocence,
Brake with a wet wind blowing, Lancelot,
Round whose sick head all night, like birds of prey,

The words of Arthur flying shriek'd, arose,
And down a streetway hung with folds of pure
White samite, and by fountains running wine,
Where children sat in white with cups of gold,
Moved to the lists, and there with slow sad steps
Ascending, fill'd his double-dragon'd chair.

He glanced and saw the stately galleries,
Dame, damsel, each thro' worship of their Queen
White-robed in honor of the stainless child,
And some with scatter'd jewels, like a bank
Of maiden snow mingled with sparks of fire.
He look'd but once, and veil'd his eyes again.

The sudden trumpet sounded as in a dream
To ears but half-awaked, then one low roll
Of autumn thunder, and the jousts began;
And ever the wind blew, and yellowing leaf,
And gloom and gleam, and shower and shorn plume
Went down it. Sighing weariedly, as one
Who sits and gazes on a faded fire,
When all the goodlier guests are past away,
Sat their great umpire looking o'er the lists.
He saw the laws that ruled the tournament
Broken, but spake not; once, a knight cast down
Before his throne of arbitration cursed
The dead babe and the follies of the King;
And once the laces of a helmet crack'd,
And show'd him, like a vermin in its hole,
Modred, a narrow face. Anon he heard
The voice that billow'd round the barriers roar
An ocean-sounding welcome to one knight,
But newly-enter'd, taller than the rest,
And armor'd all in forest green, whereon
There tript a hundred tiny silver deer,
And wearing but a holly-spray for crest,
With ever-scattering berries, and on shield
A spear, a harp, a bugle—Tristram—late
From over-seas in Brittany return'd,
And marriage with a princess of that realm,
Isolt the White—Sir Tristram of the Woods—
Whom Lancelot knew, had held sometime with pain
His own against him, and now yearn'd to shake
The burthen off his heart in one full shock

With Tristram even to death. His strong hands gript
And dinted the gilt dragons right and left,
Until he groan'd for wrath—so many of those
That ware their ladies' colors on the casque
Drew from before Sir Tristram to the bounds,
And there with gibes and flickering mockeries
Stood, while he mutter'd, "Craven crests! O shame!
What faith have these in whom they sware to love?
The glory of our Round Table is no more."

So Tristram won, and Lancelot gave, the gems,
Not speaking other word than, "Hast thou won?
Art thou the purest, brother? See, the hand
Wherewith thou takest this is red!" to whom
Tristram, half plagued by Lancelot's languorous mood,
Made answer: "Ay, but wherefore toss me this
Like a dry bone cast to some hungry hound?
Let be thy fair Queen's fantasy. Strength of heart
And might of limb, but mainly use and skill,
Are winners in this pastime of our King.
My hand—belike the lance hath dript upon it—
No blood of mine, I trow; but O chief knight,
Right arm of Arthur in the battlefield,
Great brother, thou nor I have made the world;
Be happy in thy fair Queen as I in mine."

And Tristram round the gallery made his horse
Caracole; then bow'd his homage, bluntly saying,
"Fair damsels, each to him who worships each
Sole Queen of Beauty and of love, behold
This day my Queen of Beauty is not here."
And most of these were mute, some anger'd, one
Murmuring, "All courtesy is dead," and one,
"The glory of our Round Table is no more."

Then fell thick rain, plume droopt and mantle clung,
And pettish cries awoke, and the wan day
Went glooming down in wet and weariness;
But under her black brows a swarthy one
Laugh'd shrilly, crying: "Praise the patient saints,
Our one white day of Innocence hath past,
Tho' somewhat draggled at the skirt. So be it.
The snowdrop only, flowering thro' the year,
Would make the world as blank as wintertide.
Come—let us gladden their sad eyes, our Queen's

And Lancelot's, at this night's solemnity
With all the kindlier colors of the field."

So dame and damsel glitter'd at the feast
Variously gay; for he that tells the tale
Liken'd them, saying, as when an hour of cold
Falls on the mountain in midsummer snows,
And all the purple slopes of mountain flowers
Pass under white, till the warm hour returns
With veer of wind and all are flowers again,
So dame and damsel cast the simple white,
And glowing in all colors, the live grass,
Rose-campion, bluebell, kingcup, poppy, glanced
About the revels, and with mirth so loud
Beyond all use, that, half-amazed, the Queen,
And wroth at Tristram and the lawless jousts,
Brake up their sports, then slowly to her bower
Parted, and in her bosom pain was lord.

And little Dagonet on the morrow morn,
High over all the yellow autumn-tide,
Danced like a wither'd leaf before the hall.
Then Tristram saying, "Why skip ye so, Sir Fool?"
Wheel'd round on either heel, Dagonet replied,
"Belike for lack of wiser company;
Or being fool, and seeing too much wit
Makes the world rotten, why, belike I skip
To know myself the wisest knight of all."
"Ay, fool," said Tristram, "but 't is eating dry
To dance without a catch, a roundelay
To dance to." Then he twangled on his harp,
And while he twangled little Dagonet stood
Quiet as any water-sodden log
Stay'd in the wandering warble of a brook,
But when the twangling ended, skipt again;
And being ask'd, "Why skipt ye not, Sir Fool?"
Made answer, "I had liefer twenty years
Skip to the broken music of my brains
Than any broken music thou canst make."
Then Tristram, waiting for the quip to come,
"Good now, what music have I broken, fool?"
And little Dagonet, skipping, "Arthur, the King's;
For when thou playest that air with Queen Isolt,
Thou makest broken music with thy bride,
Her daintier namesake down in Brittany—

And so thou breakest Arthur's music too."
"Save for that broken music in thy brains,
Sir Fool," said Tristram, "I would break thy head.
Fool, I came late, the heathen wars were o'er,
The life had flown, we sware but by the shell —
I am but a fool to reason with a fool—
Come, thou art crabb'd and sour; but lean me down,
Sir Dagonet, one of thy long asses' ears,
And harken if my music be not true.

    " 'Free love—free field—we love but while we may.
The woods are hush'd, their music is no more;
The leaf is dead, the yearning past away.
New leaf, new life—the days of frost are o'er;
New life, new love, to suit the newer day;
New loves are sweet as those that went before.
Free love—free field—we love but while we may.'

    "Ye might have moved slow-measure to my tune,
Not stood stock-still. I made it in the woods,
And heard it ring as true as tested gold."

    But Dagonet with one foot poised in his hand:
"Friend, did ye mark that fountain yesterday,
Made to run wine?—but this had run itself
All out like a long life to a sour end—
And them that round it sat with golden cups
To hand the wine to whosoever came—
The twelve small damosels white as Innocence,
In honor of poor Innocence the babe,
Who left the gems which Innocence the Queen
Lent to the King, and Innocence the King
Gave for a prize—and one of those white slips
Handed her cup and piped, the pretty one,
'Drink, drink, Sir Fool,' and thereupon I drank,
Spat—pish—the cup was gold, the draught was mud."

    And Tristram: "Was it muddier than thy gibes?
Is all the laughter gone dead out of thee?—
Not marking how the knighthood mock thee, fool—
'Fear God: honor the King—his one true knight—
Sole follower of the vows'—for here be they
Who knew thee swine enow before I came,
Smuttier than blasted grain. But when the King
Had made thee fool, thy vanity so shot up
It frighted all free fool from out thy heart;

Which left thee less than fool, and less than swine,
A naked aught—yet swine I hold thee still,
For I have flung thee pearls and find thee swine."

And little Dagonet mincing with his feet:
"Knight, an ye fling those rubies round my neck
In lieu of hers, I'll hold thou hast some touch
Of music, since I care not for thy pearls.
Swine? I have wallow'd, I have wash'd—the world
Is flesh and shadow—I have had my day.
The dirty nurse, Experience, in her kind
Hath foul'd me—an I wallow'd, then I wash'd—
I have had my day and my philosophies—
And thank the Lord I am King Arthur's fool.
Swine, say ye? swine, goats, asses, rams, and geese
Troop'd round a Paynim harper once, who thrumm'd
On such a wire as musically as thou
Some such fine song—but never a king's fool."

And Tristram, "Then were swine, goats, asses, geese
The wiser fools, seeing thy Paynim bard
Had such a mastery of his mystery
That he could harp his wife up out of hell."

Then Dagonet, turning on the ball of his foot,
"And whither harp'st thou thine? down! and thyself
Down! and two more; a helpful harper thou,
That harpest downward! Dost thou know the star
We call the Harp of Arthur up in heaven?"

And Tristram, "Ay, Sir Fool, for when our King
Was victor wellnigh day by day, the knights,
Glorying in each new glory, set his name
High on all hills and in the signs of heaven."

And Dagonet answer'd: "Ay, and when the land
Was freed, and the Queen false, ye set yourself
To babble about him, all to show your wit—
And whether he were king by courtesy,
Or king by right—and so went harping down
The black king's highway, got so far and grew
So witty that ye play'd at ducks and drakes
With Arthur's vows on the great lake of fire.
Tuwhoo! do ye see it? do ye see the star?"

"Nay, fool," said Tristram, "not in open day."
And Dagonet: "Nay, nor will; I see it and hear.

It makes a silent music up in heaven,
And I and Arthur and the angels hear,
And then we skip." "Lo, fool," he said, "ye talk
Fool's treason; is the King thy brother fool?"
Then little Dagonet clapt his hands and shrill'd:
"Ay, ay, my brother fool, the king of fools!
Conceits himself as God that he can make
Figs out of thistles, silk from bristles, milk
From burning spurge, honey from hornet-combs,
And men from beasts—Long live the king of fools!"

And down the city Dagonet danced away;
But thro' the slowly-mellowing avenues
And solitary passes of the wood
Rode Tristram toward Lyonnesse and the west.
Before him fled the face of Queen Isolt
With ruby-circled neck, but evermore
Past, as a rustle or twitter in the wood
Made dull his inner, keen his outer eye
For all that walk'd, or crept, or perch'd, or flew.
Anon the face, as, when a gust hath blown,
Unruffling waters re-collect the shape
Of one that in them sees himself, return'd;
But at the slot or fewmets of a deer,
Or even a fallen feather, vanish'd again.

So on for all that day from lawn to lawn
Thro' many a league-long bower he rode. At length
A lodge of intertwisted beechen-boughs,
Furze-cramm'd and bracken-rooft, the which himself
Built for a summer day with Queen Isolt
Against a shower, dark in the golden grove
Appearing, sent his fancy back to where
She lived a moon in that low lodge with him;
Till Mark her lord had past, the Cornish King,
With six or seven, when Tristram was away,
And snatch'd her thence, yet, dreading worse than shame
Her warrior Tristram, spake not any word,
But bode his hour, devising wretchedness.

And now that desert lodge to Tristram lookt
So sweet that, halting, in he past and sank
Down on a drift of foliage random-blown;
But could not rest for musing how to smooth
And sleek his marriage over to the queen.

Perchance in lone Tintagil far from all
The tonguesters of the court she had not heard.
But then what folly had sent him overseas
After she left him lonely here? a name?
Was it the name of one in Brittany,
Isolt, the daughter of the King? "Isolt
Of the White Hands" they call'd her: the sweet name
Allured him first, and then the maid herself,
Who served him well with those white hands of hers,
And loved him well, until himself had thought
He loved her also, wedded easily,
But left her all as easily, and return'd.
The black-blue Irish hair and Irish eyes
Had drawn him home—what marvel? then he laid
His brows upon the drifted leaf and dream'd.

He seem'd to pace the strand of Brittany
Between Isolt of Britain and his bride,
And show'd them both the ruby-chain, and both
Began to struggle for it, till his queen
Graspt it so hard that all her hand was red.
Then cried the Breton, "Look, her hand is red!
These be no rubies, this is frozen blood,
And melts within her hand—her hand is hot
With ill desires, but this I gave thee, look,
Is all as cool and white as any flower."
Follow'd a rush of eagle's wings, and then
A whimpering of the spirit of the child,
Because the twain had spoil'd her carcanet.

He dream'd: but Arthur with a hundred spears
Rode far, till o'er the illimitable reed,
And many a glancing plash and sallowy isle,
The wide-wing'd sunset of the misty marsh
Glared on a huge machicolated tower
That stood with open doors, whereout was roll'd
A roar of riot, as from men secure
Amid their marshes, ruffians at their ease
Among their harlot-brides, an evil song.
"Lo there," said one of Arthur's youth, for there
High on a grim dead tree before the tower,
A goodly brother of the Table Round
Swung by the neck; and on the boughs a shield
Showing a shower of blood in a field noir,
And therebeside a horn, inflamed the knights

At that dishonor done the gilded spur,
Till each would clash the shield and blow the horn,
But Arthur waved them back. Alone he rode.
Then at the dry harsh roar of the great horn,
That sent the face of all the marsh aloft
An ever upward-rushing storm and cloud
Of shriek and plume, the Red Knight heard, and all,
Even to tipmost lance and topmost helm,
In blood-red armor sallying, howl'd to the King:

"The teeth of Hell flay bare and gnash thee flat!—
Lo! art thou not that eunuch-hearted king
Who fain had clipt free manhood from the world—
The woman-worshipper? Yea, God's curse, and I!
Slain was the brother of my paramour
By a knight of thine, and I that heard her whine
And snivel, being eunuch-hearted too,
Sware by the scorpion-worm that twists in hell
And stings itself to everlasting death,
To hang whatever knight of thine I fought
And tumbled. Art thou king?—Look to thy life!"

He ended. Arthur knew the voice; the face
Wellnigh was helmet-hidden, and the name
Went wandering somewhere darkling in his mind.
And Arthur deign'd not use of word or sword,
But let the drunkard, as he stretch'd from horse
To strike him, overbalancing his bulk,
Down from the causeway heavily to the swamp
Fall, as the crest of some slow-arching wave,
Heard in dead night along that table-shore,
Drops flat, and after the great waters break
Whitening for half a league, and thin themselves,
Far over sands marbled with moon and cloud,
From less and less to nothing; thus he fell
Head-heavy. Then the knights, who watch'd him, roar'd
And shouted and leapt down upon the fallen,
There trampled out his face from being known,
And sank his head in mire, and slimed themselves;
Nor heard the King for their own cries, but sprang
Thro' open doors, and swording right and left
Men, women, on their sodden faces, hurl'd
The tables over and the wines, and slew
Till all the rafters rang with woman-yells,
And all the pavement stream'd with massacre.
Then, echoing yell with yell, they fired the tower,

Which half that autumn night, like the live North,
Red-pulsing up thro' Alioth and Alcor,
Made all above it, and a hundred meres
About it, as the water Moab saw
Come round by the east, and out beyond them flush'd
The long low dune and lazy-plunging sea.

So all the ways were safe from shore to shore,
But in the heart of Arthur pain was lord.

Then, out of Tristram waking, the red dream
Fled with a shout, and that low lodge return'd,
Mid-forest, and the wind among the boughs,
He whistled his good war-horse left to graze
Among the forest greens, vaulted upon him,
And rode beneath an ever-showering leaf,
Till one lone woman, weeping near a cross,
Stay'd him. "Why weep ye?" "Lord," she said, "my man
Hath left me or is dead;" whereon he thought—
"What, if she hate me now? I would not this.
What, if she love me still? I would not that.
I know not what I would"—but said to her,
"Yet weep not thou, lest, if thy mate return,
He find thy favor changed and love thee not"—
Then pressing day by day thro' Lyonnesse
Last in a roky hollow, belling, heard
The hounds of Mark, and felt the goodly hounds
Yelp at his heart, but, turning, past and gain'd
Tintagil, half in sea and high on land,
A crown of towers.

                    Down in a casement sat,
A low sea-sunset glorying round her hair
And glossy-throated grace, Isolt the Queen.
And when she heard the feet of Tristram grind
The spiring stone that scaled about her tower,
Flush'd, started, met him at the doors, and there
Belted his body with her white embrace,
Crying aloud: "Not Mark—not Mark, my soul!
The footstep flutter'd me at first—not he!
Catlike thro' his own castle steals my Mark.
But warrior-wise thou stridest thro' his halls
Who hates thee, as I him—even to the death.
My soul, I felt my hatred for my Mark
Quicken within me, and knew that thou wert nigh."

To whom Sir Tristram smiling, "I am here;
Let be thy Mark, seeing he is not thine."

And drawing somewhat backward she replied:
"Can he be wrong'd who is not even his own,
But save for dread of thee had beaten me,
Scratch'd, bitten, blinded, marr'd me somehow—Mark?
What rights are his that dare not strike for them?
Not lift a hand—not, tho' he found me thus!
But harken! have ye met him? hence he went
To-day for three days' hunting—as he said—
And so returns belike within an hour.
Mark's way, my soul!—but eat not thou with Mark,
Because he hates thee even more than fears,
Nor drink; and when thou passest any wood
Close vizor, lest an arrow from the bush
Should leave me all alone with Mark and hell.
My God, the measure of my hate for Mark
Is as the measure of my love for thee!"

So, pluck'd one way by hate and one by love,
Drain'd of her force, again she sat, and spake
To Tristram, as he knelt before her, saying:
"O hunter, and O blower of the horn,
Harper, and thou hast been a rover too,
For, ere I mated with my shambling king,
Ye twain had fallen out about the bride
Of one—his name is out of me—the prize,
If prize she were—what marvel?—she could see—
Thine, friend; and ever since my craven seeks
To wreck thee villainously—but, O Sir Knight,
What dame or damsel have ye kneel'd to last?"

And Tristram, "Last to my Queen Paramount,
Here now to my queen paramount of love
And loveliness—ay, lovelier than when first
Her light feet fell on our rough Lyonnesse,
Sailing from Ireland."

Softly laugh'd Isolt:
"Flatter me not, for hath not our great Queen
My dole of beauty trebled?" and he said:
"Her beauty is her beauty, and thine thine,
And thine is more to me—soft, gracious, kind—
Save when thy Mark is kindled on thy lips
Most gracious; but she, haughty, even to him,

Lancelot; for I have seen him wan enow
To make one doubt if ever the great Queen
Have yielded her love."

                    To whom Isolt:
"Ah, then, false hunter and false harper, thou
Who brakest thro' the scruple of my bond,
Calling me thy white hind, and saying to me
That Guinevere had sinn'd against the highest,
And I—misyoked with such a want of man—
That I could hardly sin against the lowest."

    He answer'd: "O my soul, be comforted!
If this be sweet, to sin in leading-strings,
If here be comfort, and if ours be sin,
Crown'd warrant had we for the crowning sin
That made us happy; but how ye greet me—fear
And fault and doubt—no word of that fond tale—
Thy deep heart-yearnings, thy sweet memories
Of Tristram in that year he was away."

    And, saddening on the sudden, spake Isolt:
"I had forgotten all in my strong joy
To see thee—yearnings?—ay! for, hour by hour,
Here in the never-ended afternoon,
O, sweeter than all memories of thee,
Deeper than any yearnings after thee
Seem'd those far-rolling, westward-smiling seas,
Watch'd from this tower. Isolt of Britain dash'd
Before Isolt of Brittany on the strand,
Would that have chill'd her bride-kiss? Wedded her?
Fought in her father's battles? wounded there?
The King was all fulfill'd with gratefulness,
And she, my namesake of the hands, that heal'd
Thy hurt and heart with unguent and caress—
Well—can I wish her any huger wrong
Than having known thee? her too hast thou left
To pine and waste in those sweet memories.
O, were I not my Mark's, by whom all men
Are noble, I should hate thee more than love."

    And Tristram, fondling her light hands, replied:
"Grace, queen, for being loved; she loved me well.
Did I love her? the name at least I loved.
Isolt?—I fought his battles, for Isolt!
The night was dark; the true star set. Isolt!

The name was ruler of the dark—Isolt?
Care not for her! patient, and prayerful, meek,
Pale-blooded, she will yield herself to God."

And Isolt answer'd: "Yea, and why not I?
Mine is the larger need, who am not meek,
Pale-blooded, prayerful. Let me tell thee now.
Here one black, mute midsummer night I sat,
Lonely, but musing on thee, wondering where,
Murmuring a light song I had heard thee sing,
And once or twice I spake thy name aloud.
Then flash'd a levin-brand; and near me stood,
In fuming sulphur blue and green, a fiend—
Mark's way to steal behind one in the dark—
For there was Mark: 'He has wedded her,' he said,
Not said, but hiss'd it; then this crown of towers
So shook to such a roar of all the sky,
That here in utter dark I swoon'd away,
And woke again in utter dark, and cried,
'I will flee hence and give myself to God'—
And thou wert lying in thy new leman's arms."

Then Tristram, ever dallying with her hand,
"May God be with thee, sweet, when old and gray,
And past desire!" a saying that anger'd her.
" 'May God be with thee, sweet, when thou art old,
And sweet no more to me!' I need Him now.
For when had Lancelot utter'd aught so gross
Even to the swineherd's malkin in the mast?
The greater man the greater courtesy.
Far other was the Tristram, Arthur's knight!
But thou thro' ever harrying thy wild beasts—
Save that to touch a harp, tilt with a lance
Becomes thee well—art grown wild beast thyself.
How darest thou, if lover, push me even
In fancy from thy side, and set me far
In the gray distance, half a life away,
Her to be loved no more? Unsay it, unswear!
Flatter me rather, seeing me so weak,
Broken with Mark and hate and solitude,
Thy marriage and mine own, that I should suck
Lies like sweet wines. Lie to me; I believe.
Will ye not lie? not swear, as there ye kneel,
And solemnly as when ye sware to him,
The man of men, our King—My God, the power

Was once in vows when men believed the King!
They lied not then who sware, and thro' their vows
The King prevailing made his realm—I say,
Swear to me thou wilt love me even when old,
Gray-hair'd, and past desire, and in despair."

Then Tristram, pacing moodily up and down:
"Vows! did you keep the vow you made to Mark
More than I mine? Lied, say ye? Nay, but learnt,
The vow that binds too strictly snaps itself—
My knighthood taught me this—ay, being snapt—
We run more counter to the soul thereof
Than had we never sworn. I swear no more.
I swore to the great King, and am forsworn.
For once—even to the height—I honor'd him.
'Man, is he man at all?' methought, when first
I rode from our rough Lyonnesse, and beheld
That victor of the Pagan throned in hall—
His hair, a sun that ray'd from off a brow
Like hill-snow high in heaven, the steel-blue eyes,
The golden beard that clothed his lips with light—
Moreover, that weird legend of his birth,
With Merlin's mystic babble about his end
Amazed me; then, his foot was on a stool
Shaped as a dragon; he seem'd to me no man,
But Michael trampling Satan; so I sware,
Being amazed. But this went by—The vows!
O, ay—the wholesome madness of an hour—
They served their use, their time; for every knight
Believed himself a greater than himself,
And every follower eyed him as a God;
Till he, being lifted up beyond himself,
Did mightier deeds than elsewise he had done,
And so the realm was made. But then their vows—
First mainly thro' that sullying of our Queen—
Began to gall the knighthood, asking whence
Had Arthur right to bind them to himself?
Dropt down from heaven? wash'd up from out the deep?
They fail'd to trace him thro' the flesh and blood
Of our old kings. Whence then? a doubtful lord
To bind them by inviolable vows,
Which flesh and blood perforce would violate;
For feel this arm of mine—the tide within
Red with free chase and heather-scented air,
Pulsing full man. Can Arthur make me pure

As any maiden child? lock up my tongue
From uttering freely what I freely hear?
Bind me to one? The wide world laughs at it.
And worldling of the world am I, and know
The ptarmigan that whitens ere his hour
Woos his own end; we are not angels here
Nor shall be. Vows—I am woodman of the woods,
And hear the garnet-headed yaffingale
Mock them—my soul, we love but while we may;
And therefore is my love so large for thee,
Seeing it is not bounded save by love."

Here ending, he moved toward her, and she said:
"Good: an I turn'd away my love for thee
To some one thrice as courteous as thyself—
For courtesy wins woman all as well
As valor may, but he that closes both
Is perfect, he is Lancelot—taller indeed,
Rosier and comelier, thou—but say I loved
This knightliest of all knights, and cast thee back
Thine own small saw, 'We love but while we may,'
Well then, what answer?"

                        He that while she spake,
Mindful of what he brought to adorn her with,
The jewels, had let one finger lightly touch
The warm white apple of her throat, replied,
"Press this a little closer, sweet, until—
Come, I am hunger'd and half-anger'd—meat,
Wine, wine—and I will love thee to the death,
And out beyond into the dream to come."

So then, when both were brought to full accord,
She rose, and set before him all he will'd;
And after these had comforted the blood
With meats and wines, and satiated their hearts—
Now talking of their woodland paradise,
The deer, the dews, the fern, the founts, the lawns;
Now mocking at the much ungainliness,
And craven shifts, and long crane legs of Mark—
Then Tristram laughing caught the harp and sang:

"Ay, ay, O, ay—the winds that bend the brier!
A star in heaven, a star within the mere!
Ay, ay, O, ay—a star was my desire,
And one was far apart and one was near.

Ay, ay, O, ay—the winds that bow the grass!
And one was water and one star was fire,
And one will ever shine and one will pass.
Ay, ay, O, ay—the winds that move the mere!"

Then in the light's last glimmer Tristram show'd
And swung the ruby carcanet. She cried,
"The collar of some Order, which our King
Hath newly founded, all for thee, my soul,
For thee, to yield thee grace beyond thy peers."

"Not so, my queen," he said, "but the red fruit
Grown on a magic oak-tree in mid-heaven,
And won by Tristram as a tourney-prize
And hither brought by Tristram for his last
Love-offering and peace-offering unto thee."

He spoke, he turn'd, then, flinging round her neck,
Claspt it, and cried, "Thine Order, O my queen!"
But, while he bow'd to kiss the jewell'd throat,
Out of the dark, just as the lips had touch'd,
Behind him rose a shadow and a shriek—
"Mark's way," said Mark, and clove him thro' the brain.

That night came Arthur home, and while he climb'd,
All in a death-dumb autumn-dripping gloom,
The stairway to the hall, and look'd and saw
The great Queen's bower was dark,—about his feet
A voice clung sobbing till he question'd it,
"What art thou?" and the voice about his feet
Sent up an answer, sobbing, "I am thy fool,
And I shall never make thee smile again."

╾╅╾╅╾╅╾╅╾╅ GUINEVERE ╾╅╾╅╾╅╾╅╾╅

Queen Guinevere had fled the court, and sat
There in the holy house at Almesbury
Weeping, none with her save a little maid,
A novice. One low light betwixt them burn'd
Blurr'd by the creeping mist, for all abroad,
Beneath a moon unseen albeit at full,

The white mist, like a face-cloth to the face,
Clung to the dead earth, and the land was still.

For hither had she fled, her cause of flight
Sir Modred; he that like a subtle beast
Lay couchant with his eyes upon the throne,
Ready to spring, waiting a chance. For this
He chill'd the popular praises of the King
With silent smiles of slow disparagement;
And tamper'd with the Lords of the White Horse,
Heathen, the brood by Hengist left; and sought
To make disruption in the Table Round
Of Arthur, and to splinter it into feuds
Serving his traitorous end; and all his aims
Were sharpen'd by strong hate for Lancelot.

For thus it chanced one morn when all the court,
Green-suited, but with plumes that mock'd the may,
Had been—their wont—a-maying and return'd,
That Modred still in green, all ear and eye,
Climb'd to the high top of the garden-wall
To spy some secret scandal if he might,
And saw the Queen who sat betwixt her best
Enid and lissome Vivien, of her court
The wiliest and the worst; and more than this
He saw not, for Sir Lancelot passing by
Spied where he couch'd, and as the gardener's hand
Picks from the colewort a green caterpillar,
So from the high wall and the flowering grove
Of grasses Lancelot pluck'd him by the heel,
And cast him as a worm upon the way;
But when he knew the prince tho' marr'd with dust,
He, reverencing king's blood in a bad man,
Made such excuses as he might, and these
Full knightly without scorn. For in those days
No knight of Arthur's noblest dealt in scorn;
But, if a man were halt, or hunch'd, in him
By those whom God had made full-limb'd and tall,
Scorn was allow'd as part of his defect,
And he was answer'd softly by the King
And all his Table. So Sir Lancelot holp
To raise the prince, who rising twice or thrice
Full sharply smote his knees, and smiled, and went;
But, ever after, the small violence done
Rankled in him and ruffled all his heart,

As the sharp wind that ruffles all day long
A little bitter pool about a stone
On the bare coast.

                    But when Sir Lancelot told
This matter to the Queen, at first she laugh'd
Lightly, to think of Modred's dusty fall,
Then shudder'd, as the village wife who cries,
"I shudder, some one steps across my grave;"
Then laugh'd again, but faintlier, for indeed
She half-foresaw that he, the subtle beast,
Would track her guilt until he found, and hers
Would be for evermore a name of scorn.
Henceforward rarely could she front in hall
Or elsewhere, Modred's narrow foxy face,
Heart-hiding smile and gray persistent eye.
Henceforward too, the Powers that tend the soul,
To help it from the death that cannot die,
And save it even in extremes, began
To vex and plague her. Many a time for hours,
Beside the placid breathings of the King,
In the dead night, grim faces came and went
Before her, or a vague spiritual fear—
Like to some doubtful noise of creaking doors,
Heard by the watcher in a haunted house,
That keeps the rust of murder on the walls—
Held her awake; or if she slept she dream'd
An awful dream, for then she seem'd to stand
On some vast plain before a setting sun,
And from the sun there swiftly made at her
A ghastly something, and its shadow flew
Before it till it touch'd her, and she turn'd—
When lo! her own, that broadening from her feet,
And blackening, swallow'd all the land, and in it
Far cities burnt, and with a cry she woke.
And all this trouble did not pass but grew,
Till even the clear face of the guileless King,
And trustful courtesies of household life,
Became her bane; and at the last she said:
"O Lancelot, get thee hence to thine own land,
For if thou tarry we shall meet again,
And if we meet again some evil chance
Will make the smouldering scandal break and blaze
Before the people and our lord the King."

And Lancelot ever promised, but remain'd,
And still they met and met. Again she said,
"O Lancelot, if thou love me get thee hence."
And then they were agreed upon a night—
When the good King should not be there—to meet
And part for ever. Vivien, lurking, heard.
She told Sir Modred. Passion-pale they met
And greeted. Hands in hands, and eye to eye,
Low on the border of her couch they sat
Stammering and staring. It was their last hour,
A madness of farewells. And Modred brought
His creatures to the basement of the tower
For testimony; and crying with full voice,
"Traitor, come out, ye are trapt at last," aroused
Lancelot, who rushing outward lion-like
Leapt on him, and hurl'd him headlong, and he fell
Stunn'd, and his creatures took and bare him off,
And all was still. Then she, "The end is come,
And I am shamed for ever;" and he said:
"Mine be the shame, mine was the sin; but rise,
And fly to my strong castle over-seas.
There will I hide thee till my life shall end,
There hold thee with my life against the world."
She answer'd: "Lancelot, wilt thou hold me so?
Nay, friend, for we have taken our farewells.
Would God that thou couldst hide me from myself!
Mine is the shame, for I was wife, and thou
Unwedded; yet rise now, and let us fly,
For I will draw me into sanctuary,
And bide my doom." So Lancelot got her horse,
Set her thereon, and mounted on his own,
And then they rode to the divided way,
There kiss'd, and parted weeping; for he past,
Love-loyal to the least wish of the Queen,
Back to his land; but she to Almesbury
Fled all night long by glimmering waste and weald,
And heard the spirits of the waste and weald,
Moan as she fled, or thought she heard them moan.
And in herself she moan'd, "Too late, too late!"
Till in the cold wind that foreruns the morn,
A blot in heaven, the raven, flying high,
Croak'd, and she thought, "He spies a field of death;
For now the heathen of the Northern Sea,

Lured by the crimes and frailties of the court,
Begin to slay the folk and spoil the land."

And when she came to Almesbury she spake
There to the nuns, and said, "Mine enemies
Pursue me, but O peaceful Sisterhood,
Receive and yield me sanctuary, nor ask
Her name to whom ye yield it till her time
To tell you;" and her beauty, grace, and power
Wrought as a charm upon them, and they spared
To ask it.

      So the stately Queen abode
For many a week, unknown, among the nuns,
Nor with them mix'd, nor told her name, nor sought,
Wrapt in her grief, for housel or for shrift,
But communed only with the little maid,
Who pleased her with a babbling heedlessness
Which often lured her from herself; but now,
This night, a rumor wildly blown about
Came that Sir Modred had usurp'd the realm
And leagued him with the heathen, while the King
Was waging war on Lancelot. Then she thought,
"With what a hate the people and the King
Must hate me," and bow'd down upon her hands
Silent, until the little maid, who brook'd
No silence, brake it, uttering "Late! so late!
What hour, I wonder now?" and when she drew
No answer, by and by began to hum
An air the nuns had taught her: "Late, so late!"
Which when she heard, the Queen look'd up, and said,
"O maiden, if indeed ye list to sing,
Sing, and unbind my heart that I may weep."
Whereat full willingly sang the little maid.

"Late, late, so late! and dark the night and chill!
Late, late, so late! but we can enter still.
Too late, too late! ye cannot enter now.

"No light had we; for that we do repent,
And learning this, the bridegroom will relent.
Too late, too late! ye cannot enter now.

"No light! so late! and dark and chill the night!
O, let us in, that we may find the light!
Too late, too late! ye cannot enter now.

"Have we not heard the bridegroom is so sweet?
O, let us in, tho' late, to kiss his feet!
No, no, too late! ye cannot enter now."

So sang the novice, while full passionately,
Her head upon her hands, remembering
Her thought when first she came, wept the sad Queen.
Then said the little novice prattling to her:

"O pray you, noble lady, weep no more;
But let my words—the words of one so small,
Who knowing nothing knows but to obey,
And if I do not there is penance given—
Comfort your sorrows, for they do not flow
From evil done; right sure am I of that,
Who see your tender grace and stateliness.
But weigh your sorrows with our lord the King's,
And weighing find them less; for gone is he
To wage grim war against Sir Lancelot there,
Round that strong castle where he holds the Queen;
And Modred whom he left in charge of all,
The traitor—Ah, sweet lady, the King's grief
For his own self, and his own Queen, and realm,
Must needs be thrice as great as any of ours!
For me, I thank the saints, I am not great;
For if there ever come a grief to me
I cry my cry in silence, and have done;
None knows it, and my tears have brought me good.
But even were the griefs of little ones
As great as those of great ones, yet this grief
Is added to the griefs the great must bear,
That, howsoever much they may desire
Silence, they cannot weep behind a cloud;
As even here they talk at Almesbury
About the good King and his wicked Queen,
And were I such a King with such a Queen,
Well might I wish to veil her wickedness,
But were I such a King it could not be."

Then to her own sad heart mutter'd the Queen,
"Will the child kill me with her innocent talk?"
But openly she answered, "Must not I,
If this false traitor have displaced his lord,
Grieve with the common grief of all the realm?"

"Yea," said the maid, "this all is woman's grief,
That *she* is woman, whose disloyal life
Hath wrought confusion in the Table Round
Which good King Arthur founded, years ago,
With signs and miracles and wonders, there
At Camelot, ere the coming of the Queen."

Then thought the Queen within herself again,
"Will the child kill me with her foolish prate?"
But openly she spake and said to her,
"O little maid, shut in by nunnery walls,
What canst thou know of Kings and Tables Round,
Or what of signs and wonders, but the signs
And simple miracles of thy nunnery?"

To whom the little novice garrulously:
"Yea, but I know; the land was full of signs
And wonders ere the coming of the Queen.
So said my father, and himself was knight
Of the great Table—at the founding of it,
And rode thereto from Lyonnese; and he said
That as he rode, an hour or maybe twain
After the sunset, down the coast, he heard
Strange music, and he paused, and turning—there,
All down the lonely coast of Lyonnesse,
Each with a beacon-star upon his head,
And with a wild sea-light about his feet,
He saw them—headland after headland flame
Far on into the rich heart of the west.
And in the light the white mermaiden swam,
And strong man-breasted things stood from the sea,
And sent a deep sea-voice thro' all the land,
To which the little elves of chasm and cleft
Made answer, sounding like a distant horn.
So said my father—yea, and furthermore,
Next morning, while he past the dimlit woods
Himself beheld three spirits mad with joy
Come dashing down on a tall wayside flower,
That shook beneath them as the thistle shakes
When three gray linnets wrangle for the seed.
And still at evenings on before his horse
The flickering fairy-circle wheel'd and broke
Flying, and link'd again, and wheel'd and broke
Flying, for all the land was full of life.

And when at last he came to Camelot,
A wreath of airy dancers hand-in-hand
Swung round the lighted lantern of the hall;
And in the hall itself was such a feast
As never man had dream'd; for every knight
Had whatsoever meat he long'd for served
By hands unseen; and even as he said
Down in the cellars merry bloated things
Shoulder'd the spigot, straddling on the butts
While the wine ran; so glad were spirits and men
Before the coming of the sinful Queen."

Then spake the Queen and somewhat bitterly,
"Were they so glad? ill prophets were they all,
Spirits and men. Could none of them foresee,
Not even thy wise father with his signs
And wonders, what has fallen upon the realm?"

To whom the novice garrulously again:
"Yea, one, a bard, of whom my father said,
Full many a noble war-song had he sung,
Even in the presence of an enemy's fleet,
Between the steep cliff and the coming wave;
And many a mystic lay of life and death
Had chanted on the smoky mountain-tops,
When round him bent the spirits of the hills
With all their dewy hair blown back like flame.
So said my father—and that night the bard
Sang Arthur's glorious wars, and sang the King
As wellnigh more than man, and rail'd at those
Who call'd him the false son of Gorloïs.
For there was no man knew from whence he came;
But after tempest, when the long wave broke
All down the thundering shores of Bude and Bos,
There came a day as still as heaven, and then
They found a naked child upon the sands
Of dark Tintagil by the Cornish sea,
And that was Arthur, and they foster'd him
Till he by miracle was approven King;
And that his grave should be a mystery
From all men, like his birth; and could he find
A woman in her womanhood as great
As he was in his manhood, then, he sang,
The twain together well might change the world.
But even in the middle of his song

He falter'd, and his hand fell from the harp,
And pale he turn'd, and reel'd, and would have fallen,
But that they stay'd him up; nor would he tell
His vision; but what doubt that he foresaw
This evil work of Lancelot and the Queen?"

Then thought the Queen, "Lo! they have set her on,
Our simple-seeming abbess and her nuns,
To play upon me," and bow'd her head nor spake.
Whereat the novice crying, with clasp'd hands,
Shame on her own garrulity garrulously,
Said the good nuns would check her gadding tongue
Full often, "and, sweet lady, if I seem
To vex an ear too sad to listen to me,
Unmannerly, with prattling and the tales
Which my good father told me, check me too
Nor let me shame my father's memory, one
Of noblest manners, tho' himself would say
Sir Lancelot had the noblest; and he died,
Kill'd in a tilt, come next, five summers back,
And left me; but of others who remain,
And of the two first-famed for courtesy—
And pray you check me if I ask amiss—
But pray you, which had noblest, while you moved
Among them, Lancelot or our lord the King?"

Then the pale Queen look'd up and answer'd her:
"Sir Lancelot, as became a noble knight,
Was gracious to all ladies, and the same
In open battle or the tilting-field
Forbore his own advantage, and the King
In open battle or the tilting-field
Forbore his own advantage, and these two
Were the most nobly-manner'd men of all;
For manners are not idle, but the fruit
Of loyal nature and of noble mind."

"Yea," said the maid, "be manners such fair fruit?
Then Lancelot's needs must be a thousand-fold
Less noble, being, as all rumor runs,
The most disloyal friend in all the world."

To which a mournful answer made the Queen:
"O, closed about by narrowing nunnery-walls,
What knowest thou of the world and all its lights
And shadows, all the wealth and all the woe?

If ever Lancelot, that most noble knight,
Were for one hour less noble than himself,
Pray for him that he scape the doom of fire,
And weep for her who drew him to his doom."

"Yea," said the little novice, "I pray for both;
But I should all as soon believe that his,
Sir Lancelot's, were as noble as the King's,
As I could think, sweet lady, yours would be
Such as they are, were you the sinful Queen."

So she, like many another babbler, hurt
Whom she would soothe, and harm'd where she would heal;
For here a sudden flush of wrathful heat
Fired all the pale face of the Queen, who cried:
"Such as thou art be never maiden more
For ever! thou their tool, set on to plague
And play upon and harry me, petty spy
And traitress!" When that storm of anger brake
From Guinevere, aghast the maiden rose,
White as her veil, and stood before the Queen
As tremulously as foam upon the beach
Stands in a wind, ready to break and fly,
And when the Queen had added, "Get thee hence!"
Fled frightened. Then that other left alone
Sigh'd, and began to gather heart again,
Saying in herself: "The simple, fearful child
Meant nothing, but my own too-fearful guilt,
Simpler than any child, betrays itself.
But help me, Heaven, for surely I repent!
For what is true repentance but in thought—
Not even in inmost thought to think again
The sins that made the past so pleasant to us?
And I have sworn never to see him more,
To see him more."

And even in saying this,
Her memory from old habit of the mind
Went slipping back upon the golden days
In which she saw him first, when Lancelot came,
Reputed the best knight and goodliest man,
Ambassador, to lead her to his lord
Arthur, and led her forth, and far ahead
Of his and her retinue moving, they,
Rapt in sweet talk or lively, all on love

And sport and tilts and pleasure,—for the time
Was may-time, and as yet no sin was dream'd,—
Rode under groves that look'd a paradise
Of blossom, over sheets of hyacinth
That seem'd the heavens upbreaking thro' the earth,
And on from hill to hill, and every day
Beheld at noon in some delicious dale
The silk pavilions of King Arthur raised
For brief repast or afternoon repose
By couriers gone before; and on again,
Till yet once more ere set of sun they saw
The Dragon of the great Pendragon-ship
That crown'd the state pavilion of the King,
Blaze by the rushing brook or silent well.

But when the Queen immersed in such a trance,
And moving thro' the past unconsciously,
Came to that point where first she saw the King
Ride toward her from the city, sigh'd to find
Her journey done, glanced at him, thought him cold,
High, self-contain'd, and passionless, not like him,
"Not like my Lancelot"—while she brooded thus
And grew half-guilty in her thoughts again,
There rode an armed warrior to the doors.
A murmuring whisper thro' the nunnery ran,
Then on a sudden a cry, "The King!" She sat
Stiff-stricken, listening; but when armed feet
Thro' the long gallery from the outer doors
Rang coming, prone from off her seat she fell,
And grovell'd with her face against the floor.
There with her milk-white arms and shadowy hair
She made her face a darkness from the King,
And in the darkness heard his armed feet
Pause by her; then came silence, then a voice,
Monotonous and hollow like a ghost's
Denouncing judgment, but, tho' changed, the King's:

"Liest thou here so low, the child of one
I honor'd, happy, dead before thy shame?
Well is it that no child is born of thee.
The children born of thee are sword and fire,
Red ruin, and the breaking up of laws,
The craft of kindred and the godless hosts
Of heathen swarming o'er the Northern Sea;
Whom I, while yet Sir Lancelot, my right arm,

The mightiest of my knights, abode with me,
Have everywhere about this land of Christ
In twelve great battles ruining overthrown.
And knowest thou now from whence I come—from him,
From waging bitter war with him; and he,
That did not shun to smite me in worse way,
Had yet that grace of courtesy in him left,
He spared to lift his hand against the King
Who made him knight. But many a knight was slain;
And many more and all his kith and kin
Clave to him, and abode in his own land.
And many more when Modred raised revolt,
Forgetful of their troth and fealty, clave
To Modred, and a remnant stays with me.
And of this remnant will I leave a part,
True men who love me still, for whom I live,
To guard thee in the wild hour coming on,
Lest but a hair of this low head be harm'd.
Fear not; thou shalt be guarded till my death.
Howbeit I know, if ancient prophecies
Have err'd not, that I march to meet my doom.
Thou hast not made my life so sweet to me,
That I the King should greatly care to live;
For thou hast spoilt the purpose of my life.
Bear with me for the last time while I show,
Even for thy sake, the sin which thou hast sinn'd.
For when the Roman left us, and their law
Relax'd its hold upon us, and the ways
Were fill'd with rapine, here and there a deed
Of prowess done redress'd a random wrong.
But I was first of all the kings who drew
The knighthood-errant of this realm and all
The realms together under me, their Head,
In that fair Order of my Table Round,
A glorious company, the flower of men,
To serve as model for the mighty world,
And be the fair beginning of a time.
I made them lay their hands in mine and swear
To reverence the King, as if he were
Their conscience, and their conscience as their King,
To break the heathen and uphold the Christ,
To ride abroad redressing human wrongs,
To speak no slander, no, nor listen to it,
To honor his own word as if his God's,

To lead sweet lives in purest chastity,
To love one maiden only, cleave to her,
And worship her by years of noble deeds,
Until they won her; for indeed I knew
Of no more subtle master under heaven
Than is the maiden passion for a maid,
Not only to keep down the base in man,
But teach high thought, and amiable words
And courtliness, and the desire of fame,
And love of truth, and all that makes a man.
And all this throve before I wedded thee,
Believing, 'Lo, mine helpmate, one to feel
My purpose and rejoicing in my joy!'
Then came thy shameful sin with Lancelot;
Then came the sin of Tristram and Isolt;
Then others, following these my mightiest knights,
And drawing foul ensample from fair names,
Sinn'd also, till the loathsome opposite
Of all my heart had destined did obtain,
And all thro' thee! so that this life of mine
I guard as God's high gift from scathe and wrong,
Not greatly care to lose; but rather think
How sad it were for Arthur, should he live,
To sit once more within his lonely hall,
And miss the wonted number of my knights,
And miss to hear high talk of noble deeds
As in the golden days before thy sin.
For which of us who might be left could speak
Of the pure heart, nor seem to glance at thee?
And in thy bowers of Camelot or of Usk
Thy shadow still would glide from room to room,
And I should evermore be vext with thee
In hanging robe or vacant ornament,
Or ghostly footfall echoing on the stair.
For think not, tho' thou wouldst not love thy lord,
Thy lord has wholly lost his love for thee.
I am not made of so slight elements.
Yet must I leave thee, woman, to thy shame.
I hold that man the worst of public foes
Who either for his own or children's sake,
To save his blood from scandal, lets the wife
Whom he knows false abide and rule the house:
For being thro' his cowardice allow'd
Her station, taken everywhere for pure,

She like a new disease, unknown to men,
Creeps, no precaution used, among the crowd,
Makes wicked lightnings of her eyes, and saps
The fealty of our friends, and stirs the pulse
With devil's leaps, and poisons half the young.
Worst of the worst were that man he that reigns!
Better the King's waste hearth and aching heart
Than thou reseated in thy place of light,
The mockery of my people and their bane!"

He paused, and in the pause she crept an inch
Nearer, and laid her hands about his feet.
Far off a solitary trumpet blew.
Then waiting by the doors the war-horse neigh'd
As at a friend's voice, and he spake again:

"Yet think not that I come to urge thy crimes;
I did not come to curse thee, Guinevere,
I, whose vast pity almost makes me die
To see thee, laying there thy golden head,
My pride in happier summers, at my feet.
The wrath which forced my thoughts on that fierce law,
The doom of treason and the flaming death,—
When first I learnt thee hidden here,—is past.
The pang—which, while I weigh'd thy heart with one
Too wholly true to dream untruth in thee,
Made my tears burn—is also past—in part.
And all is past, the sin is sinn'd, and I,
Lo, I forgive thee, as Eternal God
Forgives! do thou for thine own soul the rest.
But how to take last leave of all I loved?
O golden hair, with which I used to play
Not knowing! O imperial-moulded form,
And beauty such as never woman wore,
Until it came a kingdom's curse with thee—
I cannot touch thy lips, they are not mine,
But Lancelot's; nay, they never were the King's.
I cannot take thy hand; that too is flesh,
And in the flesh thou hast sinn'd; and mine own flesh,
Here looking down on thine polluted, cries,
'I loathe thee;' yet not less, O Guinevere,
For I was ever virgin save for thee,
My love thro' flesh hath wrought into my life
So far that my doom is, I love thee still.
Let no man dream but that I love thee still.

Perchance, and so thou purify thy soul,
And so thou lean on our fair father Christ,
Hereafter in that world where all are pure
We two may meet before high God, and thou
Wilt spring to me, and claim me thine, and know
I am thine husband—not a smaller soul,
Nor Lancelot, nor another. Leave me that,
I charge thee, my last hope. Now must I hence.
Thro' the thick night I hear the trumpet blow.
They summon me their King to lead mine hosts
Far down to that great battle in the west,
Where I must strike against the man they call
My sister's son—no kin of mine, who leagues
With Lords of the White House, heathen, and knights,
Traitors—and strike him dead, and meet myself
Death, or I know not what mysterious doom.
And thou remaining here wilt learn the event;
But hither shall I never come again,
Never lie by thy side, see thee no more—
Farewell!"

      And while she grovell'd at his feet,
She felt the King's breath wander o'er her neck,
And in the darkness o'er her fallen head
Perceived the waving of his hands that blest.

      Then, listening till those armed steps were gone,
Rose the pale Queen, and in her anguish found
The casement: "peradventure," so she thought,
"If I might see his face, and not be seen."
And lo, he sat on horseback at the door!
And near him the sad nuns with each a light
Stood, and he gave them charge about the Queen,
To guard and foster her for evermore.
And while he spake to these his helm was lower'd,
To which for crest the golden dragon clung
Of Britain; so she did not see the face,
Which then was as an angel's but she saw,
Wet with the mists and smitten by the lights,
The Dragon of the great Pendragon-ship
Blaze, making all the night a steam of fire.
And even then he turn'd; and more and more
The moony vapor rolling round the King,
Who seem'd the phantom of a giant in it,
Enwound him fold by fold, and made him gray

And grayer, till himself became as mist
Before her, moving ghostlike to his doom.

    Then she stretch'd out her arms and cried aloud,
"O Arthur!" there her voice brake suddenly,
Then—as a stream that spouting from a cliff
Fails in mid air, but gathering at the base
Re-makes itself, and flashes down the vale—
Went on in passionate utterance:

               "Gone—my lord!
Gone thro' my sin to slay and to be slain!
And he forgave me, and I could not speak.
Farewell? I should have answer'd his farewell.
His mercy choked me. Gone, my lord the King,
My own true lord! how dare I call him mine?
The shadow of another cleaves to me,
And makes me one pollution. He, the King,
Call'd me polluted. Shall I kill myself?
What help in that? I cannot kill my sin,
If soul be soul, nor can I kill my shame;
No, nor by living can I live it down.
The days will grow to weeks, the weeks to months,
The months will add themselves and make the years,
The years will roll into the centuries,
And mine will ever be a name of scorn.
I must not dwell on that defeat of fame.
Let the world be; that is but of the world—
What else? what hope? I think there was a hope,
Except he mock'd me when he spake of hope;
His hope he call'd it; but he never mocks,
For mockery is the fume of little hearts.
And blessed be the King, who hath forgiven
My wickedness to him, and left me hope
That in mine own heart I can live down sin
And be his mate hereafter in the heavens
Before high God! Ah great and gentle lord,
Who wast, as is the conscience of a saint
Among his warring senses, to thy knights—
To whom my false voluptuous pride, that took
Full easily all impressions from below,
Would not look up, or half-despised the height
To which I would not or I could not climb—
I thought I could not breathe in that fine air,
That pure severity of perfect light—
I yearn'd for warmth and color which I found

In Lancelot—now I see thee what thou art,
Thou art the highest and most human too,
Not Lancelot, nor another. Is there none
Will tell the King I love him tho' so late?
Now—ere he goes to the great battle? none!
Myself must tell him in that purer life,
But now it were too daring. Ah my God,
What might I not have made of thy fair world,
Had I but loved thy highest creature here?
It was my duty to have loved the highest;
It surely was my profit had I known;
It would have been my pleasure had I seen.
We needs must love the highest when we see it,
Not Lancelot, nor another."

                   Here her hand
Grasp'd made her vail her eyes. She look'd and saw
The novice, weeping, suppliant, and said to her,
"Yea, little maid, for am I not forgiven?"
Then glancing up beheld the holy nuns
All round her, weeping; and her heart was loosed
Within her, and she wept with these and said:

   "Ye know me then, that wicked one, who broke
The vast design and purpose of the King.
O, shut me round with narrowing nunnery-walls,
Meek maidens, from the voices crying, 'Shame!'
I must not scorn myself; he loves me still.
Let no one dream but that he loves me still.
So let me, if you do not shudder at me,
Nor shun to call me sister, dwell with you;
Wear black and white, and be a nun like you,
Fast with your fasts, not feasting with your feasts;
Grieve with your griefs, not grieving at your joys,
But not rejoicing; mingle with your rites;
Pray and be pray'd for; lie before your shrines;
Do each low office of your holy house;
Walk your dim cloister, and distribute dole
To poor sick people, richer in His eyes
Who ransom'd us, and haler too than I;
And treat their loathsome hurts and heal mine own;
And so wear out in alms-deed and in prayer
The sombre close of that voluptuous day
Which wrought the ruin of my lord the King."

She said. They took her to themselves; and she
Still hoping, fearing "Is it yet too late?"
Dwelt with them, till in time their abbess died.
Then she, for her good deeds and her pure life,
And for the power of ministration in her,
And likewise for the high rank she had borne,
Was chosen abbess, there, an abbess, lived
For three brief years, and there, an abbess, past
To where beyond these voices there is peace.

The Passing of Arthur

❖❖❖❖❖❖❖❖❖❖❖❖❖❖❖❖❖❖❖❖❖❖❖❖❖❖❖❖❖

THAT story which the bold Sir Bedivere,
First made and latest left of all the knights,
Told, when the man was no more than a voice
In the white winter of his age, to those
With whom he dwelt, new faces, other minds.

For on their march to westward, Bedivere,
Who slowly paced among the slumbering host,
Heard in his tent the moanings of the King:

"I found Him in the shining of the stars,
I mark'd Him in the flowering of His fields,
But in His ways with men I find Him not.
I waged His wars, and now I pass and die.
O me! for why is all around us here
As if some lesser god had made the world,
But had not force to shape it as he would,
Till the High God behold it from beyond,
And enter it, and make it beautiful?
Or else as if the world were wholly fair,
But that these eyes of men are dense and dim,
And have not power to see it as it is—
Perchance, because we see not to the close;—
For I, being simple, thought to work His will,
And have but stricken with the sword in vain,
And all whereon I lean'd in wife and friend
Is traitor to my peace, and all my realm
Reels back into the beast, and is no more.
My God, thou hast forgotten me in my death!
Nay—God my Christ—I pass but shall not die."

Then, ere that last weird battle in the west,
There came on Arthur sleeping, Gawain kill'd
In Lancelot's war, the ghost of Gawain blown
Along a wandering wind, and past his ear
Went shrilling: "Hollow, hollow all delight!
Hail, King! to-morrow thou shalt pass away.

Farewell! there is an isle of rest for thee.
And I am blown along a wandering wind,
And hollow, hollow, hollow all delight!"
And fainter onward, like wild birds that change
Their season in the night and wail their way
From cloud to cloud, down the long wind the dream
Shrill'd; but in going mingled with dim cries
Far in the moonlit haze among the hills,
As of some lonely city sack'd by night,
When all is lost, and wife and child with wail
Pass to new lords; and Arthur woke and call'd:
"Who spake? A dream. O, light upon the wind,
Thine, Gawain, was the voice—are these dim cries
Thine? or doth all that haunts the waste and wild
Mourn, knowing it will go along with me?"

This heard the bold Sir Bedivere and spake:
"O me, my King, let pass whatever will,
Elves, and the harmless glamour of the field;
But in their stead thy name and glory cling
To all high places like a golden cloud
For ever; but as yet thou shalt not pass.
Light was Gawain in life, and light in death
Is Gawain, for the ghost is as the man;
And care not thou for dreams from him, but rise—
I hear the steps of Modred in the west,
And with him many of thy people, and knights
Once thine, whom thou hast loved, but grosser grown
Than heathen, spitting at their vows and thee.
Right well in heart they know thee for the King.
Arise, go forth and conquer as of old."

Then spake King Arthur to Sir Bedivere:
"Far other is this battle in the west
Whereto we move than when we strove in youth,
And brake the petty kings, and fought with Rome,
Or thrust the heathen from the Roman wall,
And shook him thro' the north. Ill doom is mine
To war against my people and my knights.
The king who fights his people fights himself.
And they my knights, who loved me once, the stroke
That strikes them dead is as my death to me.
Yet let us hence, and find or feel a way
Thro' this blind haze which, ever since I saw
One lying in the dust at Almesbury,
Hath folded in the passes of the world."

Then rose the King and moved his host by night,
And ever push'd Sir Modred, league by league,
Back to the sunset bound of Lyonnesse—
A land of old upheaven from the abyss
By fire, to sink into the abyss again;
Where fragments of forgotten peoples dwelt,
And the long mountains ended in a coast
Of ever-shifting sand, and far away
The phantom circle of a moaning sea.
There the pursuer could pursue no more,
And he that fled no further fly the King;
And there, that day when the great light of heaven
Burn'd at his lowest in the rolling year,
On the waste sand by the waste sea they closed.
Nor ever yet had Arthur fought a fight
Like this last, dim, weird battle of the west.
A death-white mist slept over sand and sea,
Whereof the chill, to him who breathed it, drew
Down with his blood, till all his heart was cold
With formless fear; and even on Arthur fell
Confusion, since he saw not whom he fought.
For friend and foe were shadows in the mist,
And friend slew friend not knowing whom he slew;
And some had visions out of golden youth,
And some beheld the faces of old ghosts
Look in upon the battle; and in the mist
Was many a noble deed, many a base,
And chance and craft and strength in single fights,
And ever and anon with host to host
Shocks, and the splintering spear, the hard mail hewn,
Shield-breakings, and the clash of brands, the crash
Of battle-axes on shatter'd helms, and shrieks
After the Christ, of those who falling down
Look'd up for heaven, and only saw the mist;
And shouts of heathen and the traitor knights,
Oaths, insult, filth, and monstrous blasphemies,
Sweat, writhings, anguish, laboring of the lungs
In that close mist, and cryings for the light,
Moans of the dying, and voices of the dead.

Last, as by some one death-bed after wail
Of suffering, silence follows, or thro' death
Or death-like swoon, thus over all that shore,
Save for some whisper of the seething seas,
A dead hush fell; but when the dolorous day
Grew drearier toward twilight falling, came

A bitter wind, clear from the north, and blew
The mist aside, and with that wind the tide
Rose, and the pale King glanced across the field
Of battle. But no man was moving there;
Nor any cry of Christian heard thereon,
Nor yet of heathen; only the wan wave
Brake in among dead faces, to and fro
Swaying the helpless hands, and up and down
Tumbling the hollow helmets of the fallen,
And shiver'd brands that once had fought with Rome,
And rolling far along the gloomy shores
The voice of days of old and days to be.

Then spake King Arthur to Sir Bedivere,
And whiter than the mist that all day long
Had held the field of battle was the King:

"Hearest thou this great voice that shakes the world,
And wastes the narrow realm whereon we move,
And beats upon the faces of the dead,
My dead, as tho' they had not died for me?—
O Bedivere, for on my heart hath fallen
Confusion, till I know not what I am,
Nor whence I am, nor whether I be king;
Behold, I seem but king among the dead."

Then spake the bold Sir Bedivere: "My King!
King everywhere! and so the dead have kings,
There also will I worship thee as king.
Yet still thy life is whole, and still I live
Who love thee; but who hates thee, he that brought
The heathen back among us, yonder stands,
Modred, unharm'd the traitor of thine house."

Then spake the King: "My house hath been my doom.
But call not thou this traitor of my house
Who hath but dwelt beneath one roof with me.
My house are rather they who sware my vows,
Yea, even while they brake them, own'd me king.
And well for thee, saying in my dark hour,
When all the purport of my throne hath fail'd,
That quick or dead thou holdest me for king.
King am I, whatsoever be their cry;
And one last act of kinghood shalt thou see
Yet, ere I pass." And uttering this the King
Made at the man. Then Modred smote his liege
Hard on that helm which many a heathen sword

Had beaten thin; while Arthur at one blow,
Striking the last stroke with Excalibur,
Slew him, and, all but slain himself, he fell.

So all day long the noise of battle roll'd
Among the mountains by the winter sea,
Until King Arthur's Table, man by man,
Had fallen in Lyonnesse about their lord,
King Arthur; then, because his wound was deep,
The bold Sir Bedivere uplifted him,
And bore him to a chapel nigh the field,
A broken chancel with a broken cross,
That stood on a dark strait of barren land.
On one side lay the Ocean, and on one
Lay a great water, and the moon was full.

Then spake King Arthur to Sir Bedivere:
"The sequel of to-day unsolders all
The goodliest fellowship of famous knights
Whereof this world holds record. Such a sleep
They sleep—the men I loved. I think that we
Shall never more, at any future time,
Delight our souls with talk of knightly deeds,
Walking about the gardens and the halls
Of Camelot, as in the days that were.
I perish by this people which I made,—
Tho' Merlin sware that I should come again
To rule once more—but let what will be be,
I am so deeply smitten thro' the helm
That without help I cannot last till morn.
Thou therefore take my brand Excalibur,
Which was my pride; for thou rememberest how
In those old days, one summer noon, an arm
Rose up from out the bosom of the lake,
Clothed in white samite, mystic, wonderful,
Holding the sword—and how I row'd across
And took it, and have worn it, like a king;
And, wheresoever I am sung or told
In aftertime, this also shall be known.
But now delay not; take Excalibur,
And fling him far into the middle mere;
Watch what thou seest, and lightly bring me word."

To him replied the bold Sir Bedivere:
"It is not meet, Sir King, to leave thee thus,
Aidless, alone, and smitten thro' the helm—
A little thing may harm a wounded man;

Yet I thy hest will all perform at full,
Watch what I see, and lightly bring thee word."

So saying, from the ruin'd shrine he stept,
And in the moon athwart the place of tombs,
Where lay the mighty bones of ancient men,
Old knights, and over them the sea-wind sang
Shrill, chill, with flakes of foam. He, stepping down
By zigzag paths and juts of pointed rock,
Came on the shining levels of the lake.

There drew he forth the brand Excalibur,
And o'er him, drawing it, the winter moon,
Brightening the skirts of a long cloud, ran forth
And sparkled keen with frost against the hilt;
For all the haft twinkled with diamond sparks,
Myriads of topaz-lights, and jacinth-work
Of subtlest jewellery. He gazed so long
That both his eyes were dazzled as he stood,
This way and that dividing the swift mind,
In act to throw; but at last it seem'd
Better to leave Excalibur conceal'd
There in the many-knotted water-flags,
That whistled stiff and dry about the marge.
So strode he back slow to the wounded King.

Then spake King Arthur to Sir Bedivere:
"Hast thou perform'd my mission which I gave?
What is it thou hast seen? or what hast heard?"

And answer made the bold Sir Bedivere:
"I heard the ripple washing in the reeds,
And the wild water lapping on the crag."

To whom replied King Arthur, faint and pale:
"Thou hast betray'd thy nature and thy name,
Not rendering true answer, as beseem'd
Thy fealty, nor like a noble knight;
For surer sign had follow'd, either hand,
Or voice, or else a motion of the mere.
This is a shameful thing for men to lie.
Yet now, I charge thee, quickly go again,
As thou art lief and dear, and do the thing
I bade thee, watch, and lightly bring me word."

Then went Sir Bedivere the second time
Across the ridge, and paced beside the mere,
Counting the dewy pebbles, fixt in thought;

But when he saw the wonder of the hilt,
How curiously and strangely chased, he smote
His palms together, and he cried aloud:

"And if indeed I cast the brand away,
Surely a precious thing, one worthy note,
Should thus be lost for ever from the earth,
Which might have pleased the eyes of many men.
What good should follow this, if this were done?
What harm, undone? Deep harm to disobey,
Seeing obedience is the bond of rule.
Were it well to obey then, if a king demand
An act unprofitable, against himself?
The King is sick, and knows not what he does.
What record or what relic of my lord
Should be to aftertime, but empty breath
And rumors of a doubt? But were this kept,
Stored in some treasure-house of mighty kings,
Some one might show it at a joust of arms,
Saying: 'King Arthur's sword, Excalibur,
Wrought by the lonely Maiden of the Lake.
Nine years she wrought it, sitting in the deeps
Upon the hidden bases of the hills.'
So might some old man speak in the aftertime
To all the people, winning reverence.
But now much honor and much fame were lost."

So spake he, clouded with his own conceit,
And hid Excalibur the second time,
And so strode back slow to the wounded King.

Then spoke King Arthur, breathing heavily:
"What is it thou hast seen? or what hast heard?"

And answer made the bold Sir Bedivere:
"I heard the water lapping on the crag,
And the long ripple washing in the reeds."

To whom replied King Arthur, much in wrath:
"Ah miserable, and unkind, untrue,
Unknightly, traitor-hearted! Woe is me!
Authority forgets a dying king,
Laid widow'd of the power in his eye
That bow'd the will. I see thee what thou art,
For thou, the latest-left of all my knights,
In whom should meet the offices of all,
Thou wouldst betray me for the precious hilt;

Either from lust of gold, or like a girl
Valuing the giddy pleasure of the eyes.
Yet, for a man may fail in duty twice,
And the third time may prosper, get thee hence;
But, if thou spare to fling Excalibur,
I will arise and slay thee with my hands."

Then quickly rose Sir Bedivere, and ran,
And, leaping down the ridges lightly, plunged
Among the bulrush beds, and clutch'd the sword,
And strongly wheel'd and threw it. The great brand
Made lightnings in the splendor of the moon,
And flashing round and round, and whirl'd in an arch,
Shot like a streamer of the northern morn,
Seen where the moving isles of winter shock
By night, with noises of the Northern Sea.
So flash'd and fell the brand Excalibur;
But ere he dipt the surface, rose an arm
Clothed in white samite, mystic, wonderful,
And caught him by the hilt, and brandish'd him
Three times, and drew him under in the mere.
And lightly went the other to the King.

Then spoke King Arthur, drawing thicker breath:
"Now see I by thine eyes that this is done.
Speak out; what is it thou hast heard, or seen?"

And answer made the bold Sir Bedivere:
"Sir King, I closed mine eyelids, lest the gems
Should blind my purpose, for I never saw,
Nor shall see, here or elsewhere, till I die,
Not tho' I live three lives of mortal men,
So great a miracle as yonder hilt.
Then with both hands I flung him, wheeling him;
But when I look'd again, behold an arm,
Clothed in white samite, mystic, wonderful,
That caught him by the hilt, and brandish'd him
Three times, and drew him under in the mere."

And answer made King Arthur, breathing hard:
"My end draws nigh; 't is time that I were gone.
Make broad thy shoulders to receive my weight,
And bear me to the margin; yet I fear
My wound hath taken cold, and I shall die."

So saying, from the pavement he half rose,
Slowly, with pain, reclining on his arm,
And looking wistfully with wide blue eyes

As in a picture. Him Sir Bedivere
Remorsefully regarded thro' his tears,
And would have spoken, but he found not words;
Then took with care, and kneeling on one knee,
O'er both his shoulders drew the languid hands,
And rising bore him thro' the place of tombs.

But, as he walk'd, King Arthur panted hard,
Like one that feels a nightmare on his bed
When all the house is mute. So sigh'd the King,
Muttering and murmuring at his ear, "Quick, quick!
I fear it is too late, and I shall die."
But the other swiftly strode from ridge to ridge,
Clothed with his breath, and looking, as he walk'd,
Larger than human on the frozen hills.
He heard the deep behind him, and a cry
Before. His own thought drove him like a goad.
Dry clash'd his harness in the icy caves
And barren chasms, and all to left and right
The bare black cliff clang'd round him, as he based
His feet on juts of slippery crag that rang
Sharp-smitten with the dint of armed heels—
And on a sudden, lo, the level lake,
And the long glories of the winter moon!

Then saw they how there hove a dusky barge,
Dark as a funeral scarf from stem to stern,
Beneath them; and descending they were ware
That all the decks were dense with stately forms,
Black-stoled, black-hooded, like a dream—by these
Three queens with crowns of gold—and from them rose
A cry that shiver'd to the tingling stars,
And, as it were one voice, an agony
Of lamentation, like a wind that shrills
All night in a waste land, where no one comes,
Or hath come, since the making of the world.

Then murmur'd Arthur, "Place me in the barge."
So to the barge they came. There those three queens
Put forth their hands, and took the King, and wept.
But she that rose the tallest of them all
And fairest laid his head upon her lap,
And loosed the shatter'd casque, and chafed his hands,
And call'd him by his name, complaining loud,
And dropping bitter tears against a brow
Striped with dark blood; for all his face was white
And colorless, and like the wither'd moon

Smote by the fresh beam of the springing east;
And all his greaves and cuisses dash'd with drops
Of onset; and the light and lustrous curls—
That made his forehead like a rising sun
High from the dais-throne—were parch'd with dust,
Or, clotted into points and hanging loose,
Mixt with the knightly growth that fringed his lips.
So like a shatter'd column lay the King;
Not like that Arthur who, with lance in rest,
From spur to plume a star of tournament,
Shot thro' the lists at Camelot, and charged
Before the eyes of ladies and of kings.

Then loudly cried the bold Sir Bedivere:
"Ah! my Lord Arthur, whither shall I go?
Where shall I hide my forehead and my eyes?
For now I see the true old times are dead,
When every morning brought a noble chance,
And every chance brought out a noble knight.
Such times have been not since the light that led
The holy Elders with the gift of myrrh.
But now the whole Round Table is dissolved
Which was an image of the mighty world;
And I, the last, go forth companionless,
And the days darken round me, and the years,
Among new men, strange faces, other minds."

And slowly answer'd Arthur from the barge;
"The old order changeth, yielding place to new,
And God fulfils himself in many ways,
Lest one good custom should corrupt the world.
Comfort thyself; what comfort is in me?
I have lived my life, and that which I have done
May He within himself make pure! but thou,
If thou shouldst never see my face again,
Pray for my soul. More things are wrought by prayer
Than this world dreams of. Wherefore, let thy voice
Rise like a fountain for me night and day.
For what are men better than sheep or goats
That nourish a blind life within the brain,
If, knowing God, they lift not hands of prayer
Both for themselves and those who call them friend?
For so the whole round earth is every way
Bound by gold chains about the feet of God.
But now farewell. I am going a long way
With these thou seest—if indeed I go—

For all my mind is clouded with a doubt—
To the island-valley of Avilion;
Where falls not hail, or rain, or any snow,
Nor ever wind blows loudly; but it lies
Deep-meadow'd, happy, fair with orchard lawns
And bowery hollows crown'd with summer sea,
Where I will heal me of my grievous wound."

So said he, and the barge with oar and sail
Moved from the brink, like some full-breasted swan
That, fluting a wild carol ere her death,
Ruffles her pure cold plume, and takes the flood
With swarthy webs. Long stood Sir Bedivere
Revolving many memories, till the hull
Look'd one black dot against the verge of dawn,
And on the mere the wailing died away.

But when that moan had past for evermore,
The stillness of the dead world's winter dawn
Amazed him, and he groan'd, "The King is gone."
And therewithal came on him the weird rhyme,
"From the great deep to the great deep he goes."

Whereat he slowly turn'd and slowly clomb
The last hard footstep of that iron crag,
Thence mark'd the black hull moving yet, and cried:
"He passes to be king among the dead,
And after healing of his grievous wound
He comes again; but—if he come no more—
O me, be yon dark queens in yon black boat,
Who shriek'd and wail'd, the three whereat we gazed
On that high day, when, clothed with living light,
They stood before his throne in silence, friends
Of Arthur, who should help him at his need?"

Then from the dawn it seem'd there came, but faint
As from beyond the limit of the world,
Like the last echo born of a great cry,
Sounds, as if some fair city were one voice
Around a king returning from his wars.

Thereat once more he moved about, and clomb
Even to the highest he could climb, and saw,
Straining his eyes beneath an arch of hand,
Or thought he saw, the speck that bare the King,
Down that long water opening on the deep

Somewhere far off, pass on and on, and go
From less to less, and vanish into light,
And the new sun rose bringing the new year.

O LOYAL to the royal in thyself,
And loyal to thy land, as this to thee—
Bear witness, that rememberable day,
When, pale as yet and fever-worn, the Prince
Who scarce had pluck'd his flickering life again
From halfway down the shadow of the grave
Past with thee thro' thy people and their love,
And London roll'd one tide of joy thro' all
Her trebled millions, and loud leagues of man
And welcome! witness, too, the silent cry,
The prayer of many a race and creed, and clime—
Thunderless lightnings striking under sea
From sunset and sunrise of all thy realm,
And that true North, whereof we lately heard
A strain to shame us, "Keep you to yourselves;
So loyal is too costly! friends—your love
Is but a burthen; loose the bond, and go."
Is this the tone of empire? here the faith
That made us rulers? this, indeed, her voice
And meaning whom the roar of Hougoumont
Left mightiest of all peoples under heaven?
What shock has fool'd her since, that she should speak
So feebly? wealthier—wealthier—hour by hour!
The voice of Britain, or a sinking land,
Some third-rate isle half-lost among her seas?
There rang her voice, when the full city peal'd
Thee and thy Prince! The loyal to their crown
Are loyal to their own far sons, who love
Our ocean-empire with her boundless homes
For ever-broadening England, and her throne
In our vast Orient, and one isle, one isle,
That knows not her own greatness; if she knows
And dreads it we are fallen.—But thou, my Queen,
Not for itself, but thro' thy living love
For one to whom I made it o'er his grave
Sacred, accept this old imperfect tale,
New-old, and shadowing Sense at war with Soul,
Ideal manhood closed in real man,
Rather than that gray king whose name, a ghost,

Streams like a cloud, man-shaped from mountain peak,
And cleaves to cairn and cromlech still; or him
Of Geoffrey's book, or him of Malleor's, one
Touch'd by the adulterous finger of a time
That hover'd between war and wantonness,
And crownings and dethronements. Take withal
Thy poet's blessing, and his trust that Heaven
Will blow the tempest in the distance back
From thine and ours; for some are scared, who mark,
Or wisely or unwisely, signs of storm,
Waverings of every vane with every wind,
And wordy trucklings to the transient hour,
And fierce or careless looseners of the faith,
And Softness breeding scorn of simple life,
Or Cowardice, the child of lust for gold,
Or Labor, with a groan and not a voice,
Or Art with poisonous honey stolen from France,
And that which knows, but careful for itself,
And that which knows not, ruling that which knows
To its own harm. The goal of this great world
Lies beyond sight; yet—if our slowly-grown
And crown'd Republic's crowning common sense,
That saved her many times, not fail—their fears
Are morning shadows huger than the shapes
That cast them, not those gloomier which forego
The darkness of that battle in the west
Where all of high and holy dies away.

A SELECTION OF

Poems

CHOSEN BY OSCAR WILLIAMS

◆ ◆

THE KRAKEN

BELOW the thunders of the upper deep,
Far, far beneath in the abysmal sea,
His ancient, dreamless, uninvaded sleep,
The Kraken sleepeth: faintest sunlights flee
About his shadowy sides: above him swell
Huge sponges of millennial growth and height;
And far away into the sickly light,
From many a wondrous grot and secret cell
Unnumbered and enormous polypi
Winnow with giant fins the slumbering green.
There hath he lain for ages and will lie
Battening upon huge seaworms in his sleep,
Until the latter fire shall heat the deep;
Then once by man and angels to be seen,
In roaring he shall rise and on the surface die.

[publ. 1830]

MARIANA

"Mariana in the moated grange."
MEASURE FOR MEASURE.

WITH blackest moss the flower-plots
    Were thickly crusted, one and all;
The rusted nails fell from the knots

257

That held the pear to the gable-wall.
The broken sheds look'd sad and strange;
    Unlifted was the clinking latch;
    Weeded and worn the ancient thatch
Upon the lonely moated grange.
        She only said, "My life is dreary,
            He cometh not," she said;
        She said, "I am aweary, aweary,
            I would that I were dead!"

Her tears fell with the dews at even;
    Her tears fell ere the dews were dried;
She could not look on the sweet heaven,
    Either at morn or eventide.
After the flitting of the bats,
    When thickest dark did trance the sky,
    She drew her casement-curtain by,
And glanced athwart the glooming flats.
        She only said, "The night is dreary,
            He cometh not," she said;
        She said, "I am aweary, aweary,
            I would that I were dead!"

Upon the middle of the night,
    Waking she heard the night-fowl crow:
The cock sung out an hour ere light:
    From the dark fen the oxen's low
Came to her: without hope of change,
    In sleep she seem'd to walk forlorn,
    Till cold winds woke the gray-eyed morn
About the lonely moated grange.
        She only said, "The day is dreary,
            He cometh not," she said;
        She said, "I am aweary, aweary,
            I would that I were dead!"

About a stone-cast from the wall
    A sluice with blacken'd waters slept,
And o'er it many, round and small,
    The cluster'd marish-mosses crept.
Hard by a poplar shook alway,
    All silver-green with gnarled bark:
    For leagues no other tree did mark
The level waste, the rounding gray.
        She only said, "My life is dreary,
            He cometh not," she said;
        She said, "I am aweary, aweary,
            I would that I were dead!"

And ever when the moon was low,
   And the shrill winds were up and away,
In the white curtain, to and fro,
   She saw the gusty shadow sway.
But when the moon was very low,
   And wild winds bound within their cell,
   The shadow of the poplar fell
Upon her bed, across her brow.
     She only said, "The night is dreary,
       He cometh not," she said;
     She said, "I am aweary, aweary,
       I would that I were dead!"

All day within the dreamy house,
   The doors upon their hinges creak'd;
The blue fly sung in the pane; the mouse
   Behind the mouldering wainscot shriek'd,
Or from the crevice peer'd about.
   Old faces glimmer'd thro' the doors,
   Old footsteps trod the upper floors,
Old voices called her from without.
     She only said, "My life is dreary,
       He cometh not," she said;
     She said, "I am aweary, aweary,
       I would that I were dead!"

The sparrow's chirrup on the roof,
   The slow clock ticking, and the sound
Which to the wooing wind aloof
   The poplar made, did all confound
Her sense; but most she loathed the hour
   When the thick-moted sunbeam lay
   Athwart the chambers, and the day
Was sloping toward his western bower.
     Then, said she, "I am very dreary,
       He will not come," she said;
     She wept, "I am aweary, aweary,
       Oh God, that I were dead!"

                   [publ. 1830]

SONG

i

A SPIRIT haunts the year's last hours
Dwelling amid these yellowing bowers:
   To himself he talks;

For at eventide, listening earnestly,
At his work you may hear him sob and sigh
    In the walks;
    Earthward he boweth the heavy stalks
Of the mouldering flowers:
    Heavily hangs the broad sunflower
       Over its grave i' the earth so chilly;
    Heavily hangs the hollyhock,
       Heavily hangs the tiger-lily.

ii

The air is damp, and hush'd, and close,
As a sick man's room when he taketh repose
    An hour before death;
My very heart faints and my whole soul grieves
At the moist rich smell of the rotting leaves,
    And the breath
    Of the fading edges of box beneath,
And the year's last rose.
    Heavily hangs the broad sunflower
       Over its grave i' the earth so chilly;
    Heavily hangs the hollyhock,
       Heavily hangs the tiger-lily.

                  [publ. 1830]

THE POET

THE poet in a golden clime was born,
    With golden stars above;
Dower'd with the hate of hate, the scorn of scorn,
    The love of love.

He saw thro' life and death, thro' good and ill,
    He saw thro' his own soul.
The marvel of the everlasting will,
    An open scroll,

Before him lay: with echoing feet he threaded
    The secretest walks of fame:
The viewless arrows of his thoughts were headed
    And wing'd with flame,

Like Indian reeds blown from his silver tongue,
    And of so fierce a flight,
From Calpe unto Caucasus they sung,
      Filling with light

And vagrant melodies the winds which bore
    Then earthward till they lit;
Then, like the arrow-seeds of the field flower,
      The fruitful wit

Cleaving, took root, and springing forth anew
    Where'er they fell, behold,
Like to the mother plant in semblance, grew
      A flower all gold,

And bravely furnish'd all abroad to fling
    The winged shafts of truth,
To throng with stately blooms the breathing spring
      Of Hope and Youth.

So many minds did gird their orbs with beams,
    Tho' one did fling the fire.
Heaven flow'd upon the soul in many dreams
      Of high desire.

Thus truth was multiplied on truth, the world
    Like one great garden show'd,
And thro' the wreaths of floating dark upcurl'd,
      Rare sunrise flow'd.

And Freedom rear'd in that august sunrise
    Her beautiful bold brow,
When rites and forms before his burning eyes
      Melted like snow.

There was no blood upon her maiden robes
    Sunn'd by those orient skies;
But round about the circles of the globes
      Of her keen eyes

And in her raiment's hem was traced in flame
    WISDOM, a name to shake
All evil dreams of power—a sacred name.
      And when she spake,

Her words did gather thunder as they ran,
    And as the lightning to the thunder
Which follows it, riving the spirit of man,
      Making earth wonder,

So was their meaning to her words. No sword
    Of wrath her right arm whirl'd,
But one poor poet's scroll, and with *his* word
    She shook the world.

[publ. 1830]

THE LADY OF SHALOTT

Part i

On EITHER side the river lie
Long fields of barley and of rye,
That clothe the wold and meet the sky;
And thro' the field the road runs by
    To many-tower'd Camelot;
And up and down the people go,
Gazing where the lilies blow
Round an island there below,
    The island of Shalott.

Willows whiten, aspens quiver,
Little breezes dusk and shiver
Thro' the wave that runs for ever
By the island in the river
    Flowing down to Camelot.
Four gray walls, and four gray towers,
Overlook a space of flowers,
And the silent isle imbowers
    The Lady of Shalott.

By the margin, willow-veil'd,
Slide the heavy barges trail'd
By slow horses; and unhail'd
The shallop flitteth silken-sail'd
    Skimming down to Camelot:
But who hath seen her wave her hand?
Or at the casement seen her stand?
Or is she known in all the land,
    The Lady of Shalott?

Only reapers, reaping early
In among the bearded barley,

Hear a song that echoes cheerly
From the river winding clearly,
    Down to tower'd Camelot:
And by the moon the reaper weary,
Piling sheaves in uplands airy,
Listening, whispers " 'Tis the fairy
    Lady of Shalott."

Part ii

There she weaves by night and day
A magic web with colors gay.
She has heard a whisper say,
A curse is on her if she stay
    To look down to Camelot.
She knows not what the curse may be,
And so she weaveth steadily,
And little other care hath she,
    The Lady of Shalott.

And moving thro' a mirror clear
That hangs before her all the year,
Shadows of the world appear.
There she sees the highway near
    Winding down to Camelot:
There the river eddy whirls.
And there the surly village-churls,
And the red cloaks of market girls,
    Pass onward from Shalott.

Sometimes a troop of damsels glad,
An abbot on an ambling pad,
Sometimes a curly shepherd-lad,
Or long-hair'd page in crimson clad,
    Goes by to tower'd Camelot;
And sometimes thro' the mirror blue
The knights come riding two and two:
She hath no loyal knight and true,
    The Lady of Shalott.

But in her web she still delights
To weave the mirror's magic sights,
For often thro' the silent nights

A funeral, with plumes and lights
    And music, went to Camelot:
Or when the moon was overhead,
Came two young lovers lately wed;
"I am half sick of shadows," said
    The Lady of Shalott.

Part iii

A bow-shot from her bower-eaves,
He rode between the barley-sheaves,
The sun came dazzling thro' the leaves,
And flamed upon the brazen greaves
    Of bold Sir Lancelot.
A red-cross knight for ever kneel'd
To a lady in his shield,
That sparkled on the yellow field,
    Beside remote Shalott.

The gemmy bridle glitter'd free,
Like to some branch of stars we see
Hung in the golden Galaxy.
The bridle bells rang merrily
    As he rode down to Camelot:
And from his blazon'd baldric slung
A mighty silver bugle hung,
And as he rode his armor rung,
    Beside remote Shalott.

All in blue unclouded weather
Thick-jewell'd shone the saddle-leather,
The helmet and the helmet-feather
Burned like one burning flame together,
    As he rode down to Camelot.
As often thro' the purple night,
Below the starry clusters bright,
Some bearded meteor, trailing light,
    Moves over still Shalott.

His broad clear brow in sunlight glow'd;
On burnish'd hooves his war-horse trode;
From underneath his helmet flow'd
His coal-black curls as on he rode,
    As he rode down to Camelot.

From the bank and from the river
He flash'd into the crystal mirror,
"Tirra lirra," by the river
        Sang Sir Lancelot.

She left the web, she left the loom,
She made three paces thro' the room,
She saw the water-lily bloom,
She saw the helmet and the plume,
        She look'd down to Camelot.
Out flew the web and floated wide;
The mirror crack'd from side to side;
"The curse is come upon me," cried
        The Lady of Shalott.

Part iv

In the stormy east-wind straining,
The pale yellow woods were waning,
The broad stream in his banks complaining,
Heavily the low sky raining
        Over tower'd Camelot;
Down she came and found a boat
Beneath a willow left afloat,
And round about the prow she wrote
        The Lady of Shalott.

And down the river's dim expanse—
Like some bold seer in a trance,
Seeing all his own mischance—
With a glassy countenance
        Did she look to Camelot.
And at the closing of the day
She loosed the chain, and down she lay;
The broad stream bore her far away,
        The Lady of Shalott.

Lying, robed in snowy white
That loosely flew to left and right—
The leaves upon her falling light—
Thro' the noises of the night
        She floated down to Camelot:
And as the boat-head wound along
The willowy hills and fields among,
They heard her singing her last song,
        The Lady of Shalott.

Heard a carol, mournful, holy,
Chanted loudly, chanted lowly,
Till her blood was frozen slowly,
And her eyes were darken'd wholly,
    Turn'd to tower'd Camelot;
For ere she reach'd upon the tide
The first house by the water-side,
Singing in her song she died,
    The Lady of Shalott.

Under tower and balcony,
By garden-wall and gallery,
A gleaming shape she floated by,
Dead-pale between the houses high,
    Silent into Camelot.
Out upon the wharfs they came,
Knight and burgher, lord and dame,
And round the prow they read her name,
    The Lady of Shalott.

Who is this? and what is here?
And in the lighted palace near
Died the sound of royal cheer;
And they cross'd themselves for fear,
    All the knights at Camelot:
But Lancelot mused a little space;
He said, "She has a lovely face;
God in His mercy lend her grace,
    The Lady of Shalott."

                          [publ. 1832, 1842]

THE LOTOS-EATERS

"Courage!" he said, and pointed toward the land,
"This mounting wave will roll us shoreward soon."
In the afternoon they came unto a land,
In which it seemed always afternoon.
All round the coast the languid air did swoon,
Breathing like one that hath a weary dream.
Full-faced above the valley stood the moon;
And like a downward smoke, the slender stream
Along the cliff to fall and pause and fall did seem.

A land of streams! some, like a downward smoke,
Slow-dropping veils of thinnest lawn, did go;
And some thro' wavering lights and shadows broke,

Rolling a slumbrous sheet of foam below.
They saw the gleaming river seaward flow
From the inner land; far off, three mountain-tops,
Three silent pinnacles of aged snow,
Stood sunset-flush'd; and, dew'd with showery drops,
Up-clomb the shadowy pine above the woven copse.

The charmed sunset linger'd low adown
In the red West; thro' mountain clefts the dale
Was seen far inland, and the yellow down
Border'd with palm, and many a winding vale
And meadow, set with slender galingale;
A land where all things always seem'd the same!
And round about the keel with faces pale,
Dark faces pale against that rosy flame,
The mild-eyed melancholy Lotos-eaters came.

Branches they bore of that enchanted stem,
Laden with flower and fruit, whereof they gave
To each, but whoso did receive of them,
And taste, to him the gushing of the wave
Far far away did seem to mourn and rave
On alien shores; and if his fellow spake,
His voice was thin, as voices from the grave;
And deep-asleep he seem'd, yet all awake,
And music in his ears his beating heart did make.

They sat them down upon the yellow sand,
Between the sun and moon upon the shore;
And sweet it was to dream of Father-land,
Of child, and wife, and slave; but evermore
Most weary seem'd the sea, weary the oar,
Weary the wandering fields of barren foam.
Then some one said, "We will return no more";
And all at once they sang, "Our island home
Is far beyond the wave; we will no longer roam."

CHORIC SONG

i

THERE is sweet music here that softer falls
Than petals from blown roses on the grass,

Or night-dews on still waters between walls
Of shadowy granite, in a gleaming pass;
Music that gentlier on the spirit lies,
Than tir'd eyelids upon tir'd eyes;
Music that brings sweet sleep down from the blissful skies.
Here are cool mosses deep,
And thro' the moss the ivies creep,
And in the stream the long-leaved flowers weep,
And from the craggy ledge the poppy hangs in sleep.

ii

Why are we weigh'd upon with heaviness,
And utterly consumed with sharp distress,
While all things else have rest from weariness?
All things have rest: why should we toil alone,
We only toil, who are the first of things,
And make perpetual moan,
Still from one sorrow to another thrown;
Nor ever fold our wings,
And cease from wanderings,
Nor steep our brows in slumber's holy balm;
Nor harken what the inner spirit sings,
"There is no joy but calm!"
Why should we only toil, the roof and crown of things?

iii

Lo! in the middle of the wood,
The folded leaf is woo'd from out the bud
With winds upon the branch, and there
Grows green and broad, and takes no care,
Sun-steep'd at noon, and in the moon
Nightly dew-fed; and turning yellow
Falls, and floats adown the air.
Lo! sweeten'd with the summer light,
The full-juiced apple, waxing over-mellow,

Drops in a silent autumn night.
All its allotted length of days,
The flower ripens in its place,
Ripens and fades, and falls, and hath no toil,
Fast-rooted in the fruitful soil.

iv

Hateful is the dark-blue sky,
Vaulted o'er the dark-blue sea.
Death is the end of life; ah, why
Should life all labor be?
Let us alone. Time driveth onward fast,
And in a little while our lips are dumb.
Let us alone. What is it that will last?
All things are taken from us, and become
Portions and parcels of the dreadful Past.
Let us alone. What pleasure can we have
To war with evil? Is there any peace
In ever climbing up the climbing wave?
All things have rest, and ripen toward the grave
In silence; ripen, fall and cease:
Give us long rest or death, dark death, or dreamful ease.

v

How sweet it were, hearing the downward stream,
With half-shut eyes ever to seem
Falling asleep in a half-dream!
To dream and dream, like yonder amber light,
Which will not leave the myrrh-bush on the height;
To hear each other's whisper'd speech;
Eating the Lotos day by day,
To watch the crisping ripples on the beach,
And tender curving lines of creamy spray;
To lend our hearts and spirits wholly
To the influence of mild-minded melancholy;

To muse and brood and live again in memory,
With those old faces of our infancy
Heap'd over with a mound of grass,
Two handfuls of white dust, shut in an urn of brass!

vi

Dear is the memory of our wedded lives,
And dear the last embraces of our wives
And their warm tears; but all hath suffer'd change;
For surely now our household hearths are cold:
Our sons inherit us; our looks are strange;
And we should come like ghosts to trouble joy.
Or else the island princes over-bold
Have eat our substance, and the minstrel sings
Before them of the ten years' war in Troy,
And our great deeds, as half-forgotten things.
Is there confusion in the little isle?
Let what is broken so remain.
The Gods are hard to reconcile;
'Tis hard to settle order once again.
There is confusion worse than death,
Trouble on trouble, pain on pain,
Long labor unto aged breath,
Sore tasks to hearts worn out by many wars
And eyes grown dim with gazing on the pilot-stars.

vii

But, propt on beds of amaranth and moly,
How sweet (while warm airs lull us, blowing lowly)
With half-dropt eyelids still,
Beneath a heaven dark and holy,
To watch the long bright river drawing slowly
His waters from the purple hill—
To hear the dewy echoes calling

From cave to cave thro' the thick-twined vine—
To watch the emerald-color'd water falling
Thro' many a wov'n acanthus-wreath divine!
Only to hear and see the far-off sparkling brine,
Only to hear were sweet, stretch'd out beneath the pine.

viii

The Lotos blooms below the barren peak;
The Lotos blows by every winding creek;
All day the wind breathes low with mellower tone;
Thro' every hollow cave and alley lone
Round and round the spicy downs the yellow Lotos-dust is
    blown.
We have had enough of action, and of motion we,
Roll'd to starboard, roll'd to larboard, when the surge was
    seething free,
Where the wallowing monster spouted his foam-fountains in
    the sea.
Let us swear an oath, and keep it with an equal mind,
In the hollow Lotos-land to live and lie reclined
On the hills like Gods together, careless of mankind.
For they lie beside their nectar, and the bolts are hurl'd
Far below them in the valleys, and the clouds are lightly curl'd
Round their golden houses, girdled with the gleaming world;
Where they smile in secret, looking over wasted lands,
Blight and famine, plague and earthquake, roaring deeps and
    fiery sands,
Clanging fights, and flaming towns, and sinking ships, and
    praying hands.
But they smile, they find a music centred in a doleful song
Steaming up, a lamentation and an ancient tale of wrong,
Like a tale of little meaning tho' the words are strong;
Chanted from an ill-used race of men that cleave the soil,
Sow the seed, and reap the harvest with enduring toil,
Storing yearly little dues of wheat, and wine and oil;
Till they perish and they suffer—some, 'tis whisper'd—down
    in hell
Suffer endless anguish, others in Elysian valleys dwell,
Resting weary limbs at last on beds of asphodel.
Surely, surely, slumber is more sweet than toil, the shore

Than labor in the deep mid-ocean, wind and wave and oar;
O rest ye, brother mariners, we will not wander more.

[*publ. 1832, 1842*]

BREAK, BREAK, BREAK

BREAK, break, break,
  On thy cold gray stones, O Sea!
And I would that my tongue could utter
  The thoughts that arise in me.

O well for the fisherman's boy,
  That he shouts with his sister at play!
O well for the sailor lad,
  That he sings in his boat on the bay!

And the stately ships go on
  To their haven under the hill;
But O for the touch of a vanish'd hand,
  And the sound of a voice that is still!

Break, break, break,
  At the foot of thy crags, O Sea!
But the tender grace of a day that is dead
  Will never come back to me.

[*1833–34; publ. 1842*]

THE TWO VOICES

A STILL small voice spake unto me,
  "Thou art so full of misery,
Were it not better not to be?"

Then to the still small voice I said:
  "Let me not cast in endless shade
What is so wonderfully made."

To which the voice did urge reply;
  "To-day I saw the dragon-fly
Come from the wells where he did lie.

"An inner impulse rent the veil
Of his old husk; from head to tail
Came out clear plates of sapphire mail.

"He dried his wings; like gauze they grew;
Thro' crofts and pastures wet with dew
A living flash of light he flew."

I said, "When first the world began,
Young Nature thro' five cycles ran,
And in the sixth she moulded man.

"She gave him mind, the lordliest
Proportion, and, above the rest,
Dominion in the head and breast."

Thereto the silent voice replied;
"Self-blinded are you by your pride;
Look up thro' night; the world is wide.

"This truth within thy mind rehearse,
That in a boundless universe
Is boundless better, boundless worse.

"Think you this mould of hopes and fears
Could find no statelier than his peers
In yonder hundred million spheres?"

It spake, moreover, in my mind:
"Tho' thou wert scatter'd to the wind,
Yet is there plenty of the kind."

Then did my response clearer fall:
"No compound of this earthly ball
Is like another, all in all."

To which he answer'd scoffingly:
"Good soul! suppose I grant it thee,
Who'll weep for thy deficiency?

"Or will one beam be less intense,
When thy peculiar difference
Is cancell'd in the world of sense?"

I would have said, "Thou canst not know,"
But my full heart, that work'd below,
Rain'd thro' my sight its overflow.

Again the voice spake unto me:
"Thou art so steep'd in misery,
Surely 't were better not to be.

"Thine anguish will not let thee sleep,
Nor any train of reason keep;
Thou canst not think, but thou wilt weep."

I said, "The years with change advance;
If I make dark my countenance,
I shut my life from happier chance.

"Some turn this sickness yet might take,
Ev'n yet." But he: "What drug can make
A wither'd palsy cease to shake?"

I wept, "Tho' I should die, I know
That all about the thorn will blow
In tufts of rosy-tinted snow;

"And men, thro' novel spheres of thought
Still moving after truth long sought,
Will learn new things when I am not."

"Yet," said the secret voice, "some time,
Sooner or later, will gray prime
Make thy grass hoar with early rime.

"Not less swift souls that yearn for light,
Rapt after heaven's starry flight,
Would sweep the tracts of day and night.

"Not less the bee would range her cells,
The furzy prickle fire the dells,
The foxglove cluster dappled bells."

I said that "All the years invent;
Each month is various to present
The world with some development.

"Were this not well, to bide mine hour,
Tho' watching from a ruin'd tower
How grows the day of human power?"

"The highest-mounted mind," he said,
"Still sees the sacred morning spread
The silent summit overhead.

"Will thirty seasons render plain
Those lonely lights that still remain,
Just breaking over land and main?

"Or make that morn, from his cold crown
And crystal silence creeping down,
Flood with full daylight glebe and town?

"Forerun thy peers, thy time, and let
Thy feet, millenniums hence, be set
In midst of knowledge, dream'd not yet.

"Thou hast not gain'd a real height,
Nor art thou nearer to the light,
Because the scale is infinite.

" 'T were better not to breathe or speak,
Than cry for strength, remaining weak,
And seem to find, but still to seek.

"Moreover, but to seem to find
Asks what thou lackest, thought resign'd,
A healthy frame, a quiet mind."

I said, "When I am gone away,
'He dared not tarry,' men will say,
Doing dishonor to my clay."

"This is more vile," he made reply,
"To breathe and loathe, to live and sigh,
Than once from dread of pain to die.

"Sick art thou—a divided will
Still heaping on the fear of ill
The fear of men, a coward still.

"Do men love thee? Art thou so bound
To men, that how thy name may sound
Will vex thee lying underground?

"The memory of the wither'd leaf
In endless time is scarce more brief
Than of the garner'd Autumn-sheaf.

"Go, vexed Spirit, sleep in trust;
The right ear, that is fill'd with dust,
Hears little of the false or just."

"Hard task, to pluck resolve," I cried,
"From emptiness and the waste wide
Of that abyss, or scornful pride!

"Nay—rather yet that I could raise
One hope that warm'd me in the days
While still I yearn'd for human praise.

"When, wide in soul and bold of tongue,
Among the tents I paused and sung,
The distant battle flash'd and rung.

"I sung the joyful Pæan clear,
And, sitting, burnish'd without fear
The brand, the buckler, and the spear—

"Waiting to strive a happy strife,
To war with falsehood to the knife,
And not to lose the good of life—

"Some hidden principle to move,
To put together, part and prove,
And mete the bounds of hate and love—

"As far as might be, to carve out
Free space for every human doubt,
That the whole mind might orb about—

"To search thro' all I felt or saw,
The springs of life, the depths of awe,
And reach the law within the law;

"At least, not rotting like a weed,
But, having sown some generous seed,
Fruitful of further thought and deed,

"To pass, when Life her light withdraws,
Not void of righteous self-applause,
Nor in a merely selfish cause—

"In some good cause, not in mine own,
To perish, wept for, honor'd, known,
And like a warrior overthrown;

"Whose eyes are dim with glorious tears,
When, soil'd with noble dust, he hears
His country's war-song thrill his ears:

"Then dying of a mortal stroke,
What time the foeman's line is broke,
And all the war is roll'd in smoke."

"Yea!" said the voice, "thy dream was good,
While thou abodest in the bud.
It was the stirring of the blood.

"If Nature put not forth her power
About the opening of the flower,
Who is it that could live an hour?

"Then comes the check, the change, the fall,
Pain rises up, old pleasures pall.
There is one remedy for all.

"Yet hadst thou, thro' enduring pain,
Link'd month to month with such a chain
Of knitted purport, all were vain.

"Thou hadst not between death and birth
Dissolved the riddle of the earth.
So were thy labor little-worth.

"That men with knowledge merely play'd,
I told thee—hardly nigher made,
Tho' scaling slow from grade to grade;

"Much less this dreamer, deaf and blind,
Named man, may hope some truth to find,
That bears relation to the mind.

"For every worm beneath the moon
Draws different threads, and late and soon
Spins, toiling out his own cocoon.

"Cry, faint not; either Truth is born
Beyond the polar gleam forlorn,
Or in the gateways of the morn.

"Cry, faint not, climb: the summits slope
Beyond the furthest flights of hope,
Wrapt in dense cloud from base to cope.

"Sometimes a little corner shines,
As over rainy mist inclines
A gleaming crag with belts of pines.

"I will go forward, sayest thou,
I shall not fail to find her now.
Look up, the fold is on her brow.

"If straight thy track, or if oblique,
Thou know'st not. Shadows thou dost strike,
Embracing cloud, Ixion-like;

"And owning but a little more
Than beasts, abidest lame and poor,
Calling thyself a little lower

"Than angels. Cease to wail and brawl!
Why inch by inch to darkness crawl?
There is one remedy for all."

"O dull, one-sided voice," said I,
"Wilt thou make everything a lie,
To flatter me that I may die?

"I know that age to age succeeds,
Blowing a noise of tongues and deeds,
A dust of systems and of creeds.

"I cannot hide that some have striven,
Achieving calm, to whom was given
The joy that mixes man with Heaven;

"Who, rowing hard against the stream,
Saw distant gates of Eden gleam,
And did not dream it was a dream;

"But heard, by secret transport led,
Ev'n in the charnels of the dead,
The murmur of the fountain-head—

"Which did accomplish their desire,
Bore and forebore, and did not tire,
Like Stephen, an unquenched fire.

"He heeded not reviling tones,
Nor sold his heart to idle moans,
Tho' cursed and scorn'd, and bruised with stones;

"But looking upward, full of grace,
He pray'd, and from a happy place
God's glory smote him on the face."

The sullen answer slid betwixt:
"Not that the grounds of hope were fix'd,
The elements were kindlier mix'd."

I said, "I toil beneath the curse,
But, knowing not the universe,
I fear to slide from bad to worse.

"And that, in seeking to undo
One riddle, and to find the true,
I knit a hundred others new.

"Or that this anguish fleeting hence,
Unmanacled from bonds of sense,
Be fix'd and froz'n to permanence:

"For I go, weak from suffering here;
Naked I go, and void of cheer:
What is it that I may not fear?"

"Consider well," the voice replied,
"His face, that two hours since hath died;
Wilt thou find passion, pain or pride?

"Will he obey when one commands?
Or answer should one press his hands?
He answers not, nor understands.

"His palms are folded on his breast;
There is no other thing express'd
But long disquiet merged in rest.

"His lips are very mild and meek;
Tho' one should smite him on the cheek,
And on the mouth, he will not speak.

"His little daughter, whose sweet face
He kiss'd, taking his last embrace,
Becomes dishonor to her race—

"His sons grow up that bear his name,
Some grow to honor, some to shame,—
But he is chill to praise or blame.

"He will not hear the north-wind rave,
Nor, moaning, household shelter crave
From winter rains that beat his grave.

"High up the vapors fold and swim;
About him broods the twilight dim;
The place he knew forgetteth him."

"If all be dark, vague voice," I said,
"These things are wrapt in doubt and dread,
Nor canst thou show the dead are dead.

"The sap dries up: the plant declines.
A deeper tale my heart divines.
Know I not Death? the outward signs?

"I found him when my years were few;
A shadow on the graves I knew,
And darkness in the village yew.

"From grave to grave the shadow crept;
In her still place the morning wept;
Touch'd by his feet the daisy slept.

"The simple senses crown'd his head:
'Omega! thou art Lord,' they said,
'We find no motion in the dead.'

"Why, if man rot in dreamless ease,
Should that plain fact, as taught by these,
Not make him sure that he shall cease?

"Who forged that other influence,
That heat of inward evidence,
By which he doubts against the sense?

"He owns the fatal gift of eyes,
That read his spirit blindly wise,
Not simple as a thing that dies.

"Here sits he shaping wings to fly;
His heart forebodes a mystery;
He names the name Eternity.

"That type of Perfect in his mind
In Nature can he nowhere find.
He sows himself on every wind.

"He seems to hear a Heavenly Friend,
And thro' thick veils to apprehend
A labor working to an end.

"The end and the beginning vex
His reason: many things perplex,
With motions, checks, and counterchecks.

"He knows a baseness in his blood
At such strange war with something good,
He may not do the thing he would.

"Heaven opens inward, chasms yawn,
Vast images in glimmering dawn,
Half shown, are broken and withdrawn.

"Ah! sure within him and without,
Could his dark wisdom find it out,
There must be answer to his doubt.

"But thou canst answer not again.
With thine own weapon art thou slain,
Or thou wilt answer but in vain.

"The doubt would rest, I dare not solve,
In the same circle we revolve.
Assurance only breeds resolve."

As when a billow, blown against,
Falls back, the voice with which I fenced
A little ceased, but recommenced.

"Where wert thou when thy father play'd
In his free field, and pastime made,
A merry boy in sun and shade?

"A merry boy they call'd him then,
He sat upon the knees of men
In days that never come again.

"Before the little ducts began
To feed thy bones with lime, and ran
Their course, till thou wert also man:

"Who took a wife, who rear'd his race,
Whose wrinkles gather'd on his face,
Whose troubles number with his days.

"A life of nothings, nothing worth,
From that first nothing ere his birth
To the last nothing under earth!"

"These words," I said, "are like the rest,
No certain clearness, but at best
A vague suspicion of the breast:

"But if I grant, thou might'st defend
The thesis which thy words intend—
That to begin implies to end;

"Yet how should I for certain hold,
Because my memory is so cold,
That I first was in human mould?

"I cannot make this matter plain,
But I would shoot, howe'er in vain,
A random arrow from the brain.

"It may be that no life is found,
Which only to one engine bound
Falls off, but cycles always round.

"As old mythologies relate,
Some draught of Lethe might await
The slipping thro' from state to state.

"As here we find in trances, men
Forget the dream that happens then,
Until they fall in trance again.

"So might we, if our state were such
As one before, remember much,
For those two likes might meet and touch.

"But, if I lapsed from nobler place,
Some legend of a fallen race
Alone might hint of my disgrace;

"Some vague emotion of delight
In gazing up an Alpine height,
Some yearning toward the lamps of night;

"Or if thro' lower lives I came—
Tho' all experience past became
Consolidate in mind and frame—

"I might forget my weaker lot;
For is not our first year forgot?
The haunts of memory echo not.

"And men, whose reason long was blind,
From cells of madness unconfined,
Oft lose whole years of darker mind.

"Much more, if first I floated free,
As naked essence, must I be
Incompetent of memory;

"For memory dealing but with time,
And he with matter, could she climb
Beyond her own material prime?

"Moreover, something is or seems,
That touches me with mystic gleams,
Like glimpses of forgotten dreams—

"Of something felt, like something here;
Of something done, I know not where;
Such as no language may declare."

The still voice laugh'd. "I talk," said he,
"Not with thy dreams. Suffice it thee
Thy pain is a reality."

"But thou," said I, "hast miss'd thy mark,
Who sought'st to wreck my mortal ark,
By making all the horizon dark.

"Why not set forth, if I should do
This rashness, that which might ensue
With this old soul in organs new?

"Whatever crazy sorrow saith,
No life that breathes with human breath
Has ever truly long'd for death.

" 'Tis life, whereof our nerves are scant,
O life, not death, for which we pant;
More life, and fuller, that I want."

I ceased, and sat as one forlorn.
Then said the voice, in quiet scorn,
"Behold, it is the Sabbath morn."

And I arose, and I released
The casement, and the light increased
With freshness in the dawning east.

Like soften'd airs that blowing steal,
When meres begin to uncongeal,
The sweet church bells began to peal.

On to God's house the people prest;
Passing the place where each must rest,
Each enter'd like a welcome guest.

One walk'd between his wife and child,
With measured footfall firm and mild,
And now and then he gravely smiled.

The prudent partner of his blood
Lean'd on him, faithful, gentle, good,
Wearing the rose of womanhood.

And in their double love secure,
The little maiden walk'd demure,
Pacing with downward eyelids pure.

These three made unity so sweet,
My frozen heart began to beat,
Remembering its ancient heat.

I blest them, and they wander'd on;
I spoke, but answer came there none;
The dull and bitter voice was gone.

A second voice was at mine ear,
A little whisper silver-clear,
A murmur, "Be of better cheer."

As from some blissful neighborhood,
A notice faintly understood,
"I see the end, and know the good."

A little hint to solace woe,
A hint, a whisper breathing low,
"I may not speak of what I know."

Like an Æolian harp that wakes
No certain air, but overtakes
Far thought with music that it makes;

Such seem'd the whisper at my side:
"What is it thou knowest, sweet voice?" I cried.
"A hidden hope," the voice replied;

So heavenly-toned, that in that hour
From out my sullen heart a power
Broke, like the rainbow from the shower,

To feel, altho' no tongue can prove,
That every cloud, that spreads above
And veileth love, itself is love.

And forth into the fields I went,
And Nature's living motion lent
The pulse of hope to discontent.

I wonder'd at the bounteous hours,
The slow result of winter showers;
You scarce could see the grass for flowers.

I wonder'd, while I paced along;
The woods were fill'd so full with song,
There seem'd no room for sense of wrong.

So variously seem'd all things wrought,
I marvell'd how the mind was brought
To anchor by one gloomy thought;

And wherefore rather I made choice
To commune with that barren voice,
Than him that said, "Rejoice! rejoice!"

[1833; publ. 1842]

ULYSSES

IT LITTLE profits that an idle king,
By this still hearth, among these barren crags,
Match'd with an aged wife, I mete and dole
Unequal laws unto a savage race,
That hoard, and sleep, and feed, and know not me.
I cannot rest from travel; I will drink
Life to the lees: all times I have enjoy'd
Greatly, have suffer'd greatly, both with those
That loved me, and alone; on shore, and when

Thro' scudding drifts the rainy Hyades
Vex the dim sea: I am become a name;
For always roaming with a hungry heart
Much have I seen and known; cities of men
And manners, climates, councils, governments,
Myself not least, but honor'd of them all;
And drunk delight of battle with my peers,
Far on the ringing plains of windy Troy.
I am a part of all that I have met;
Yet all experience is an arch wherethro'
Gleams that untravell'd world, whose margin fades
For ever and for ever when I move.
How dull it is to pause, to make an end,
To rust unburnish'd, not to shine in use!
As tho' to breathe were life. Life piled on life
Were all too little, and of one to me
Little remains; but every hour is saved
From that eternal silence, something more,
A bringer of new things; and vile it were
For some three suns to store and hoard myself,
And this gray spirit yearning in desire
To follow knowledge like a sinking star,
Beyond the utmost bound of human thought.

This is my son, mine own Telemachus,
To whom I leave the sceptre and the isle—
Well-loved of me, discerning to fulfil
This labor, by slow prudence to make mild
A rugged people, and thro' soft degrees
Subdue them to the useful and the good.
Most blameless is he, centred in the sphere
Of common duties, decent not to fail
In offices of tenderness, and pay
Meet adoration to my household gods,
When I am gone. He works his work, I mine.

There lies the port; the vessel puffs her sail;
There gloom the dark broad seas. My mariners,
Souls that have toil'd, and wrought, and thought with me—
That ever with a frolic welcome took
The thunder and the sunshine, and opposed
Free hearts, free foreheads—you and I are old;
Old age hath yet his honor and his toil;
Death closes all; but something ere the end,
Some work of noble note, may yet be done,
Not unbecoming men that strove with Gods.
The lights begin to twinkle from the rocks;

The long day wanes; the slow moon climbs; the deep
Moans round with many voices. Come, my friends,
'Tis not too late to seek a newer world.
Push off, and sitting well in order smite
The sounding furrows; for my purpose holds
To sail beyond the sunset, and the baths
Of all the western stars, until I die.
It may be that the gulfs will wash us down;
It may be we shall touch the Happy Isles,
And see the great Achilles, whom we knew.
Tho' much is taken, much abides; and tho'
We are not now that strength which in old days
Moved earth and heaven; that which we are, we are;
One equal temper of heroic hearts,
Made weak by time and fate, but strong in will
To strive, to seek, to find, and not to yield.

[1833; publ. 1842]

TITHONUS

The woods decay, the woods decay and fall,
The vapors weep their burden to the ground,
Man comes and tills the field and lies beneath,
And after many a summer dies the swan.
Me only cruel immortality
Consumes; I wither slowly in thine arms,
Here at the quiet limit of the world,
A white-hair'd shadow roaming like a dream
The ever silent spaces of the East,
Far-folded mists, and gleaming halls of morn.

Alas! for this gray shadow, once a man—
So glorious in his beauty and thy choice,
Who madest him thy chosen, that he seem'd
To his great heart none other than a God!
I ask'd thee, "Give me immortality."
Then didst thou grant mine asking with a smile,
Like wealthy men who care not how they give.
But thy strong Hours indignant work'd their wills,
And beat me down and marr'd and wasted me,
And tho' they could not end me, left me maim'd
To dwell in presence of immortal youth,

Immortal age beside immortal youth,
And all I was, in ashes. Can thy love,
Thy beauty, make amends, tho' even now,
Close over us, the silver star, thy guide,
Shines in those tremulous eyes that fill with tears
To hear me? Let me go; take back thy gift:
Why should a man desire in any way
To vary from the kindly race of men,
Or pass beyond the goal of ordinance
Where all should pause, as is most meet for all?

A soft air fans the cloud apart; there comes
A glimpse of that dark world where I was born.
Once more the old mysterious glimmer steals
From thy pure brows, and from thy shoulders pure,
And bosom beating with a heart renew'd.
Thy cheek begins to redden thro' the gloom,
Thy sweet eyes brighten slowly close to mine,
Ere yet they blind the stars, and the wild team
Which love thee, yearning for thy yoke, arise,
And shake the darkness from their loosen'd manes,
And beat the twilight into flakes of fire.

Lo! ever thus thou growest beautiful
In silence, then before thine answer given
Departest, and thy tears are on my cheek.

Why wilt thou ever scare me with thy tears,
And make me tremble lest a saying learnt,
In days far-off, on that dark earth, be true?
"The Gods themselves cannot recall their gifts."

Ay me! ay me! with what another heart
In days far-off, and with what other eyes
I used to watch—if I be he that watch'd—
The lucid outline forming round thee; saw
The dim curls kindle into sunny rings;
Changed with thy mystic change, and felt my blood
Glow with the glow that slowly crimson'd all
Thy presence and thy portals, while I lay,
Mouth, forehead, eyelids, growing dewy-warm
With kisses balmier than half-opening buds
Of April, and could hear the lips that kiss'd
Whispering I knew not what of wild and sweet,
Like that strange song I heard Apollo sing,
While Ilion like a mist rose into towers.

Yet hold me not for ever in thine East;
How can my nature longer mix with thine?

Coldly thy rosy shadows bathe me, cold
Are all thy lights, and cold my wrinkled feet
Upon thy glimmering thresholds, when the steam
Floats up from those dim fields about the homes
Of happy men that have the power to die,
And grassy barrows of the happier dead.
Release me, and restore me to the ground;
Thou seëst all things, thou wilt see my grave;
Thou wilt renew thy beauty morn by morn;
I earth in earth forget these empty courts,
And thee returning on thy silver wheels.

[1833–34; rev. 1859; publ. 1860]

OF OLD SAT FREEDOM ON THE HEIGHTS

OF OLD sat Freedom on the heights,
  The thunders breaking at her feet;
Above her shook the starry lights;
  She heard the torrents meet.

There in her place she did rejoice,
  Self-gather'd in her prophet-mind,
But fragments of her mighty voice
  Came rolling on the wind.

Then stept she down thro' town and field
  To mingle with the human race,
And part by part to men reveal'd
  The fullness of her face—

Grave mother of majestic works,
  From her isle-altar gazing down,
Who, God-like, grasps the triple forks,
  And, King-like, wears the crown:

Her open eyes desire the truth.
  The wisdom of a thousand years
Is in them. May perpetual youth
  Keep dry their light from tears;

That her fair form may stand and shine,
  Make bright our days and light our dreams,
Turning to scorn with lips divine
  The falsehood of extremes!

[1833–34; publ. 1842]

ST. AGNES' EVE

DEEP on the convent-roof the snows
  Are sparkling to the moon;

My breath to heaven like vapor goes;
  May my soul follow soon!
The shadows of the convent-towers
  Slant down the snowy sward,
Still creeping with the creeping hours
  That lead me to my Lord:
Make Thou my spirit pure and clear
  As are the frosty skies,
Or this first snowdrop of the year .
  That in my bosom lies.

As these white robes are soil'd and dark,
  To yonder shining ground;
As this pale taper's earthly spark,
  To yonder argent round;
So shows my soul before the Lamb,
  My spirit before Thee;
So in mine earthly house I am,
  To that I hope to be.
Break up the heavens, O Lord! and far,
  Thro' all yon starlight keen,
Draw me, thy bride, a glittering star,
  In raiment white and clean.

He lifts me to the golden doors;
  The flashes come and go;
All heaven bursts her starry floors,
  And strows her lights below,
And deepens on and up! the gates
  Roll back, and far within
For me the Heavenly Bridegroom waits,
  To make me pure of sin.
The Sabbaths of Eternity,
  One Sabbath deep and wide—
A light upon the shining sea—
  The Bridegroom with his bride!

                              [1834; publ. 1836]

LOCKSLEY HALL

COMRADES, leave me here a little, while as yet 'tis early morn;
Leave me here, and when you want me, sound upon the bugle
  horn.

'Tis the place, and all around it, as of old, the curlews call,
Dreary gleams about the moorland flying over Locksley Hall;

Locksley Hall, that in the distance overlooks the sandy tracts,
And the hollow ocean-ridges roaring into cataracts.

Many a night from yonder ivied casement, ere I went to rest,
Did I look on great Orion sloping slowly to the west.

Many a night I saw the Pleiads, rising thro' the mellow shade,
Glitter like a swarm of fire-flies tangled in a silver braid.

Here about the beach I wander'd, nourishing a youth sublime
With the fairy tales of science, and the long result of Time;

When the centuries behind me like a fruitful land reposed;
When I clung to all the present for the promise that it closed:

When I dipt into the future far as human eye could see;
Saw the Vision of the world, and all the wonder that would be.

In the Spring a fuller crimson comes upon the robin's breast;
In the Spring the wanton lapwing gets himself another crest;

In the Spring a livelier iris changes on the burnish'd dove;
In the Spring a young man's fancy lightly turns to thoughts of
    love.

Then her cheek was pale and thinner than should be for one so
    young,
And her eyes on all my motions with a mute observance hung.

And I said, "My cousin Amy, speak, and speak the truth to
    me,
Trust me, cousin, all the current of my being sets to thee."

On her pallid cheek and forehead came a color and a light,
As I have seen the rosy red flushing in the northern night.

And she turn'd—her bosom shaken with a sudden storm of
    sighs—
All the spirit deeply dawning in the dark of hazel eyes—

Saying, "I have hid my feelings, fearing they should do me
    wrong;"
Saying, "Dost thou love me, cousin?" weeping, "I have loved
    thee long."

Love took up the glass of Time, and turn'd it in his glowing
    hands;
Every moment, lightly shaken, ran itself in golden sands.

Love took up the harp of Life, and smote on all the chords
  with might;
Smote the chord of Self, that, trembling, pass'd in music out
  of sight.

Many a morning on the moorland did we hear the copses ring,
And her whisper throng'd my pulses with the fullness of the
  Spring.

Many an evening by the waters did we watch the stately ships,
And our spirits rush'd together at the touching of the lips.

O my cousin, shallow-hearted! O my Amy, mine no more!
O the dreary, dreary moorland! O the barren, barren shore!

Falser than all fancy fathoms, falser than all songs have sung,
Puppet to a father's threat, and servile to a shrewish tongue!

Is it well to wish thee happy?—having known me—to decline
On a range of lower feelings and a narrower heart than mine!

Yet it shall be; thou shalt lower to his level day by day,
What is fine within thee growing coarse to sympathize with
  clay.

As the husband is, the wife is; thou art mated with a clown,
And the grossness of his nature will have weight to drag thee
  down.

He will hold thee, when his passion shall have spent its novel
  force,
Something better than his dog, a little dearer than his horse.

What is this? his eyes are heavy: think not they are glazed with
  wine.
Go to him; it is thy duty; kiss him; take his hand in thine.

It may be my lord is weary, that his brain is overwrought;
Soothe him with thy finer fancies, touch him with thy lighter
  thought.

He will answer to the purpose, easy things to understand—
Better thou wert dead before me, tho' I slew thee with my
  hand!

Better thou and I were lying, hidden from the heart's disgrace,
Roll'd in one another's arms, and silent in a last embrace.

Cursed be the social wants that sin against the strength of
  youth!
Cursed be the social lies that warp us from the living truth!

Cursed be the sickly forms that err from honest Nature's rule!
Cursed be the gold that gilds the straiten'd forehead of the
fool!

Well—'t is well that I should bluster!—Hadst thou less
unworthy proved—
Would to God—for I had loved thee more than ever wife was
loved.

Am I mad, that I should cherish that which bears but bitter
fruit?
I will pluck it from my bosom, tho' my heart be at the root.

Never, tho' my mortal summers to such length of years should
come
As the many-winter'd crow that leads the clanging rookery
home.

Where is comfort? in division of the records of the mind?
Can I part her from herself, and love her, as I knew her, kind?

I remember one that perish'd; sweetly did she speak and move:
Such a one do I remember, whom to look at was to love.

Can I think of her as dead, and love her for the love she bore?
No—she never loved me truly; love is love for evermore.

Comfort? comfort scorn'd of devils! this is truth the poet sings,
That a sorrow's crown of sorrow is remembering happier
things.

Drug thy memories, lest thou learn it, lest thy heart be put to
proof,
In the dead unhappy night, and when the rain is on the roof.

Like a dog, he hunts in dreams, and thou art staring at the
wall,
Where the dying night-lamp flickers and the shadows rise and
fall.

Then a hand shall pass before thee, pointing to his drunken
sleep,
To thy widow'd marriage-pillows, to the tears that thou wilt
weep.

Thou shalt hear the "Never, never," whisper'd by the phan-
tom years,
And a song from out the distance in the ringing of thine ears;

And an eye shall vex thee, looking ancient kindness on thy
    pain.
Turn thee, turn thee on thy pillow; get thee to thy rest again.

Nay, but Nature brings thee solace; for a tender voice will cry.
'T is a purer life than thine; a lip to drain thy trouble dry.

Baby lips will laugh me down; my latest rival brings thee rest.
Baby fingers, waxen touches, press me from the mother's
    breast.

O, the child too clothes the father with a dearness not his due.
Half is thine and half is his; it will be worthy of the two.

O, I see thee old and formal, fitted to thy petty part,
With a little hoard of maxims preaching down a daughter's
    heart.

"They were dangerous guides the feelings—she herself was
    not exempt—
Truly, she herself had suffer'd"—Perish in thy self-contempt!

Overlive it—lower yet—be happy! wherefore should I care?
I myself must mix with action, lest I wither by despair.

What is that which I should turn to, lighting upon days like
    these?
Every door is barr'd with gold, and opens but to golden keys.

Every gate is throng'd with suitors, all the markets overflow.
I have but an angry fancy; what is that which I should do?

I had been content to perish, falling on the foeman's ground,
When the ranks are roll'd in vapor, and the winds are laid with
    sound.

But the jingling of the guinea helps the hurt that Honor feels,
And the nations do but murmur, snarling at each other's heels.

Can I but relive in sadness? I will turn that earlier page.
Hide me from my deep emotion, O thou wondrous Mother-
    Age!

Make me feel the wild pulsation that I felt before the strife,
When I heard my days before me, and the tumult of my life;

Yearning for the large excitement that the coming years would
    yield,
Eager-hearted as a boy when first he leaves his father's field,

And at night along the dusky highway near and nearer drawn,
Sees in heaven the light of London flaring like a dreary dawn;

And his spirit leaps within him to be gone before him then,
Underneath the light he looks at, in among the throngs of men;

Men, my brothers, men the workers, ever reaping something
    new;
That which they have done but earnest of the things that they
    shall do:

For I dipt into the future, far as human eye could see,
Saw the Vision of the world, and all the wonder that would be;

Saw the heavens fill with commerce, argosies of magic sails,
Pilots of the purple twilight, dropping down with costly bales;

Heard the heavens fill with shouting, and there rain'd a ghastly
    dew
From the nations' airy navies grappling in the central blue;

Far along the world-wide whisper of the south-wind rushing
    warm,
With the standards of the peoples plunging thro' the thunder-
    storm;

Till the war-drum throbb'd no longer, and the battle-flags were
    furl'd
In the Parliament of man, the Federation of the world.

There the common sense of most shall hold a fretful realm in
    awe,
And the kindly earth shall slumber, lapt in universal law.

So I triumph'd ere my passion sweeping thro' me left me dry,
Left me with the palsied heart, and left me with the jaundiced
    eye;

Eye, to which all order festers, all things here are out of joint.
Science moves, but slowly, slowly, creeping on from point to
    point;

Slowly comes a hungry people, as a lion, creeping nigher,
Glares at one that nods and winks behind a slowly-dying fire.

Yet I doubt not thro' the ages one increasing purpose runs,
And the thoughts of men are widen'd with the process of the
    suns.

What is that to him that reaps not harvest of his youthful joys,
Tho' the deep heart of existence beat for ever like a boy's?

Knowledge comes, but wisdom lingers, and I linger on the
    shore,
And the individual withers, and the world is more and more.

Knowledge comes, but wisdom lingers, and he bears a laden
    breast,
Full of sad experience, moving toward the stillness of his rest.

Hark, my merry comrades call me, sounding on the bugle-horn,
They to whom my foolish passion were a target for their scorn;

Shall it not be scorn to me to harp on such a moulder'd string?
I am shamed thro' all my nature to have loved so slight a thing.

Weakness to be wroth with weakness! woman's pleasure, wom-
    an's pain—
Nature made them blinder motions bounded in a shallower
    brain:

Woman is the lesser man, and all thy passions, match'd with
    mine,
Are as moonlight unto sunlight, and as water unto wine—

Here at least, where nature sickens, nothing. Ah, for some
    retreat
Deep in yonder shining Orient, where my life began to beat;

Where in wild Mahratta-battle fell my father evil-starr'd;—
I was left a trampled orphan, and a selfish uncle's ward.

Or to burst all links of habit—there to wander far away,
On from island unto island at the gateways of the day.

Larger constellations burning, mellow moons and happy skies,
Breadths of tropic shade and palms in cluster, knots of Para-
    dise.

Never comes the trader, never floats an European flag,
Slides the bird o'er lustrous woodland, swings the trailer from
    the crag;

Droops the heavy-blossom'd bower, hangs the heavy-fruited
    tree—
Summer isles of Eden lying in dark-purple spheres of sea.

There methinks would be enjoyment more than in this march
    of mind,
In the steamship, in the railways, in the thoughts that shake
    mankind.

There the passions cramp'd no longer shall have scope and
    breathing space;
I will take some savage woman, she shall rear my dusky race.

Iron-jointed, supple-sinew'd, they shall dive, and they shall
    run,
Catch the wild goat by the hair, and hurl their lances in the
    sun;

Whistle back the parrot's call, and leap the rainbows of the
    brooks,
Not with blinded eyesight poring over miserable books—

Fool, again the dream, the fancy! but I know my words are
    wild,
But I count the gray barbarian lower than the Christian child.

I, to herd with narrow foreheads, vacant of our glorious gains,
Like a beast with lower pleasures, like a beast with lower pains!

Mated with a squalid savage—what to me were sun or clime?
I the heir of all the ages, in the foremost files of time—

I that rather held it better men should perish one by one,
Than that earth should stand at gaze like Joshua's moon in
    Ajalon!

Not in vain the distance beacons. Forward, forward let us
    range,
Let the great world spin for ever down the ringing grooves of
    change.

Thro' the shadow of the globe we sweep into the younger day:
Better fifty years of Europe than a cycle of Cathay.

Mother-Age (for mine I knew not) help me as when life
    begun;
Rift the hills, and roll the waters, flash the lightnings, weigh
    the Sun—

O, I see the crescent promise of my spirit hath not set.
Ancient founts of inspiration well thro' all my fancy yet.

Howsoever these things be, a long farewell to Locksley Hall!
Now for me the woods may wither, now for me the roof-tree
    fall.

Comes a vapor from the margin, blackening over heath and
    holt,
Cramming all the blast before it, in its breast a thunderbolt.

Let it fall on Locksley Hall, with rain or hail, or fire or snow;
For the mighty wind arises, roaring seaward, and I go.

[1835–42; publ. 1842]

✠✠✠ From THE PRINCESS: A MEDLEY ✠✠✠

THE SPLENDOR FALLS

THE splendor falls on castle walls
    And snowy summits old in story.
The long light shakes across the lakes,
    And the wild cataract leaps in glory.
Blow, bugle, blow, set the wild echoes flying,
Blow, bugle; answer, echoes, dying, dying, dying.

O, hark, O hear! how thin and clear,
    And thinner, clearer, farther going!
O, sweet and far from cliff and scaur
    The horns of Elfland faintly blowing!
Blow, let us hear the purple glens replying:
Blow, bugle; answer, echoes, dying, dying, dying.

O love, they die in yon rich sky,
    They faint on hill or field or river;
Our echoes roll from soul to soul,
    And grow for ever and for ever.
Blow, bugle, blow, set the wild echoes flying,
And answer, echoes, answer, dying, dying, dying.

[publ. 1850]

TEARS, IDLE TEARS

TEARS, idle tears, I know not what they mean,
Tears from the depth of some divine depair
Rise in the heart, and gather to the eyes,
In looking on the happy Autumn-fields,
And thinking of the days that are no more.

Fresh as the first beam glittering on a sail,
That brings our friends up from the underworld,

Sad as the last which reddens over one
That sinks with all we love below the verge;
So sad, so fresh, the days that are no more.

Ah, sad and strange as in dark summer dawns
The earliest pipe of half-awaken'd birds
To dying ears, when unto dying eyes
The casement slowly grows a glimmering square;
So sad, so strange, the days that are no more.

Dear as remember'd kisses after death,
And sweet as those by hopeless fancy feign'd
On lips that are for others; deep as love,
Deep as first love, and wild with all regret;
O Death in Life, the days that are no more.

                      [publ. 1847]

ASK ME NO MORE

Ask me no more: the moon may draw the sea;
   The cloud may stoop from heaven and take the shape,
   With fold to fold, of mountain or of cape;
But O too fond, when have I answer'd thee?
               Ask me no more.

Ask me no more: what answer should I give?
   I love not hollow cheek or faded eye:
   Yet, O my friend, I will not have thee die!
Ask me no more, lest I should bid thee live;
               Ask me no more.

Ask me no more: thy fate and mine are seal'd;
   I strove against the stream and all in vain:
   Let the great river take me to the main:
No more, dear love, for at a touch I yield;
               Ask me no more.
                      [publ. 1850]

NOW SLEEPS THE CRIMSON PETAL

Now sleeps the crimson petal, now the white;
Nor waves the cypress in the palace walk;
Nor winks the gold fin in the porphyry font:
The fire-fly wakens: waken thou with me.

Now droops the milkwhite peacock like a ghost,
And like a ghost she glimmers on to me.

Now lies the Earth all Danaë to the stars,
And all thy heart lies open unto me.

Now slides the silent meteor on, and leaves
A shining furrow, as thy thoughts in me.

Now folds the lily all her sweetness up,
And slips into the bosom of the lake:
So fold thyself, my dearest, thou, and slip
Into my bosom and be lost in me.

                        [publ. 1847]

THE EAGLE
(FRAGMENT)

HE CLASPS the crag with crooked hands;
Close to the sun in lonely lands,
Ring'd with the azure world, he stands.

The wrinkled sea beneath him crawls;
He watches from his mountain walls,
And like a thunderbolt he falls.

             [1846–51?; publ. 1851]

✠✠ From IN MEMORIAM A. H. H. ✠✠

OBIIT MDCCCXXXIII

STRONG Son of God, immortal Love,
   Whom we, that have not seen thy face,
   By faith, and faith alone, embrace,
Believing where we cannot prove;

Thine are these orbs of light and shade;
   Thou madest Life in man and brute;
   Thou madest Death; and lo, thy foot
Is on the skull which thou hast made.

Thou wilt not leave us in the dust:
   Thou madest man, he knows not why;
   He thinks he was not made to die;
And thou has made him: thou art just.

Thou seemest human and divine,
    The highest, holiest manhood, thou:
    Our wills are ours, we know not how;
Our wills are ours, to make them thine.

Our little systems have their day;
    They have their day and cease to be;
    They are but broken lights of thee,
And thou, O Lord, art more than they.

We have but faith: we cannot know;
    For knowledge is of things we see;
    And yet we trust it comes from thee,
A beam in darkness: let it grow.

Let knowledge grow from more to more,
    But more of reverence in us dwell;
    That mind and soul, according well,
May make one music as before,

But vaster. We are fools and slight;
    We mock thee when we do not fear:
    But help thy foolish ones to bear;
Help thy vain worlds to bear thy light.

Forgive what seem'd my sin in me,
    What seem'd my worth since I began;
    For merit lives from man to man,
And not from man, O Lord, to thee.

Forgive my grief for one removed,
    Thy creature, whom I found so fair.
    I trust he lives in thee, and there
I find him worthier to be loved.

Forgive these wild and wandering cries,
    Confusions of a wasted youth;
    Forgive them where they fail in truth,
And in thy wisdom make me wise.
    1849.

---

i

I held it truth, with him who sings
    To one clear harp in divers tones,

That men may rise on stepping-stones
Of their dead selves to higher things.

But who shall so forecast the years
    And find in loss a gain to match?
    Or reach a hand thro' time to catch
The far-off interest of tears?

Let Love clasp Grief lest both be drown'd,
    Let darkness keep her raven gloss:
    Ah, sweeter to be drunk with loss,
To dance with Death, to beat the ground,

Than that the victor Hours should scorn
    The long result of love, and boast,
    "Behold the man that loved and lost,
But all he was is overworn."

vii

Dark house, by which once more I stand
    Here in the long unlovely street,
    Doors, where my heart was used to beat
So quickly, waiting for a hand,

A hand that can be clasp'd no more,
    Behold me, for I cannot sleep,
    And like a guilty thing I creep
At earliest morning to the door.

He is not here; but far away
    The noise of life begins again,
    And ghastly thro' the drizzling rain
On the bald street breaks the blank day.

xiv

If one should bring me this report,
    That thou hadst touch'd the land to-day,
    And I went down unto the quay,
And found thee lying in the port;

And standing, muffled round with woe,
    Should see thy passengers in rank

Come stepping lightly down the plank,
And beckoning unto those they know;

And if along with these should come
The man I held as half-divine,
Should strike a sudden hand in mine,
And ask a thousand things of home;

And I should tell him all my pain,
And how my life had droop'd of late,
And he should sorrow o'er my state
And marvel what possess'd my brain;

And I perceived no touch of change,
No hint of death in all his frame,
But found him all in all the same,
I should not feel it to be strange.

xxvii

I envy not in any moods
The captive void of noble rage,
The linnet born within the cage,
That never knew the summer woods;

I envy not the beast that takes
His license in the field of time,
Unfetter'd by the sense of crime,
To whom a conscience never wakes;

Nor, what may count itself as blest,
The heart that never plighted troth,
But stagnates in the weeds of sloth;
Nor any want-begotten rest.

I hold it true, whate'er befall;
I feel it, when I sorrow most;
'Tis better to have loved and lost
Than never to have loved at all.

xliii

If Sleep and Death be truly one,
And every spirit's folded bloom

Thro' all its interval gloom
In some long trance should slumber on;

Unconscious of the sliding hour,
    Bare of the body, might it last,
    And silent traces of the past
Be all the color of the flower:

So then were nothing lost to man,
    So that still garden of the souls
    In many a figured leaf enrolls
The total world since life begun;

And love will last as pure and whole
    As when he loved me here in Time,
    And at the spiritual prime
Reawaken with the dawning soul.

xlv

The baby new to earth and sky,
    What time his tender palm is prest
    Against the circle of the breast,
Has never thought that "this is I;"

But as he grows he gathers much,
    And learns the use of "I," and "me,"
    And finds "I am not what I see,
And other than the things I touch."

So rounds he to a separate mind
    From whence clear memory may begin,
    As thro' the frame that binds him in
His isolation grows defined.

This use may lie in blood and breath,
    Which else were fruitless of their due,
    Had man to learn himself anew
Beyond the second birth of Death.

l

Be near me when my light is low,
    When the blood creeps, and the nerves prick
    And tingle; and the heart is sick,
And all the wheels of Being slow.

Be near me when the sensuous frame
   Is rack'd with pangs that conquer trust;
   And Time, a maniac scattering dust,
And Life, a Fury slinging flame.

Be near me when my faith is dry,
   And men the flies of latter spring,
   That lay their eggs, and sting and sing
And weave their petty cells and die.

Be near me when I fade away,
   To point the term of human strife,
   And on the low dark verge of life
The twilight of eternal day.

liv

O yet we trust that somehow good
   Will be the final goal of ill,
   To pangs of nature, sins of will,
Defects of doubt, and taints of blood;

That nothing walks with aimless feet;
   That not one life shall be destroy'd,
   Or cast as rubbish to the void,
When God hath made the pile complete;

That not a worm is cloven in vain;
   That not a moth with vain desire
   Is shrivell'd in a fruitless fire,
Or but subserves another's gain.

Behold, we know not anything;
   I can but trust that good shall fall
   At last—far off—at last, to all,
And every winter change to spring.

So runs my dream; but what am I?
   An infant crying in the night;
   An infant crying for the light;
And with no language but a cry.

lxvii

When on my bed the moonlight falls,
   I know that in thy place of rest,

By that broad water of the west,
There comes a glory on the walls:

Thy marble bright in dark appears,
   As slowly steals a silver flame
   Along the letters of thy name,
And o'er the number of thy years.

The mystic glory swims away;
   From off my bed the moonlight dies;
   And closing eaves of wearied eyes
I sleep till dusk is dipt in gray:

And then I know the mist is drawn
   A lucid veil from coast to coast,
   And in the dark church like a ghost
Thy tablet glimmers to the dawn.

lxx

I cannot see the features right,
   When on the gloom I strive to paint
   The face I know; the hues are faint
And mix with hollow masks of night;

Cloud-towers by ghostly masons wrought,
   A gulf that ever shuts and gapes,
   A hand that points, and palled shapes
In shadowy thoroughfares of thought;

And crowds that stream from yawning doors,
   And shoals of pucker'd faces drive;
   Dark bulks that tumble half alive,
And lazy lengths on boundless shores;

Till all at once beyond the will
   I hear a wizard music roll,
   And thro' a lattice on the soul
Looks thy fair face and makes it still.

lxxvii

What hope is here for modern rhyme
   To him, who turns a musing eye

On songs, and deeds, and lives, that lie
Foreshorten'd in the tract of time?

These mortal lullabies of pain
  May bind a book, may line a box,
  May serve to curl a maiden's locks;
Or when a thousand moons shall wane

A man upon a stall may find,
  And, passing, turn the page that tells
  A grief, then changed to something else,
Sung by a long-forgotten mind.

But what of that? My darken'd ways
  Shall ring with music all the same;
  To breathe my loss is more than fame,
To utter love more sweet than praise.

xciv

How pure at heart and sound in head,
  With what divine affections bold
  Should be the man whose thought would hold
An hour's communion with the dead.

In vain shalt thou, or any, call
  The spirits from their golden day,
  Except, like them, thou too canst say,
My spirit is at peace with all.

They haunt the silence of the breast,
  Imaginations calm and fair,
  The memory like a cloudless air,
The conscience as a sea at rest;

But when the heart is full of din,
  And doubt beside the portal waits,
  They can but listen at the gates,
And hear the household jar within.

cvi

Ring out, wild bells, to the wild sky,
  The flying cloud, the frosty light;

The year is dying in the night;
Ring out, wild bells, and let him die.

Ring out the old, ring in the new,
   Ring, happy bells, across the snow:
   The year is going, let him go;
Ring out the false, ring in the true.

Ring out the grief that saps the mind,
   For those that here we see no more;
   Ring out the feud of rich and poor,
Ring in redress to all mankind.

Ring out a slowly dying cause,
   And ancient forms of party strife;
   Ring in the nobler modes of life,
With sweeter manners, purer laws.

Ring out the want, the care, the sin,
   The faithless coldness of the times;
   Ring out, ring out my mournful rhymes,
But ring the fuller minstrel in.

Ring out false pride in place and blood,
   The civic slander and the spite;
   Ring in the love of truth and right,
Ring in the common love of good.

Ring out old shapes of foul disease;
   Ring out the narrowing lust of gold;
   Ring out the thousand wars of old,
Ring in the thousand years of peace.

Ring in the valiant man and free,
   The larger heart, the kindlier hand;
   Ring out the darkness of the land,
Ring in the Christ that is to be.

cxxii

O, wast thou with me, dearest, then,
   While I rose up against my doom,
   And yearn'd to burst the folded gloom,
To bare the eternal heavens again,

To feel once more, in placid awe,
   The strong imagination roll
     A sphere of stars about my soul,
In all her motion one with law.

If thou wert with me, and the grave
   Divide us not, be with me now,
     And enter in at breast and brow,
Till all my blood, a fuller wave,

Be quicken'd with a livelier breath,
   And like an inconsiderate boy,
     As in the former flash of joy,
I slip the thoughts of life and death;

And all the breeze of Fancy blows,
   And every dewdrop paints a bow,
     The wizard lightnings deeply glow,
And every thought breaks out a rose.

cxxxi

O living will that shalt endure
   When all that seems shall suffer shock,
     Rise in the spiritual rock,
Flow thro' our deeds and make them pure,

That we may lift from out of dust
   A voice as unto him that hears,
     A cry above the conquer'd years
To one that with us works, and trust,

With faith that comes of self-control,
   The truths that never can be proved
     Until we close with all we loved,
And all we flow from, soul in soul.

AGAIN THE FEAST*

Again the feast, the speech, the glee,
   The shade of passing thought, the wealth
     Of words and wit, the double health,
The crowning cup, the three-times-three,

* Stanzas 26 to 36 of the last poem in *In Memoriam*.

And last the dance;—till I retire:
　　Dumb is that tower which spake so loud,
　　And high in heaven the streaming cloud,
And on the downs a rising fire:

And rise, O moon, from yonder down
　　Till over down and over dale
　　All night the shining vapor sail
And pass the silent-lighted town,

The white-faced halls, the glancing rills,
　　And catch at every mountain head,
　　And o'er the friths that branch and spread
Their sleeping silver thro' the hills;

And touch with shade the bridal doors,
　　With tender gloom the roof, the wall;
　　And breaking let the splendor fall
To spangle all the happy shores

By which they rest, and ocean sounds,
　　And, star and system rolling past,
　　A soul shall draw from out the vast
And strike his being into bounds.

And, moved thro' life of lower phase,
　　Result in man, be born and think,
　　And act and love, a closer link
Betwixt us and the crowning race

Of those that, eye to eye, shall look
　　On knowledge; under whose command
　　Is Earth and Earth's, and in their hand
Is Nature like an open book;

No longer half-akin to brute,
　　For all we thought and loved and did,
　　And hoped, and suffer'd, is but seed
Of what in them is flower and fruit;

Whereof the man that with me trod
　　This planet was a noble type
　　Appearing ere the times were ripe,
That friend of mine who lives in God,

That God, which ever lives and loves,
　　One God, one law, one element,

And one far-off divine event,
To which the whole creation moves.

                                    [1833–50; publ. 1850]

THE DAISY

Written at Edinburgh

O LOVE, what hours were thine and mine
In lands of palm and southern pine;
    In lands of palm, or orange-blossom,
Of olive, aloe, and maize and vine.

What Roman strength Turbìa show'd
In ruin, by the mountain road;
    How like a gem, beneath, the city
Of little Monaco, basking, glow'd.

How richly down the rocky dell
The torrent vineyard streaming fell
    To meet the sun and sunny waters,
That only heaved with a summer swell.

What slender campanili grew
By bays, the peacock's neck in hue;
    Where, here and there, on sandy beaches
A milky-bell'd amaryllis blew.

How young Columbus seem'd to rove,
Yet present in his natal grove,
    Now watching high on mountain cornice,
And steering, now, from a purple cove,

Now pacing mute by ocean's rim;
Till, in a narrow street and dim,
    I stay'd the wheels at Cogoletto,
And drank, and loyally drank to him.

Nor knew we well what pleased us most,
Not the clipt palm of which they boast;
    But distant color, happy hamlet,
A moulder'd citadel on the coast,

Or tower, or high hill-convent, seen
A light amid its olives green;

Or olive-hoary cape in ocean;
Or rosy blossom in hot ravine,

Where oleanders flush'd the bed
Of silent torrents, gravel-spread;
    And, crossing, oft we saw the glisten
Of ice, far up on a mountain head.

We loved that hall, tho' white and cold,
Those niched shapes of noble mould,
    A princely people's awful princes,
The grave, severe Genovese of old.

At Florence too what golden hours,
In those long galleries, were ours;
    What drives about the fresh Cascinè,
Or walks in Boboli's ducal bowers!

In bright vignettes, and each complete,
Of tower or duomo, sunny-sweet,
    Or palace, how the city glitter'd,
Thro' cypress avenues, at our feet.

But when we crost the Lombard plain
Remember what a plague of rain;
    Of rain at Reggio, rain at Parma,
At Lodi rain, Piacenza rain.

And stern and sad (so rare the smiles
Of sunlight) look'd the Lombard piles;
    Porch-pillars on the lion resting,
And sombre, old, colonnaded aisles.

O Milan, O the chanting quires,
The giant windows' blazon'd fires,
    The height, the space, the gloom, the glory!
A mount of marble, a hundred spires!

I climb'd the roofs at break of day;
Sun-smitten Alps before me lay.
    I stood among the silent statues,
And statued pinnacles, mute as they.

How faintly-flush'd, how phantom-fair,
Was Monte Rosa, hanging there
    A thousand shadowy-pencill'd valleys
And snowy dells in a golden air.

Remember how we came at last
To Como; shower and storm and blast
    Had blown the lake beyond his limit,
And all was flooded; and how we past

From Como, when the light was gray,
And in my head, for half the day,
    The rich Virgilian rustic measure
Of Lari Maxume, all the way,

Like ballad-burden music, kept,
As on the Lariano crept
    To that fair port below the castle
Of Queen Theodolind, where we slept;

Or hardly slept, but watch'd awake
A cypress in the moonlight shake,
    The moonlight touching o'er a terrace
One tall Agavè above the lake.

What more? we took our last adieu,
And up the snowy Splügen drew;
    But ere we reach'd the highest summit
I pluck'd a daisy, I gave it you.

It told of England then to me,
And now it tells of Italy.
    O love, we two shall go no longer
To lands of summer across the sea;

So dear a life your arms enfold
Whose crying is a cry for gold:
    Yet here to-night in this dark city,
When ill and weary, alone and cold,

I found, tho' crush'd to hard and dry,
This nursling of another sky
    Still in the little book you lent me,
And where you tenderly laid it by:

And I forgot the clouded Forth,
The gloom that saddens Heaven and Earth,
    The bitter east, the misty summer
And gray metropolis of the North.

Perchance, to lull the throbs of pain,
Perchance, to charm a vacant brain,

Perchance, to dream you still beside me,
My fancy fled to the South again.

[1853; publ. 1855]

✠ From MAUD: A MONODRAMA ✠

xviii

I have led her home, my love, my only friend.
There is none like her, none.
And never yet so warmly ran my blood
And sweetly, on and on
Calming itself to the long-wish'd-for end,
Full to the banks, close on the promised good.

None like her, none.
Just now the dry-tongued laurels' pattering talk
Seem'd her light foot along the garden walk,
And shook my heart to think she comes once more;
But even then I heard her close the door,
The gates of Heaven are closed, and she is gone.

There is none like her, none.
Nor will be when our summers have deceased.
O, art thou sighing for Lebanon
In the long breeze that streams to thy delicious East,
Sighing for Lebanon,
Dark cedar, tho' thy limbs have here increased,
Upon a pastoral slope as fair,
And looking to the South, and fed
With honey'd rain and delicate air,
And haunted by the starry head
Of her whose gentle will has changed my fate,
And made my life a perfumed altar-flame;
And over whom thy darkness must have spread
With such delight as theirs of old, thy great
Forefathers of the thornless garden, there
Shadowing the snow-limb d Eve from whom she came.

Here will I lie, while these long branches sway,
And you fair stars that crown a happy day

Go in and out as if at merry play,
Who am no more so all forlorn,
As when it seem'd far better to be born
To labor and the mattock-harden'd hand
Than nursed at ease and brought to understand
A sad astrology, the boundless plan
That makes you tyrants in your iron skies,
Innumerable, pitiless, passionless eyes,
Cold fires, yet with power to burn and brand
His nothingness into man.

But now shine on, and what care I,
Who in this stormy gulf have found a pearl
The countercharm of space and hollow sky,
And do accept my madness, and would die
To save from some slight shame one simple girl.

Would die; for sullen-seeming Death may give
More life to Love than is or ever was
In our low world, where yet 't is sweet to live.
Let no one ask me how it came to pass;
It seems that I am happy, that to me
A livelier emerald twinkles in the grass,
A purer sapphire melts into the sea.

Not die; but live a life of truest breath,
And teach true life to fight with mortal wrongs.
O, why should Love, like men in drinking-songs,
Spice his fair banquet with the dust of death?
Make answer, Maud my bliss,
Maud made my Maud by that long lover's kiss,
Life of my life, wilt thou not answer this?
"The dusky strand of Death inwoven here
With dear Love's tie, makes Love himself more dear."

Is that enchanted moan only the swell
Of the long waves that roll in yonder bay?
And hark the clock within, the silver knell
Of twelve sweet hours that past in bridal white,
And died to live, long as my pulses play;
But now by this my love has closed her sight
And given false death her hand, and stol'n away
To dreamful wastes where footless fancies dwell

Among the fragments of the golden day.
May nothing there her maiden grace affright!
Dear heart, I feel with thee the drowsy spell.
My bride to be, my evermore delight,
My own heart's heart, my ownest own, farewell;
It is but for a little space I go:
And ye meanwhile far over moor and fell
Beat to the noiseless music of the night!
Has our whole earth gone nearer to the glow
Of your soft splendors that you look so bright?
I have climb'd nearer out of lonely Hell.
Beat, happy stars, timing with things below,
Beat with my heart more blest than heart can tell,
Blest, but for some dark undercurrent woe
That seems to draw—but it shall not be so:
Let all be well, be well.

xxii

Come into the garden, Maud,
    For the black bat, night, has flown,
Come into the garden, Maud,
    I am here at the gate alone;
And the woodbine spices are wafted abroad,
    And the musk of the rose is blown.

For a breeze of morning moves,
    And the planet of Love is on high,
Beginning to faint in the light that she loves
    On a bed of daffodil sky,
To faint in the light of the sun she loves,
    To faint in his light, and to die.

All night have the roses heard
    The flute, violin, bassoon;
All night has the casement jessamine stirr'd
    To the dancers dancing in tune;
Till a silence fell with the waking bird,
    And a hush with the setting moon.

I said to the lily, "There is but one,
    With whom she has heart to be gay.
When will the dancers leave her alone?
    She is weary of dance and play."
Now half to the setting moon are gone,
    And half to the rising day;
Low on the sand and loud on the stone
    The last wheel echoes away.

I said to the rose, "The brief night goes
    In babble and revel and wine.
O young lord-lover, what sighs are those,
    For one that will never be thine?
But mine, but mine," so I sware to the rose,
    "For ever and ever, mine."

And the soul of the rose went into my blood,
    As the music clash'd in the hall;
And long by the garden lake I stood,
    For I heard your rivulet fall
From the lake to the meadow and on to the wood,
    Our wood, that is dearer than all;

From the meadow your walks have left so sweet
    That whenever a March-wind sighs
He sets the jewel-print of your feet
    In violets blue as your eyes,
To the woody hollows in which we meet
    And the valleys of Paradise.

The slender acacia would not shake
    One long milk-bloom on the tree;
The white lake-blossom fell into the lake
    As the pimpernel dozed on the lea;
But the rose was awake all night for your sake,
    Knowing your promise to me;
The lilies and roses were all awake,
    They sigh'd for the dawn and thee.

Queen rose of the rosebud garden of girls,
    Come hither, the dances are done,
In gloss of satin and glimmer of pearls,
    Queen lily and rose in one;

Shine out, little head, sunning over with curls,
    To the flowers, and be their sun.

There has fallen a splendid tear
    From the passion-flower at the gate.
She is coming, my dove, my dear;
    She is coming, my life, my fate;
The red rose cries, "She is near, she is near;"
    And the white rose weeps, "She is late;"
The larkspur listens, "I hear, I hear;"
    And the lily whispers, "I wait."

She is coming, my own, my sweet;
    Were it ever so airy a tread,
My heart would hear her and beat,
    Were it earth in an earthy bed;
My dust would hear her and beat,
    Had I lain for a century dead;
Would start and tremble under her feet,
    And blossom in purple and red.

FLOWER IN THE CRANNIED WALL

FLOWER in the crannied wall,
I pluck you out of the crannies;—
I hold you here, root and all, in my hand,
Little flower—but if I could understand
What you are, root and all, and all in all,
I should know what God and man is.

                    [publ. 1830]

TO VIRGIL

*Written at the Request of the Mantuans for the
Nineteenth Centenary of Virgil's Death*

ROMAN VIRGIL, thou that singest
    Ilion's lofty temples robed in fire,
Ilion falling, Rome arising,
    wars, and filial faith, and Dido's pyre;

Landscape-lover, lord of language,
    more than he that sang the Works and Days,
All the chosen coin of fancy
    flashing out from many a golden phrase;

Thou that singest wheat and woodland,
    tilth and vineyard, hive and horse and herd;
All the charm of all the Muses
    often flowering in a lonely word;

Poet of the happy Tityrus
    piping underneath his beechen bowers;
Poet of the poet-satyr
    whom the laughing shepherd bound with flowers;

Chanter of the Pollio, glorying
    in the blissful years again to be,
Summers of the snakeless meadow,
    unlaborious earth and oarless sea;

Thou that seest Universal
    Nature moved by Universal Mind;
Thou majestic in thy sadness
    at the doubtful doom of human kind;

Light among the vanish'd ages;
    star that gildest yet this phantom shore;
Golden branch amid the shadows,
    kings and realms that pass to rise no more;

Now thy Forum roars no longer,
    fallen every purple Cæsar's dome—
Tho' thine ocean-roll of rhythm
    sound for ever of Imperial Rome—

Now the Rome of slaves hath perish'd,
    and the Rome of freemen holds her place,
I, from out the Northern Island,
    sunder'd once from all the human race,

I salute thee, Mantovano,
    I that loved thee since my day began,
Wielder of the stateliest measure
    ever moulded by the lips of man.

                    [publ. 1882]

CROSSING THE BAR

Sunset and evening star,
    And one clear call for me!
And may there be no moaning of the bar,
    When I put out to sea,

But such a tide as moving seems asleep,
    Too full for sound and foam,
When that which drew from out the boundless deep
    Turns again home.

Twilight and evening bell,
    And after that the dark!
And may there be no sadness of farewell,
    When I embark;

For tho' from out our bourne of Time and Place
    The flood may bear me far,
I hope to see my Pilot face to face
    When I have crost the bar.

              [1889; publ. 1889]

LEE COUNTY LIBRARY
107 Hawkins Ave.
Sanford, N. C. 27330

LEE COUNTY LIBRARY SYSTEM

||||| ||| |||| ||||| ||| ||||| ||| ||| |||||

3 3262 00104 6785

C **SIGNET** (0451)

POETRY THROUGH THE AGES

☐ **LEAVES OF GRASS by Walt Whitman.** These are the incomparable poems of one of America's greatest poets—an exuberant, passionate man who loved his country and wrote of it as no other has ever done. Emerson judged *Leaves of Grass* as "the most extraordinary piece of wit and wisdom America has yet contributed." (517024—$2.95)

☐ **PARADISE LOST AND PARADISE REGAINED by John Milton.** Edited and with Introduction and Notes by Christopher Ricks. Chronology, Bibliography and Footnotes included. (523520—$4.95)

☐ **IDYLLS OF THE KING and A Selection of Poems by Alfred Lord Tennyson.** Foreword by George Barker. Includes selections from *The Princess, In Memoriam A.H.H.* and *Maud.* (522583—$3.95)

Price is higher in Canada

_____

Buy them at your local bookstore or use this convenient coupon for ordering.

NEW AMERICAN LIBRARY
P.O. Box 999, Bergenfield, New Jersey 07621

Please send me the books I have checked above. I am enclosing $_____
(please add $1.00 to this order to cover postage and handling). Send check or money order—no cash or C.O.D.'s. Prices and numbers are subject to change without notice.

Name_____

Address_____

City _____ State _____ Zip Code _____
Allow 4-6 weeks for delivery.
This offer, prices and numbers are subject to change without notice.